Will you love me?
Cathy Glass

The story
of my adopted
daughter Lucy

Certain details in this story, including names, places and dates,
have been changed to protect the family's privacy.

HarperElement
An imprint of HarperCollins*Publishers*
77–85 Fulham Palace Road,
Hammersmith, London W6 8JB

www.harpercollins.co.uk

and HarperElement are trademarks of
HarperCollins*Publishers* Ltd

First published by HarperElement 2013

1 3 5 7 9 10 8 6 4 2

A catalogue record of this book
is available from the British Library

ISBN 978-0-00-753091-5

Printed and bound in Great Britain by
Clays Ltd, St Ives plc

Acknowledgements

A big thank-you to my editor, Holly; my literary agent Andrew; and Carole, Vicky, Laura and all the team at HarperCollins.

*'Every time I hear a newborn baby cry ...
Then I know why,
I believe.'*

'I Believe' by Ervin Drake

Prologue

I heard Pat, Lucy's carer, knock on Lucy's bedroom door, and then a slight creak as the door opened, followed by: 'Your new carer, Cathy, is on the phone for you. Can you come and talk to her?'

There was silence and then I heard the bedroom door close. A few moments later Pat's voice came on the phone again. 'I told her, but she's still refusing to even look at me. She's just sitting there on the bed staring into space.'

My worries for Lucy rose.

'What should I do now?' Pat asked, anxiously. 'Shall I ask my husband to talk to her?'

'Does Lucy have a better relationship with him?' I asked.

'No, not really,' Pat said. 'She won't speak to him, either. We might have to leave her here until Monday, when her social worker is back at work.'

'Then Lucy will have the whole weekend to brood over this,' I said. 'It will be worse. Let's try again to get her to the phone. I'm sure it will help if she hears I'm not an ogre.'

Pat gave a little snort of laughter. 'Jill said you were very good with older children,' referring to my support social worker.

'That was sweet of her,' I said. 'Now, is your phone fixed or cordless?'

'Cordless.'

'Excellent. Take the handset up with you, knock on Lucy's bedroom door, go in and tell her again I would like to talk to her, please. But this time, leave the phone on her bed facing up, so she can hear me, and then come out. I might end up talking to myself, but I'm used to that.'

Pat gave another snort of nervous laughter. 'Fingers crossed,' she said.

I heard Pat's footsteps going up the stairs again, followed by the knock on Lucy's bedroom door and the slight creak as it opened. Pat's voice trembled a little as she said: 'Cathy's still on the phone and she'd like to talk to you.'

There was a little muffled sound, presumably as Pat put the phone on Lucy's bed, and then I heard the bedroom door close. I was alone with Lucy.

Lucy and I believe we were destined to be mother and daughter; it just took us a while to find each other. Lucy was eleven years old when she came to me. I desperately wish it could have been sooner. It breaks my heart when I think of what happened to her, as I'm sure it will break yours. To tell Lucy's story – our story – properly, we need to go back to when she was a baby, before I knew her. With the help of records we've been able to piece together Lucy's early life, so here is her story, right from the start …

Will you love me?

PART ONE

PART ONE

Chapter One

Desperate

It was dark outside and, at nine o'clock on a February evening in England, bitterly cold. A cruel northeasterly wind whipped around the small parade of downbeat shops: a newsagent's, a small grocer's, a bric-a-brac shop selling everything from bags of nails to out-of-date packets of sweets and biscuits, and at the end a launderette. Four shops with flats above forming a dismal end to a rundown street of terraced houses, which had once been part of the council's regeneration project, until its budget had been cut.

Three of the four shops were in darkness and shuttered against the gangs of marauding yobs who roamed this part of town after dark. But the launderette, although closed to the public, wasn't shuttered. It was lit, and the machines were working. Fluorescent lighting flickered against a stained grey ceiling as steam from the machines condensed on the windows. The largest window over the dryers ran with rivulets of water that puddled on the sill.

Inside, Bonnie, Lucy's mother, worked alone. She was in her mid-twenties, thin, and had her fair hair pulled back into a ponytail. She was busy heaving the damp clothes from the washing machines and piling them into the dryers, then reloading the machines. She barely faltered in her work, and the

3

background noise of the machines, clicking through their programmes of washing, rinsing, spinning and drying, provided a rhythm; it was like a well-orchestrated dance. While all the machines were occupied and in mid-cycle, Bonnie went to the ironing board at the end of the room and ironed as many shirts as she could before a machine buzzed to sound the end of its cycle and needed her attention.

Bonnie now stood at the ironing board meticulously pressing the shirts of divorced businessmen who didn't know how to iron, had no inclination to learn and drove past the launderette from the better end of town on their way to and from work. Usually they gave her a tip, which was just as well, for the money her boss, Ivan, gave her wasn't enough to keep her and her baby. Nowhere near.

With her earphones in and the volume turned up high on her Discman, plus the noise coming from the machines, Bonnie didn't hear the man tapping on the window and then rattling the shop door. With her concentrating on the ironing and her back turned away from him, he could have stood there indefinitely trying to attract her attention. The door was Chubb locked and double bolted, as it was every evening when Bonnie worked alone. It was lucky, therefore, that after a few moments Bonnie set down the iron to adjust the volume on her Discman, because as she did so she caught a glimpse of movement out of the corner of her eye. Turning, she peered from the brightness of the shop into the darkness outside and was a little startled to see the silhouette of a man at the door. Then, with relief, she recognized the silhouette as that of Vince.

Bonnie crossed the shop floor, taking out her earphones and switching off her Discman as she went. She was expecting Vince; he was the reason the shutters weren't down. He'd phoned earlier and said he needed to see her urgently as he was leaving – for good. Bonnie hadn't been shocked to hear that the father of her baby was leaving. Vince (not his real name, which he'd told her was unpronounceable to English people) had come over from Thailand on a student visa four years previously, although as far as Bonnie knew he'd never been a student. His visa had long since run out, and in the fourteen months Bonnie had known Vince he'd said many times that immigration were after him and he would have to leave. But after the first few times, as with many of the other things Vince had told her – like his age and where his money came from – Bonnie had begun to doubt that it was true, and suspected it was just an excuse to come and go from her life as he pleased. However, as Bonnie now slid the bolts aside and opened the door, letting the cold night air rush in, she could see from his expression that something was different tonight. Vince's usually smooth manner was ruffled and he appeared to be sweating, despite it being cold outside.

'My sister phoned,' he said, slightly out of breath, as he stepped in and locked the door behind him. 'My mother is ill. I have to go to her.'

Bonnie looked at him. He was the same height as her – about five foot eight inches – with pale olive skin and jet-black hair; she saw his charm and appeal now as she always had, despite the way he treated her. Her mother had said it was her fault that she allowed men to treat her like a doormat, but at least Vince didn't hit her, as some men had.

'Your mother is always ill,' Bonnie said, not unkindly, but stating a fact. 'You told me your sister looks after her.'

Vince rubbed his forehead with the heel of his hand. 'My mother is in hospital. She has cancer and will not live long. I have to go home.'

Bonnie looked into his dark, almost black eyes and searched for the truth in what he said, which was also probably the key to her future.

'You're going home? On a plane?' she asked, raising her voice over the noise of the machines, for he'd never said before that he was going home, only that he was going away.

Vince nodded and stuffed his hands into the pockets of his leather jacket.

'For how long?' Bonnie asked.

He shrugged. 'Maybe for good.'

'And your daughter?' Bonnie said, irritated by his casualness, and still not fully believing him. 'What do I tell Lucy when she is old enough to ask about her father?'

'I'll write,' he said with no commitment. 'I'll write and phone on her birthday.'

'Like your father does with you?' she said bitterly, aware that Vince only ever heard from his father on his birthday. But if she was honest, she knew Vince had never wanted a baby; it had been her decision not to terminate the pregnancy.

'I have to go,' he said, glancing anxiously towards the shop door. 'I need to buy my ticket home, but I haven't the money.'

Bonnie gave a small, sharp laugh. 'So that's why you're here? To borrow money. No, Vince,' she said, before he could ask. 'The little I earn is for me and my baby. There's never any left over, as you know.'

'You live rent free here in the flat,' he said, an edge of desperation creeping into his voice. 'You must have some cash you can lend me?'

'No. I have to pay bills – heating and lighting. I have to buy food and clothes. I've told you before I have no savings. I don't have enough for Lucy and me.' She was growing angry now. A better man would have realized and not asked.

Desperate

'I'm desperate,' Vince said, almost pleading. 'You wouldn't stop me from seeing my mother when she is dying, would you?'

Bonnie heard the emotional blackmail, but it didn't stop her feeling guilty. 'I don't have any money,' she said again. 'Honestly, I don't.'

Vince's eyes grew cold, as they did sometimes, though not normally in relation to her. It made her uneasy, as though there was a side to him she didn't know.

'The till,' he said, shifting his gaze to the far end of the shop where the till sat on a table fixed to the floor. 'You have the day's takings. Please. I'm desperate. I'll repay you, I promise.'

'No. It's impossible,' Bonnie said, an icy chill running down her spine. 'I've told you what Ivan's like. He's always saying he'll beat me if the day's takings are down. He would, I'm sure. He's capable of it. You wouldn't put me in danger?'

But she could tell from Vince's eyes that he could and would. His gaze flickered to the till again as he nervously licked his bottom lip. 'You don't understand,' he said. 'It's not just about my mother. I owe people money. People who'll kill me if I don't pay them. I'm sorry, Bonnie, but I don't have any choice.'

His mother's illness or creditors? Bonnie didn't know the truth and it hardly mattered any more; his betrayal of her was complete. She watched in horror as with single-minded determination he walked the length of the shop to the till. She watched from where she stood as he opened the till draw, struggling to accept that he thought more of his own safety than hers and would put her in danger to save himself. But as he began taking out the money – the money she had collected from hand washes, dry cleaning and ironing; which could be £500 or more; and which she took to the flat each night for safe keeping, ready to give Ivan the following morning – her thoughts went to Ivan and what he would do to her if any of the money was missing. She knew she had to stop Vince.

'No, Vince!' she cried, rushing to the till. 'No!' She grabbed his arm. 'No! Stop. Think of Lucy. Ivan will hurt her as well as me if you take the money.'

'Not as much as the gang I owe will hurt me,' he sneered. He pushed her from him and continued filling his jacket pockets.

'No. Stop!' Bonnie cried again. In desperation she grabbed his hands and tried to stop him from taking the money, but he shook her off.

She grabbed his hands again but his next push was much harder and sent her reeling backwards against the hard metal edge of a washing machine. She cried out as the impact winded her and pain shot through her. Vince quickly stuffed the last of the money into his jacket pockets and without looking back ran from the shop.

Bonnie stayed where she was, trying to catch her breath. She was also trying to come to terms with what had just happened. Vince had gone, probably for good, and he'd taken all of Ivan's money – the money Ivan would expect to collect at 8.00 the following morning. Tears stung the backs of her eyes as she stood and leant against the washing machine, trying to work out what to do.

The launderette was uncannily quiet. The dryers that had been working when Vince arrived had completed their cycles and now stood still; the washing machines were in mid-cycle, their drums gently swishing water from side to side. Bonnie looked at the shop door, which was still wide open from Vince's exit. The chill from the night was quickly replacing the previous warmth of the shop. Before long, if she didn't close the door, a drunk, druggie or yob would come in. Not that there was any money left to steal, she thought grimly; there was just her safety to worry about.

Desperate

Heaving herself away from the support of the machine, Bonnie rubbed her back and began to make her way towards the open door. Despite Vince's behaviour, Bonnie didn't condemn him for what he'd done; she believed she deserved it. Abuse was always her fault. Things like this didn't happen to nice girls. She was bad, so men treated her badly. It was as simple as that. She closed and locked the door, slid the bolts across and turned to survey the shop. Baskets of washing waited to be loaded into machines and dryers, the ironing was half done and the whole shop needed to be cleaned and tidied ready for when it opened at 7.30 a.m. the next day. Bonnie usually did all this before she went to bed. Ivan expected it and liked a clean and tidy shop when he called to collect his money at 8.00 a.m. Even if it took her until midnight to finish, she always made sure everything was done, just as Ivan liked it.

But not tonight, Bonnie thought. There's no point in finishing the laundry and cleaning the shop, for the crime of losing Ivan's money was far greater and could not be put right by a clean and tidy shop. It briefly crossed her mind that perhaps she could say they'd been broken into and the day's takings had been stolen, but with no forced entry she doubted Ivan would believe her, and she didn't dare take the risk. Bonnie lived in fear of Ivan, as she did most men who came into her life.

With a very heavy heart and her back paining her, Bonnie went to the corner of the shop and opened the internal door that led to the flat above. She pressed the light switch and the staircase was illuminated, then she turned off the lights in the shop – all except the night light, which always stayed on. Closing the door on the shop, she began up the stairs, and as she did so she heard Lucy crying. Bonnie knew from the distress in her screams that she'd been crying for a very long time.

Chapter Two

Escape

Halfway up the damp and foul-smelling staircase, with its dangerously frayed carpet, the light went out. Ivan had the light switches at the top and bottom of the stairs on timers so as not to waste electricity: he paid for the electricity on the stairs and in the shop; Bonnie paid for it in the flat. As usual, Bonnie climbed the last six steps in darkness and then groped for the light switch on the landing and pressed it, which gave her another ten seconds of light – enough to open the door to the flat and go inside.

The door opened directly into the room where Lucy lay, and her screams were deafening now. The living room was lit by a single standard lamp that Bonnie left on whenever Lucy was alone – which was often. The main overhead light had never worked, and Ivan had never offered to fix it. In the half-light Bonnie crossed to where her daughter lay in a Moses basket on the floor. Lucy's eyes were screwed shut and her mouth was open in a grimace of crying. The smell was putrid, a combination of the diarrhoea and vomit that had been festering since the last time Bonnie had checked on Lucy and changed her nappy, over five hours previously. Bonnie knew it was wrong to leave a baby unattended for so long, but she had to work. She also knew that, at six months old, Lucy was too old for a Moses basket, but she couldn't afford a cot. She kept the basket on the floor so that if Lucy did tumble out she wouldn't have far to fall.

Lucy's eyes shot open as her mother picked her up and she stopped crying. But her expression wasn't one of relaxed reassurance sensing that, as a baby, all her needs were about to be met. She didn't smile on seeing her mother, as most six-month-old babies would. No, Lucy's little brow furrowed and her eyes registered concern and anxiety, as though she shared her mother's fears and responsibilities for their future.

The sheet in the Moses basket and the Baby-gro and cardigan Lucy wore were caked with dried vomit. Round the tops of the legs of the Baby-gro were fresh brown stains where her nappy had overflowed. Lucy's sickness and diarrhoea were in their third day now and Bonnie knew she should really take her to a doctor, but if she did she would be registered on their computer system, and then it would only be a matter of time before concerns were raised and a social worker came knocking on her door. At present, no one knew where she was, not even her mother. Only the hospital where Lucy had been born – over 100 miles away – knew of her baby's existence, and that was all they knew.

Bonnie felt Lucy's forehead. Thankfully she didn't feel hot so Bonnie assumed she didn't have a temperature. Bonnie was hoping, praying, that nature would take its course and Lucy would get better of her own accord, although how long that would take she didn't know. Ignoring the squalor of the living room, Bonnie carried her daughter through to the bathroom where she pulled on the light cord. Filthy broken tiles formed the splashback to an old chipped and badly stained bath. What was left of the lino on the floor was stained from the leaking toilet and the ceiling was covered with large, dark, irregular-shaped water marks from the leaking roof above. This room, like the rest of the flat, was cold, and mould had formed between the tiles, around the edge of the bath and around the window, which couldn't be opened but rattled in the wind. Bonnie knew that this room – like the others she was allowed to use in the flat: the living room and kitchen – was unfit for human habitation. Ivan knew it too, and that she wouldn't complain, because she was desperate and had nowhere else to go. The doors to the two bedrooms were permanently locked and Ivan had the keys. He'd never told her what was in them and she'd never dared to ask.

Spreading the one towel she owned on the filthy bathroom floor, Bonnie carefully laid Lucy on top of it. Lucy immediately began to cry again, as if she anticipated what was coming next.

'There, there,' Bonnie soothed. 'I'm sorry, but I have to wash you.' Bonnie always felt a sense of panic when Lucy cried, as though she was doing something wrong.

Lucy's cries grew louder as Bonnie began taking off her dirty clothes. 'You must stop crying,' she said anxiously. 'The man next door will hear you.'

The Asian man who ran the newsagent's next door and lived in the flat above with his wife and two children had twice come into the launderette worried that they'd heard a baby crying for long periods and that there might be something wrong. Bonnie had reassured him, but now lived in dread that he would voice his concerns to the police or social services.

Bonnie placed Lucy's soiled cardigan, Baby-gro and vest to one side and then unfastened the tabs on her nappy. The smell was overpowering and Bonnie swallowed to stop herself from gagging. Before removing Lucy's nappy, in a well-practised routine she reached into the bath and turned on the hot tap. Cold water spluttered out as the pipes running through the flat creaked and banged. Bonnie held her fingers under the small stream of water until it lost its chill and became lukewarm. This was as hot as it got, so she and Lucy always washed in luke-warm water, and Lucy always cried.

Leaving the tap running, Bonnie took off Lucy's nappy and lifted her into the bath where she held her bottom under the tap. Lucy's cries escalated. 'Sssh,' Bonnie said, as she washed her with an old flannel. 'Please be quiet.' But Lucy didn't understand.

Having cleaned her back and bottom, Bonnie turned Lucy around and washed her front, finishing with her face and the little hair she had. Lucy gave a climactic scream and shivered as the water ran over her head and face. 'Finished. All done!' Bonnie said.

Turning off the tap, she lifted Lucy out of the bath and onto the towel. The comparative warmth and comfort of the fabric soothed Lucy and she finally stopped crying. 'Good girl,' Bonnie said, relieved.

She knelt on the floor in front of her daughter and patted her dry with the towel. Lucy's gaze followed her mother's move-ments apprehensively as though at any moment she might have reason to cry again. Once Lucy was dry, Bonnie wrapped the towel around her daughter like a shawl and then carried her into the half-light of the living room, where she sat on the threadbare sofa with Lucy on her lap. 'Soon have you dressed,' she said, kissing her head.

Bonnie took a disposable nappy from the packet she kept with most of her other possessions on the sofa. Bonnie owned very little; her and Lucy's belongings were easily accommodated on the sofa and armchair. At least I won't have much packing to do, she thought bitterly. Where she would go escaped her, but she knew she had no choice but to leave, now that Ivan's money had gone.

Lying Lucy flat on the sofa, Bonnie secured the clean nappy with the sticky fasteners, and then reached to the end of the sofa for Lucy's clean clothes. One advantage of working in the launderette was that she'd been able to wash and dry their clothes for free.

Taking the clean vest, Baby-gro and cardigan (bought second-hand), Bonnie dressed Lucy as quickly as she could. The only heating in the room was an electric fire, which was far too expensive to use, so Bonnie relied on the heat rising from the launderette to take the chill off the flat, but it was never warm. Lucy didn't cry as Bonnie dressed her; in fact, she didn't make any noise at all. Bonnie found that Lucy was either silent or crying; there was no contented in-between. Neither had she begun to make the babbling and chuntering noises most babies of her age do. The reason was lack of stimulation, but Bonnie didn't know that.

Once Lucy was dressed, Bonnie replaced the sheet in the Moses basket ready for later and then carried her daughter into the squalid kitchen. Balancing Lucy on her hip with one arm, she filled and plugged in the kettle with the other, and then took the carton of milk from the windowsill. There was no fridge so the windowsill, draughty from the ill-fitting window, acted as a fridge in winter. Bonnie kept her 'fridge foods' there – milk, yoghurt and cheese spread. An ancient gas cooker stood against one wall but only the hobs had ever worked, so since coming to the flat five months previously Bonnie had lived on cold baked beans, cheese spread on bread, cornflakes, crisps and biscuits. Lucy was on cow's milk – the formula was too expensive – and Bonnie wondered if this could be the reason for Lucy's sickness and diarrhoea.

Bonnie prepared the milk for Lucy in the way she usually did, by half filling the feeding bottle with milk and topping it

14

up with boiling water. Without a hob or milk pan it was all she could do, and it also made the milk go further. She made herself a mug of tea and, taking a handful of biscuits from the open packet, returned to the living room. She sat on the sofa and gave Lucy her bottle while she drank her tea and nervously ate the biscuits. She would have liked to make her escape now so she was well away from the area before Ivan returned in the morning and found his money and them gone, but the night was cold, so it made sense to stay in the flat for as long as possible. Bonnie decided that if she left at 6.00 a.m. she'd have two hours before Ivan arrived – enough time to safely make their getaway.

Physically exhausted and emotionally drained, Bonnie rested her head against the back of the grimy sofa and closed her eyes, as Lucy suckled on her bottle. She wondered if she should head north for Scotland where her mother lived, but her mother wouldn't be pleased to see her. A single parent with a procession of live-in lovers, many of whom had tried to seduce Bonnie; she had her own problems. Bonnie had tolerated her mother's lifestyle for as long as she could but had then left. Aged seventeen and carrying a single canvas holdall that contained all her belongings, Bonnie had been on the streets, sleeping rough or wherever she could find a bed. Bonnie's two older brothers had left home before her and hadn't kept in touch, so as Lucy finished the last of her bottle and fell asleep Bonnie concluded that she didn't have anywhere to go – which was how she'd ended up at Ivan's in the first place.

Dioralyte! Bonnie thought, her eyes shooting open. Wasn't that the name of the medicine you gave babies and children when they had diarrhoea or sickness? Hadn't she seen it advertised on television last year when she'd stayed in a squat where they'd had a television? She was sure it was. She had a bit of money –

the tips from the day – she'd find a chemist when they opened in the morning and buy the Dioralyte that would make Lucy well again. With her spirits rising slightly, Bonnie looked down at her daughter sleeping peacefully in her arms and felt a surge of love and pity. Poor little sod, she thought, not for the first time. She deserved better than this, but Bonnie knew that better wasn't an easy option when you were a homeless single mother.

Careful not to wake Lucy, Bonnie gently lifted her from her lap and into the Moses basket, where she tucked her in, making sure her little hands were under the blanket. The room was very cold now the machines below had stopped. It then occurred to her that tonight neither of them had to be cold – she didn't have to worry about the heating bill as she wouldn't be here to pay it. They could be warm on their last night in Ivan's disgusting flat! Crossing to the electric fire she dragged it into the centre of the room, close enough for them to feel its warmth, but not too close that it could burn or singe their clothes. She plugged it in and the two bars soon glowed red. Presently the room was warm and Bonnie began to yawn and then close her eyes. She lifted up her legs onto the sofa, kicked off the packet of nappies to make space and then curled into a foetal position on her side, resting her head on the pile of clothes, and fell asleep.

She came to with a start. Lucy was crying, and through the ill-fitting ragged curtains Bonnie could see the sky was beginning to lighten. 'Shit!' she said out loud, sitting bolt upright. 'What time is it?' Groping in her bag she took out her phone. Jesus! It was 7.00 a.m. The heat of the room must have lulled her into a deep sleep; Ivan would be here in an hour, possibly sooner!

With her heart racing and leaving Lucy crying in the Moses basket, Bonnie grabbed the empty feeding bottle from where she'd left it on the floor and tore through to the kitchen. She filled the kettle and then rinsed out the bottle under the 'hot' water tap. While the kettle boiled she returned to the living room and, ignoring Lucy's cries, changed her nappy. It was badly soiled again; she would find a chemist as soon as she could. Returning Lucy to the Moses basket, Bonnie flew into the kitchen, poured the last of the milk into Lucy's bottle and topped it up with boiling water. Back in the living room she put the teat into Lucy's mouth and then propped the bottle against the side of the basket so Lucy could feed while she packed.

Opening the canvas bag, Bonnie began stuffing in their clothes and then the nappies and towel. She put on her hoody and zipped it up; she didn't own a coat or warmer jacket. Bonnie then ran into the bathroom, quickly used the toilet, washed her hands in the lukewarm water and, taking her toothbrush and the roll of toilet paper, returned to the living room and stuffed those into the holdall. Bonnie didn't have any toiletries or cosmetics; they were too expensive and she never risked stealing non-essential items; she could live without soap and make-up.

In the kitchen Bonnie collected together the little food she had left – half a packet of biscuits, two yoghurts and a tub of cheese spread. She remembered to take a teaspoon from the drawer so she could eat the yoghurts, and then returning to the living room she put them all in the holdall. The bag was full now so she zipped it shut. She'd packed most of their belongings; all that remained were Lucy's soiled clothes and they would have to stay. There wasn't room for them and they would smell.

Bonnie checked the time again. It was now 7.15. Her heart quickened. She'd have to be careful as she left the area and keep a watchful lookout for Ivan. He arrived by car each morning, but from which direction she didn't know. With a final glance around the dismal living room and with mixed feelings about leaving – at least the place had provided a roof over their heads and a wage – Bonnie threw her bag over her shoulder and then picked up the Moses basket. She felt a stab of pain in her back from where Vince had pushed her into the washing machine.

Opening the door that led from the flat to the staircase, Bonnie switched on the timed light and then manoeuvred the Moses basket out and closed the door behind her. She began carefully down the stairs, her stomach cramping with fear. The only way out was through the launderette and if for any reason Ivan arrived early, as he had done a couple of times before, there'd be no escape. The back door was boarded shut to keep the yobs out. Halfway down the stairs the light went out and Bonnie gingerly made her way down the last few steps, tightly clutching the Moses basket and steadying herself on the wall with her elbow. At the foot of the stairs she pressed the light switch and saw the door to the launderette. Opening it, she went through and then closed it behind her. With none of the machines working the shop was eerily still and cold. She began across the shop with her eyes trained on the door to the street looking for any sign of Ivan; her heart beat wildly in her chest. With one final glance through the shop window, she opened the door. The bell clanged and, leaving the sign showing 'Closed', she let herself out.

Chapter Three

Concerned

The cruel northeasterly wind bit through Bonnie's jeans and zip-up top as she headed for town, about a mile away. She had no clear plan of what she should do, but she knew enough about being on the streets and sleeping rough to know there would be a McDonald's in the high street open from 6.00 a.m.; some even stayed open all night. It would be warm in there and as long as you bought something to eat or drink – it didn't matter how small – and sat unobtrusively in a corner, the staff usually let you stay there indefinitely. That was how she'd met Jameel last year, she remembered, sitting in a McDonald's. He'd sat at the next table and had begun talking. When he'd found out she was sleeping rough, he'd taken her back to the squat he shared with eight others – men and women in their late teens and early twenties, many of whom had been in the care system. One of the girls had had a four-year-old child with her, and at the time Bonnie had thought it was wrong that the kid should be forced to live like that and felt it would have been better off in foster care or being adopted, but now she had a baby of her own it was different; she'd do anything to keep her child. Bonnie had lived at the squat for two months and had only left when Vince had reappeared in her life. Bad move, Bonnie thought resentfully, as she continued towards the town with Lucy awake and gazing up at her.

'You all right, love?' a male voice boomed suddenly from somewhere close by.

Bonnie started, stopped walking and turned to look. A police car had drawn into the kerb and the male officer in the driver's seat was looking at her through his lowered window, waiting for a reply.

'Yes, I'm fine,' she said, immediately uneasy.

'Bit early to be out with a little one in this cold,' he said, glancing at the Moses basket she held in front of her.

Bonnie felt a familiar stab of anxiety at being stopped by the police. 'I'm going on holiday,' she said, trying to keep her voice even and raising a small smile. She could see from his expression that he doubted this, which was understandable. It was the middle of winter and she didn't exactly look like a jet-setter off to seek the sun. 'To my aunt's,' she added. 'Just for a short break while my husband's away.'

The lie was so ludicrous that Bonnie was sure he'd know. Through the open window she could see the trousered legs of a WPC sitting in the passenger seat.

'Where does your aunt live?' the officer driving asked.

'On the other side of town,' Bonnie said without hesitation. 'Not too far.'

The WPC ducked her head down so she, too, could see Bonnie through the driver's window. 'How old is the baby?' she asked.

'Six months,' Bonnie said.

'And she's yours?'

'Yes. Don't worry, she won't be out in the cold long. I'll get a bus as soon as one comes along.'

Bonnie saw the driver's hand go to the ignition keys. This was a bad sign. She knew from experience that if he switched off the engine it meant they would ask her more questions and possibly run a check through the car's computer. When that had happened before she hadn't had Lucy, so she'd legged it and run like hell. But that wasn't an option now. It would be impossible to outrun the police with the holdall and Lucy in the Moses basket.

'Where does your aunt live?' the WPC asked, as the driver cut the engine.

Shit! Bonnie thought. 'On the Birdwater Estate,' she said. She didn't know anyone on the estate, only that it existed from seeing the name in the destination window on the front of buses.

Suddenly their attention was diverted to the car's radio. A message was coming through: 'Immediate support requested for an RTA' – a multi-vehicle accident on the motorway. Bonnie watched with relief as the driver's hand returned to the ignition key and he started the engine.

'As long as you're OK then,' the WPC said, straightening in her seat and moving out of Bonnie's line of vision.

'I am,' Bonnie said. 'Thank you for asking.'

The driver raised his window and the car sped away with its lights flashing and siren wailing.

'That was close,' Bonnie said, and quickened her pace.

She knew she'd attract the attention of any police officer with child protection on his mind, being on the streets so early with her holdall and a baby. That was how she'd arrived at Ivan's launderette at 7.30 a.m. when Lucy had been one month old. Living rough, she'd dodged a police car that had been circling the area, and Bonnie had run into the launderette, which had just opened, to find Ivan cursing and swearing that the woman who should have been opening up and working for him had buggered off the day before. They'd started talking and when she'd heard that the job came with the flat above she'd said straight away she would work for him.

Now she crossed the road and waited at the bus stop. It was only a couple of stops into town, and she could just afford the fare. She also knew from experience that she was less likely to be stopped by the police while waiting at a bus stop than she was while walking.

It was a little after 8.00 a.m. when Bonnie entered the brightly lit fast-food restaurant, with its usual breakfast clientele. She was thirsty, her arms and back ached from carrying the Moses basket and bag and she desperately needed a wee. She was also hungry; apart from the handful of biscuits she'd eaten the evening before, she'd had nothing since lunch yesterday, and that had only been a cheese-spread sandwich made from the last of the bread. Although she had enough money to buy breakfast, she had no idea how long she'd be living rough, so she wasn't about to spend it until it became absolutely necessary. Bonnie opened the door to the corridor that led to the toilets and one of the staff came out. 'Oh, a baby!' she said, surprised, and then continued into the restaurant to clear tables.

Bonnie manoeuvred the Moses basket and holdall into the ladies. Fortunately it was empty, so she left the bag and Moses basket with Lucy in it outside the cubicle with the door open while she had a wee. Flushing the toilet, she came out, washed her hands and then held them under the hot-air dryer. As the dryer roared, Lucy started and cried. 'It's all right,' Bonnie soothed, and quickly moved away from the dryer.

She picked up the Moses basket and bag, and as she did she caught sight of her face in the mirror on the wall. Under the bright light she looked even paler than usual and she seemed to have lost weight; her cheekbones jutted out and there were dark circles under her eyes. With a stab of horror, Bonnie thought that if she didn't change her lifestyle soon she'd end up looking like her mother, haggard from years of drinking and smoking and being knocked around.

Returning to the restaurant, Bonnie ordered a hot chocolate for herself and a carton of milk for Lucy. 'Eat here or take-away?' the assistant asked.

'Here,' Bonnie confirmed.

She paid and then, lodging the drinks upright at the foot of the Moses basket so she could carry everything in one go, she crossed to one of the long bench seats on the far side – away from the cashiers and the draughty door. Placing the Moses basket on the seat beside her, Bonnie quickly began drinking her hot chocolate. The warmth and sweetness was comforting and reminiscent of the hot milky drinks her gran used to make for her when she'd stayed with her as a child. Bonnie wondered what her gran was doing now. Her mother had fallen out with her and they hadn't spoken for some years. Bonnie loved her gran, although she hadn't seen her since she'd left home eight years previously.

She took the packet containing the last few biscuits from her bag and kept it on her lap, out of sight of the staff, as she quickly ate them. The sugar rush lifted her spirits and helped quell her appetite for the time being. Lucy was watching her, but didn't appear to be hungry so Bonnie decided she'd keep the carton of milk she'd just bought for later and tucked it back in at the foot of the Moses basket, ready for when it was needed. She also had the yoghurts, one of which she'd give to Lucy later. She'd started giving her some soft food – yoghurt, a chip chewed by her first to soften it or a piece of bread soaked in her tea. When they were settled, she thought, and she had more money, she'd start buying the proper baby foods for weaning.

'It won't always be like this,' Bonnie said out loud, turning to her daughter and gently stroking her cheek. 'It will get better. I promise you.' Although how and when it would get better Bonnie had no idea.

At 9.00 a.m. Bonnie hitched the bag over her shoulders, picked up the Moses basket and left the fast-food restaurant in search of a chemist. Lucy was asleep now and, although she hadn't been sick or had a dirty nappy yet that morning, Bonnie wanted to buy the medicine so she had it ready in case it was needed. She tried to be a good mum, she told herself, but it was very difficult with no home, no regular income and having her own mother as a role model. When she'd been a child she'd assumed that the chaos and poverty she and her brothers were forced to live in was normal, that all families lived like that. But when she was old enough to play in other children's houses she realized not only that it was not normal but that others on the estate pitied her and criticized her mother for neglecting her and her brothers. Bonnie wondered why no one had inter-vened; perhaps it was because of her mother's ugly temper, which she'd been on the receiving end of many times and was always worse when she'd been drinking. This might also have been the reason why the social services hadn't rescued her and her brothers as they had some of the other kids on the estate, she thought; that, or they weren't worth saving – a view she still held today.

Bonnie spotted the blue-and-white cross on the chemist's shop a little further up and went in. There were two customers already inside: a lady browsing the shelves and a man being served at the counter. Bonnie scanned the shelves looking for the medicine she needed but couldn't find it. Once the man at the counter had finished, she went up to the pharmacist – a rather stern middle-aged Asian woman dressed in a colourful sari.

Concerned

'I think what I need is called Dioralyte,' Bonnie said.

'Is it for you?' the pharmacist asked, giving Bonnie the once over.

'No, for my baby.'

'How old is it?'

'Six months.'

She glanced at the Moses basket Bonnie held in front of her. 'What are the symptoms?'

'Sickness and diarrhoea.'

'How long has she been ill?'

'Two days,' Bonnie said.

'She needs to see a doctor if it continues,' the pharmacist said. Reaching up to a shelf on her right, she took down a box marked Dioralyte. 'This box contains six sachets,' she said, leaning over the counter and tapping the box with her finger. 'You follow the instructions. Mix one sachet with water or milk. You understand this doesn't cure sickness and diarrhoea? It replaces the salts and glucose lost from the body. If your baby is no better in twenty-four hours, you must take her to your doctor.'

'I will,' Bonnie said, taking her purse from her pocket.

'Four pounds twenty,' the woman said.

'That's a lot!' Bonnie exclaimed. 'Can't I just buy two sachets?'

The pharmacist paused from ringing up the item on the till and looked at Bonnie. Bonnie knew she should have kept quiet and paid. Through the dispensing hatch Bonnie could see a man, presumably the woman's husband, stop what he was doing and look at her. Then the woman came out from behind the counter and leaned over the Moses basket for a closer look at Lucy.

'I can smell sick,' she said, feeling Lucy's forehead to see if she had a temperature. Lucy stirred but didn't wake.

'It might be on the blanket,' Bonnie said defensively. 'I didn't have time to wash that before I left. Her clothes are clean.'

'Have you taken the baby's temperature?' the woman now asked.

'Yes,' Bonnie lied. 'She doesn't feel hot, does she?'

'No, but that isn't necessarily a good test. What was her temperature?'

'Normal,' Bonnie said, with no idea what that was.

The woman looked at her and then returned to behind the counter. 'Babies can become seriously ill very quickly,' she said. 'You need to watch her carefully. If you go to your doctor's, they will give you a prescription for free. Where do you live?'

'Eighty-six Hillside Gardens,' Bonnie said, giving the address of the launderette she'd just left. It was the only local address she knew by heart.

'Do you want the Dioralyte?'

'Yes,' Bonnie said, and quickly handed her a five pound note.

'Remember, you see your doctor if she's no better tomorrow,' the woman said again, and gave her the change.

'I will,' Bonnie said, just wanting to get out. Once she'd tucked the change into her purse, she dropped it along with the paper bag containing the Dioralyte into the Moses basket and hurried from the shop.

However, inside the shop Mrs Patel was concerned. The young woman she had just served looked thin and gaunt and her baby was ill. She'd appeared agitated and the basket she carried her baby in was old and grubby; she hadn't seen one like it for years. And why was the mother out on the streets with her bags packed in the middle of winter when her baby was ill? It didn't add up; something wasn't right. Mrs Patel was aware that in the past chemists had missed warning signs when intervention could have stopped suffering and even saved a life. Half an hour later, having voiced her concerns to her husband, he served in the shop while she went into their office at the back of the shop and phoned the social services.

'This may be nothing,' she began, as many callers to the duty social worker do. 'My name is Mrs Patel, I'm the chemist at 137 High Street. I've just served a young woman with a sick baby and I'm concerned. Is it possible for someone to check on her? I have an address.'

And that was the first time Lucy came to the notice of the social services – as a six-month-old baby with an address but no name.

Chapter Four

Too Late to Help

Three days later, in the early afternoon, Miranda parked her car in the first available space on the road, a little way past the launderette, and got out, extending her umbrella as she went. She was a first-year social worker, having qualified the year before, and had been assigned this relatively straightforward case. The duty social worker at the Local Authority had noted Mrs Patel's concerns and passed the referral to Miranda's team manager, who'd allotted the case to her. Miranda had duly contacted the health visitor whose patch included 86 Hillside Gardens, but having checked their records she had come back to her and said they had no record of a young mother and baby registered at that address. Now Miranda was visiting the address to investigate Mrs Patel's concerns.

It was only as Miranda stood in the street that she realized the address she'd been given wasn't a house but a launderette – the last shop in a parade of four. With the rain bouncing off her umbrella, she checked the street sign to make sure she was in the correct road, and then looked round the end of the building to the side of the launderette to see if there was a door to Number 86. There wasn't, so she returned to the front of the launderette, collapsed her umbrella and went in. Thick, dank and unhealthily humid air hit her. Although most of the machines were working, there were only two people in the shop: an elderly man sitting on the bench in front of the machines, presumably waiting for his washing to finish, and a rather large woman in her late thirties ironing at the far end of the shop. The woman looked over as Miranda entered and, seeing her hesitate, asked in a strong Eastern European accent: 'Can I help you?'

Miranda walked over to the woman before she spoke. 'Is this Number 86 Hillside Gardens?' she asked.

'Yes,' the woman confirmed, pausing from her ironing.

'Are you the owner?'

'No. I work here. Why?'

'I'm trying to find a young woman with a baby who may live here,' Miranda said.

The woman looked at her suspiciously, and Miranda thought that perhaps she hadn't fully understood her, so she rephrased: 'I would like to see the woman living here who has a baby.'

'No. I live here. Me – Alicja, with my husband,' she said, pointing to the ceiling and flat above.

'Do you have a baby?' Miranda asked. Although Alicja didn't match the description Mrs Patel had given, she was possibly a relative.

'No baby. My boy eight. He in Poland,' Alicja said.

'Does anyone else live here with you?'

'Are you the police?' Alicja asked, her eyes narrowing. 'We have right to be here. My husband has visa.'

'No, I'm not the police,' Miranda said with a smile, trying to reassure the woman. 'I am a social worker.'

Alicja frowned, puzzled.

'Social worker,' Miranda repeated, wishing that like some of her colleagues she'd mastered the basics of Polish. 'Me good lady,' she said, pointing to herself. 'I help people. I want to help the woman with the baby.'

'Not police?' Alicja asked again, seeking confirmation.

'No. Social worker. Do you have a mother and baby living with you?'

'No. No baby. Only me and husband,' Alicja confirmed.

'Do you know a woman in her early twenties with a six-month-old baby?' Miranda now asked, for it was possible that the mother she was looking for had stayed with Alicja or just visited.

'No. I show you our room?' Alicja said again, pointing to the flat above.

Miranda hadn't intended to ask to see the living accommodation; she really didn't have a right, but as Alicja had offered it made sense for her to see the flat so she could rule out the baby being there.

'Yes, please,' she said. 'That is kind of you.'

Alicja gave a small nod and, unplugging the iron, led the way to the door in the far corner of the shop. Opening it, she tapped the light switch and Miranda followed her up the dingy, damp-smelling staircase.

'Ivan very angry with the girl with baby,' Alicja said. 'Ivan own shop and she steal his money and go.'

'I see,' Miranda said. 'So there was a girl with a baby living here before you, and she left?' Then she gave a little cry and stopped dead as the lights went out.

'No worry. I press,' Alicja said, going up the last few steps and pressing the switch at the top to restore the lights.

Miranda joined her on the small landing.

'Yes. She go,' Alicja said, opening the door to the flat. 'Me and husband come last night. No unpacking yet.'

Miranda followed Alicja into the flat, which, like the staircase, smelled damp and musty. A drizzle of winter light filtered through the grimy windows, but even in the half-light Miranda could see the flat was unfit for human habitation.

'We unpack later,' Alicja said, almost apologetically, waving a hand at the bags, cardboard boxes and carrier bags that littered the floor. 'No time yet.'

Miranda gave a weak smile and nodded; her gaze had gone to the nylon sleeping bags open on the grimy, worn sofa and armchair.

'No beds,' Alicja said, following Miranda's gaze. 'Ivan say no bed. He lock door to bedrooms. He have key. Me and husband sleep here.'

Not for the first time since Miranda had begun her career in social work, she was appalled at the conditions some people were forced to live in. And while it was true that this wasn't the worse she'd seen – not by a long way – it was bad, and she felt Alicja's humiliation that she and her husband – two hard-working adults – had been reduced to living like this. She also felt anger towards the landlords who exploited immigrant labour.

'And there was a baby living here?' Miranda asked, now concerned that a baby could have been living in such conditions.

'Yes,' Alicja said. 'Mother leave dirty nappy and clothes, baby clothes. I show you.'

Miranda followed Alicja round the boxes and bags into what passed for a kitchen. Freezing cold, with crumbling plaster and filthy like the rest of the flat, Miranda noted it didn't even have the basics of storage cupboards or a fridge. Alicja went to a row of knotted bin bags propped against the old cooker, which had its oven door hanging off. Untying the top of one of the bags, Alicja tilted it towards her so she could see in. Miranda saw the soiled nappy and baby clothes among the other garbage and took a step back, away from the smell coming from the bag.

'I put these out later, and clean when I finish work,' Alicja said quickly, retying the bag.

Miranda was tempted to ask how much she and her husband were paying Ivan for this dump, but it was none of her business. She'd learnt early on in her career that social workers couldn't save every adult living in poverty; the social services budget didn't stretch that far. As there was no child or vulnerable adult living here, her involvement was effectively finished. There was nothing she could do.

'I show you bathroom?' Alicja offered. 'Then I work. Ivan angry if I not work.'

'Thank you,' Miranda said. She followed Alicja out of the kitchen, around the bags and boxes in the living room to the bathroom. It was pretty much as Miranda had expected: basic, with mould growing on the walls and around the window, an old cracked bath and sink, ripped lino, a leaking toilet and no heating. That a baby had been living here was appalling.

'Do you know where the woman and baby went?' Miranda asked, as they returned to the top of the stairs and Alicja pressed the light switch.

'No. Good that Ivan not know,' Alicja said. 'He very angry. She take his money, but he bad man. He frighten me, but not frighten my husband.'

Alicja went ahead to the bottom of the stairs and kept the light switch pressed so Miranda could complete her decent without suddenly being plunged into darkness.

'Now I work,' Alicja said, as they returned to the launderette.

'Thank you very much for your time,' Miranda said. 'You've been very helpful.' She took a social services compliment slip, which she used as a business card, from her bag and handed it to Alicja. 'That is the telephone number of where I work,' she said. 'If the girl and her baby come back, will you call me please?'

Alicja nodded and tucked the slip of paper into the pocket of her jeans and picked up the iron. 'She not come back here. She keep away from Ivan. Maybe you talk to the man in the shop next door? He come here this morning. Ask about baby. He worried – his wife hear baby crying.'

'I will,' Miranda said gratefully. 'Thank you. Take care.'

'You're welcome.'

Wishing that there was something she could do to help Alicja and her husband and the thousands like them being exploited for cheap labour, she left the launderette. Not bothering to put up her umbrella, she stepped quickly into the newsagent's next door. Being a social worker often involved detective work – asking questions of neighbours, friends and family and trying to build a picture of the person they were investigating. Some people were happy to help, others were not; some were rude and even threatening. It was part of the job.

Two teenage lads came out of the newsagent's as Miranda entered. She went up to the counter where an Asian gentleman wearing glasses and a thick jumper was serving. He looked at her and smiled. 'Can I help you?'

Miranda smiled back. 'I'm a social worker. I –'

'You've come about the baby next door?' he said, before she could get any further.

'Yes,' Miranda said, a little taken aback.

'You're too late. She's gone,' he said. 'My wife saw them go on Monday morning, at about half past seven. We have been very concerned. You should have come sooner.'

'We didn't know they were here,' Miranda said, taking her notepad and pen from her shoulder bag and making a note of the date and time.

'The mother and baby moved in about five months ago,' he continued. 'My wife and I heard the baby crying. We heard it every evening while the mother worked downstairs in the launderette. It's not right to leave a baby crying for so long. We were very worried. We have two children and when they were babies we comforted them when they cried. We never left them.'

'Do you know the woman's name?' Miranda asked, writing and then glancing up.

'No. But the baby was called Lucy. I know because when I went round to see if they were all right, the mother referred to her as Lucy. She was ironing and the washing machines were going and making such a noise, she couldn't hear the baby crying in the flat above. When I told her we could hear the baby through the wall she looked very worried and stopped ironing. She said, "I'm going to see to Lucy now." She worked very long hours, too long with the baby. I suppose she needed the money.'

'Yes. Thank you. I see,' Miranda said, frowning, and writing quickly to catch up. 'Can I take your name?'

'Mr Singh.'

Miranda made a note.

'My wife offered to look after the baby while the woman worked,' Mr Singh continued. 'But she didn't want our help. It's understandable, she didn't know us. But it would have been better for us to look after the baby than to leave it crying for hours.'

'Did the woman have a partner or boyfriend living with her?'

'Not as far as I know. There was a man, oriental origin I think, who used to visit sometimes. I don't think he was living there.'

'Did you see the baby?' Miranda now asked.

Mr Singh shook his head. 'No. The baby was always in the flat. It never went out. The only time we saw the baby was when they left on Monday morning. My wife was looking out of the window and called me over. We saw her leaving with the baby in a funny type of basket. She had a big bag with her so it was obvious she was going. Running away, I think. She seemed very anxious and kept looking behind her as she went up the road. That was the only time we saw the baby.'

'Thank you,' Miranda said again, as she wrote.

'The mother always kept herself to herself,' Mr Singh added. 'Perhaps she was in trouble with the police. I don't know.' He gave a small shrug. 'She was young, early twenties; white skin, fair hair and very thin. My wife said she looked like she needed a good meal.'

'I don't suppose you know where they might have gone?' Miranda now asked, knowing it was a long shot.

'No. As I say, she never spoke to us. We just heard the baby crying.'

'Thank you, you've been very helpful,' Miranda said again, returning her pen and pad to her bag. She took out another compliment slip and passed it to Mr Singh. 'If you see the girl again, perhaps you would phone me on that number?'

'Yes.' He nodded and placed the compliment slip beside the till. 'I hope you find them. My wife and I were very worried about the baby. Children are so precious.'

'Yes, they are,' Miranda agreed. 'I'll try my best to find them.'

Thanking him again, Miranda left the shop, more worried than when she'd arrived. Clearly baby Lucy was being badly neglected, but with no surname, national health number or address, there was very little she could do to trace and help them. Dodging the rain, she ran to her car, got in and closed the door. On her return to the office she would discuss her findings with her line manager who would make sure she hadn't overlooked anything and then she'd file her report. It was a great pity Mr and Mrs Singh hadn't called the social services or the police while Lucy and her mother had been living in the flat, then she could have been helped. But like many people who didn't report their concerns, they'd probably felt that they would be prying and hoped someone else would assume the responsibility and phone.

As Miranda returned to her office, Bonnie was three miles away boarding a train for the next big town — forty miles south — where her Aunt Maggie lived. Having spent two nights sleeping rough, desperate and worried about Lucy's health, Bonnie had reluctantly telephoned her mother and asked for help. Her mother, sober for once, was surprised to hear from her after so long, but not wholly surprised to hear she had a baby. 'I always thought you'd end up getting up the duff,' she said, with a smoker's cough. 'Like mother like daughter!'

Bonnie had stopped herself from snapping back that she wasn't like her and never would be, not in a million years, for she needed her mother's help. But Bonnie didn't get any further, for her mother said: 'And if you're thinking of asking if you can come home, forget it. My new bloke's moving in with his kids soon so there's no room.'

The rejection was no more than Bonnie expected from her mother, who'd always put her own needs first.

'What about Gran?' Bonnie asked. 'Perhaps Lucy and I could live with her like I used to?'

Her mother gave a cynical laugh. 'You're well out of touch. Gran's in a care home. Lost her marbles and on her last legs.'

Bonnie was sad to hear that her gran was poorly, and hated her mother for being so callous. She wished she'd made more of an effort to see her gran. She was about to hang up when her mother had said: 'You could try your Aunt Maggie. She's a sucker for kids.'

Apart from Gran, Maggie was the only family member her mother had any contact with, and although Bonnie had no recollection of Maggie, having not seen her since she was about three years old, Maggie always sent her mother a Christmas card with an open invitation to visit.

'Give me her address and telephone number,' Bonnie said.

'Say please,' her mother said.

'Please,' Bonnie said. Then she noted down the details that her mother read out.

'Goodbye,' her mother said, and with no 'take care' or 'stay in touch' the line went dead. Bonnie felt little resentment towards her mother, who saw nothing wrong in putting her latest boyfriend and his kids before her daughter and granddaughter; her reaction had been no more than she was used to and expected. Her mother was damaged goods, and it was doubtful she'd ever change. As long as I don't follow the same path with my daughter, Bonnie thought.

Having used the last of her money to buy the train ticket, and with no credit on her phone to call ahead and tell Maggie she was on her way, Bonnie planned to just arrive and hope for the best. All she knew of Aunt Maggie – apart from that she was married and liked kids – was that she was mixed race. She and Bonnie's mother had shared the same mother, but Maggie's father had been black. With Lucy asleep in the Moses basket on the bench seat beside her, the motion of the train soon made Bonnie doze. At some point during the journey she received a text message from Vince: *Plane leaves in 30 mins. Bye. Vince.* She didn't reply, and that was the last Bonnie heard from Lucy's father.

Chapter Five

Family

It was nearly 6.00 p.m. when Bonnie arrived at Aunt Maggie's – a mid-terrace Victorian townhouse on the outskirts of the city. She struggled up the path, cold and aching from carrying the Moses basket and the holdall all the way from the station, over a mile away. She set down the Moses basket, grateful to be able to relieve her arms of the weight, and pressed the doorbell. Already, she knew this house was very different from her mother's or any of the places she'd lived in since. The neat front garden, the freshly painted red door, the large potted plant in the porch and the doormat all suggested a house that was well looked after – and that those living inside were equally well cared for.

Bonnie pressed the bell again and felt her heart beat faster. Supposing no one was in, what would she do then? Or supposing Aunt Maggie didn't want to help her? Bonnie wasn't even sure what she wanted from Aunt Maggie, who was after all a stranger to her. But she was so desperate she'd have journeyed to any address her mother or anyone else had given her. It was impossible to sleep rough with a baby, and she prayed Aunt Maggie would help her, for she didn't know what else to do.

Eventually she heard footsteps scurrying down the hall towards the door – children's footsteps, Bonnie thought. The door sprung open and a boy and girl aged about nine and ten grinned up at her. They were of similar height, with large dark eyes and brown skin; the boy's Afro hair was cut short while the girl's was neatly plaited into cornrows.

'Who is it?' a woman called from inside the house, as the children gazed inquisitively up at Bonnie.

'Dunno, Mum!' the boy shouted. 'It's a woman.'

'What's she selling?' their mother called back.

The children's eyes fell from Bonnie to Lucy in the Moses basket.

'A baby!' the boy returned.

Both children exploded into laughter, and for the first time since Bonnie could remember she found herself actually smiling. 'No, I'm not selling my baby,' she said quietly. 'Tell your mummy I'm Bonnie.'

But there was no need for the children to relay this to their mother, for Bonnie could see she was already coming down the hall. She was of medium height, with a cuddly figure, and wore a brightly patterned blouse over black trousers.

'Can I help you?' she said, arriving at the door and taking in Bonnie, her bags and the baby in the Moses basket. Her children moved to stand either side of her.

'Are you Maggie?' Bonnie asked.

The woman nodded.

'Mum gave me your address. I'm Bonnie.'

A brief puzzled frown flickered across Maggie's face before she realized who she was looking at. 'My sister's girl!' she exclaimed. 'Good heavens! What are you doing here?' Stepping forward, she threw her arms around Bonnie and hugged her tightly. 'You should have told me you were coming. I'd no idea.'

Bonnie felt uncomfortable at being hugged; she didn't like physical contact, especially from strangers. She was relieved when Maggie released her and stepped back.

'So, what are you doing coming all this way in the cold with your bags and a baby?' Maggie began. But before Bonnie had the chance to reply, to her relief Maggie welcomed her in. 'It's freezing out there, come on in. Good heavens, girl. Let me help you.'

Maggie scooped up the Moses basket from the porch and carried it indoors, peering at Lucy as she did. Usually Bonnie was very protective of Lucy and never let anyone near her, but now she found she didn't mind Aunt Maggie holding the basket; indeed there was something comforting in having her take control.

'Leave your bag and shoes down there,' Maggie said, pointing to a place in the hall just below a row of coat pegs. 'Don't you have a coat, girl?'

'No,' Bonnie said, still shivering.

Maggie tutted. 'Well, come and warm yourself.'

Bonnie slipped off her trainers as the children watched. She saw that they and Maggie went barefoot, but unlike Bonnie's their feet were clean.

'Sorry,' she said, embarrassed. 'I've been sleeping rough.'

Maggie tutted again. 'Through here,' she said, and led the way into their neat front room.

Bonnie took in the thick-pile mauve carpet, the china ornaments that filled the shelves and the framed family photographs dotted on most of the walls. It was warm and friendly, a proper home, like no other she'd ever known.

'So my sister sent you here?' Maggie said, setting the Moses basket on the floor and pulling back the cover so she could see Lucy. Her children peered in too.

Family

'Sort of,' Bonnie said. 'I didn't have anywhere to go and she suggested you.'

'And your mother wouldn't have you home?' Maggie said.

'No.'

'All right. Let's get your baby sorted out first and then you. What's her name?'

'Lucy.'

'When was she last fed?' Maggie asked. For having pulled back the cover she could see little Lucy was sucking ravenously on her fist.

'About twelve o'clock.' Bonnie said. 'I guess she's hungry now.'

'I bet she is, poor little mite,' Maggie said. 'That's six hours ago. Too long for a baby to go without food. How old is she?'

'Just over six months.'

'It's all right, pet,' Maggie said, cradling Lucy in her arms. 'We'll soon have you fed and comfortable.' Then to her children she said: 'Go upstairs and fetch your sister. Tell Liza I need her downstairs now to keep an eye on the dinner. Tell her now, not when it suits her.'

The children scuttled off and Bonnie knew they were used to doing as their mother told them and that Maggie was used to being obeyed. Yet while Maggie was firm, Bonnie sensed she was also very caring and loving – so unlike her own mother it was difficult to believe they were blood relatives.

She heard the children's footsteps disappear upstairs and then their shouts of: 'Hey, Liza! Mum wants you now. Guess what!'

Maggie looked at Bonnie as she perched awkwardly on the edge of the sofa. 'Relax, girl. You can tell me later what's been going on. First, we need to get this little one fed and bathed. Is she ill? I can smell sick.'

'She was sick, but I gave her medicine from the chemist.'

'You didn't take her to a doctor?'

'No. She stopped being sick.'

'So what does she eat?' Maggie now asked, taking the empty milk-stained feeding bottle from the Moses basket.

'Milk, yoghurt and anything soft I have,' Bonnie said.

Maggie didn't voice her thoughts. 'OK, let's start her with a bottle of milk first and then we'll bath her. Then, once she's more comfortable we'll give her some dinner. We'll also need to wash her clothes and the covers from the basket.'

'I have some clean clothes for her in my bag,' Bonnie said, grateful that Maggie knew what to do to help them.

Footsteps sounded on the stairs and the children reappeared, with a teenage girl dressed fashionably in leggings and a long jersey top. She looked at Bonnie and then at Lucy in her mother's arms.

'Liza, this is Bonnie,' Maggie said. 'My sister's girl, your cousin. I need you to help me with dinner while I get this little one sorted out.'

Bonnie thought she saw the faintest flash of resentment cross Liza's face as she gave a small nod and then left the front room to go into the kitchen.

'You hold your baby while I fix her a bottle,' Maggie said to Bonnie, placing Lucy in her arms. She took the bottle, which was in need of a good wash, and disappeared into the kitchen, while the two younger children stayed, staring quizzically at Bonnie.

'Are you going to sleep here?' the boy asked after a moment.

Bonnie shrugged. 'I dunno.'

'Haven't you got a home?' the girl asked.

Bonnie shook her head and concentrated on Lucy, who was sucking hard on her fist.

Family

'How come?' the boy asked. 'How come you haven't got a home and a mum and dad?'

'I just haven't. That's all,' Bonnie said, niggled by their intrusive questions. She could hear muffled voices coming from the kitchen and hoped Maggie would reappear soon. These kids had so much confidence they frightened her. She felt safe with Maggie, and Lucy was going to start crying again soon and worry her further.

In the kitchen, Maggie was using boiling water and a bottle brush to thoroughly clean the bottle of congealed milk. 'Little wonder the baby was sick,' she said, scrubbing the rim of the bottle for the third time.

Milk was warming in a milk pan on the hob and Liza was keeping an eye on it while stirring the pan of food for dinner.

'Is she staying?' Liza asked, glancing at her mother.

'She'll have to tonight,' Maggie said. 'It's late and cold. She can't be out with a baby. They've nowhere else to go.'

'You weren't thinking of giving her Bett's bed?' Liza said, giving the spoon a sharp tap on the edge of the pan before setting it on the work surface.

'Yes, just for tonight.'

Liza knew better than to complain; it was her mother's decision to allow Bonnie to use her elder sister's bed while she was away at university.

'What about the baby?' Liza asked. 'Is she coming in my room too?'

'She'll have to until I get something else sorted out.'

Maggie poured the warmed milk into the clean bottle and took it into the living room where she left Bonnie to feed Lucy while she went upstairs to prepare the bedroom.

* * *

That evening, once Lucy was fed, dressed in clean clothes and asleep, and the family had eaten, Maggie had a long talk with Bonnie, from which it soon became clear that there was no point in phoning her sister as she couldn't, or wouldn't, help her daughter. So Maggie assumed the responsibility, although she made it clear from the outset that Bonnie staying was only temporary, until she could find something more suitable. The social services' records show that Bonnie and Lucy stayed for two months and that Bonnie came to view this period as the best two months of her life – living in a loving family headed by a woman who actually cared for her.

Every evening when Leon, Maggie's husband, came home from work they ate around a large circular table, with a spotlessly clean tablecloth and cutlery that gleamed. Dinner was a sociable event, with everyone talking and laughing, sharing their news and catching up on the day's events – it was unlike anything Bonnie had experienced before. To begin with she felt uneasy and slightly intimidated by this noisy family and ate in silence, but gradually she began to relax and join in the conversation, although she never had that much to say. Leon did most of the talking and was a great storyteller. Bonnie loved to listen to him; to her, he was a proper dad and far removed from the men her mother had brought home. He was from a large Jamaican family and was used to accommodating members of the extended family, so he was relaxed about Bonnie and Lucy staying. He worked at the bus depot as a mechanic, servicing and repairing the council's fleet of buses, while Maggie, primarily a homemaker, supplemented their income by working lunchtimes as a canteen supervisor at the local primary school. Liza soon forgot her grievances at having to share her room and happily traded in the lack of space and privacy for the novelty of helping to look after baby Lucy, who rarely cried at night now she was warm and fed. To Bonnie, her aunt's family was the ideal family, like the ones you saw on television at Christmas, and she would have loved to have stayed for ever.

That first morning after Bonnie had arrived, Maggie insisted they take Lucy to the doctor's for a check-up. She registered both Bonnie and Lucy at her doctor's as temporary patients, living at her address. The doctor checked Lucy's heart, chest and stomach; asked Bonnie a number of questions about the illness and if Lucy was up-to-date with her immunizations, to which Bonnie replied that she 'thought so'. The doctor said he would check on the system and a card would be sent to her if there were any vaccinations outstanding. He also said Lucy's sickness and diarrhoea was very likely 'a bug' and, as long as the vomiting and diarrhoea didn't return, she would be fine and he needn't see her again. While Bonnie was relieved that Lucy had been pronounced fit and well, she was concerned that her details were now on the system and that a health visitor might call.

'Don't worry, girl,' Maggie told her, when Bonnie voiced her concerns. 'Health visitors help mothers with their babies. It's nothing for you to worry about. You're not in any trouble.' Although, of course, Maggie wasn't aware of the shocking conditions Bonnie and Lucy had been living in prior to coming to her, nor that the social services had been alerted and that a social worker had called at the launderette and found her gone.

During Bonnie's stay, Maggie looked after her as she would a daughter. She fed and clothed her, and gave her pocket money in exchange for her helping with the chores around the house as the other children did. She showed Bonnie how to cook basic meals, established a routine for Lucy and began to teach her how to play with her daughter to stimulate her – of which Bonnie had no idea. Maggie also began weaning Lucy properly – by introducing her to small nutritious meals, which she mashed down. Bonnie was happy to accept her aunt's advice and Maggie formed the opinion that Bonnie was able to successfully parent Lucy, for as she said to Leon: 'While Bonnie isn't the sharpest pencil in the pencil case, she loves her baby and has an inbuilt survival kit.'

Staying at Maggie's not only showed Bonnie what a proper family life was, but also gave her new skills. For the first time in her life Bonnie felt wanted rather than something that had to be tolerated – as she'd felt at her mother's and later in her relationships with men. Realizing the gaping chasm between her life and that of her cousins, Bonnie grew increasingly angry with her mother, for not only had she failed to provide the basics, but she'd allowed her to be abused. She said so to Maggie and then one morning, when there was just the two of them at home, Bonnie asked Maggie if she could use the phone to call her mother, and Maggie agreed.

Maggie was in another room but she could hear Bonnie clearly as her voice quickly rose until she was shouting at her mother, ripping into her for all she had failed to do and blaming her for the abuse she'd suffered and the life she'd been forced into. Eventually Maggie stopped the call as Bonnie was nearly hysterical. She put the phone down and then held and comforted Bonnie until she was calmer. Late that night, when Bonnie was asleep, her mother phoned Maggie. Drunk and belligerent, she blamed Maggie for 'putting ideas into Bonnie's head' and turning her against her. Maggie tried reasoning with her sister but without success, and eventually Leon took the phone from her and hung up.

Although Bonnie knew that living with Aunt Maggie and her family was only ever going to be temporary, and that Maggie was actively looking for suitable accommodation for her, it was

Family

still a shock when Maggie returned home from work one afternoon and announced that she'd found a small furnished self-contained flat just right for Bonnie and Lucy. It was only a mile away, Maggie said, and had a large bedroom big enough to take a bed and a cot, and a small kitchenette and bathroom. Furthermore, and unlike many of the other landlords Maggie had contacted, this one didn't mind benefit claimants. Maggie explained to Bonnie that once she had a permanent address, and until she could find a job and sort out child-care arrangements, she could claim benefit to pay the rent and live on. Worried that the flat might go quickly, Maggie had paid the deposit and the first month's rent. Bonnie thanked her, but Maggie could see she was sad at having to go and she felt guilty, even though she didn't have the room to let Bonnie stay. Bett was due home from university for the Easter holiday and ultimately she would return to live at home when she had graduated, and Maggie's two younger children already shared a bedroom.

Out of her own money Maggie bought a cot, bedding, a pushchair, a warm coat for Bonnie and the next size of baby clothes for Lucy, and filled the cupboards in the flat with food. Then she helped Bonnie move in and gave her fifty pounds to 'see her over' until her benefit money came through. Maggie felt she had done her best for Bonnie and, having made sure she and Lucy had everything they needed at the flat, she promised to phone and look in regularly, telling Bonnie to visit whenever she wanted and phone if she had any worries.

All went reasonably well for the first few weeks; Maggie visited twice a week, and although Bonnie's flat was often untidy, Lucy appeared clean, comfortable and well fed. But then, over the next month, Maggie began to have concerns. Bonnie often wasn't up when Maggie called on her way to work at the school, although it was 11.30 a.m. When Bonnie eventually answered the door she was often still in her nightwear and Lucy was still in her cot. Although Bonnie told Maggie that she'd been up early and had fed and changed Lucy, Maggie began to doubt this. Lucy's nappy, her clothes and the cot bedding would be saturated, suggesting she hadn't been changed for some time, possibly not since the night before, and she was always hungry. A couple of times, while Maggie waited for Bonnie to answer the door, she heard Lucy crying, very distressed, from inside. Then Maggie found that there wasn't any food in the cupboards and only milk and yoghurt in the fridge, despite Bonnie now being in receipt of benefit.

'What are you two living on?' Maggie asked, concerned.

Bonnie became defensive; she shrugged and told Maggie she had to leave as she was going out soon.

Now very concerned, Maggie returned to Bonnie's flat after work with a bag of groceries for them, but Bonnie refused to answer the door. Maggie knew she was in as she could hear Lucy crying, so she called through the letter box, but Bonnie still refused to come to the door. Eventually she left the bag of groceries on the doorstep and, wondering what she'd done wrong, returned home. That evening and the following day Maggie telephoned Bonnie many times but she didn't pick up, neither did she return Maggie's messages. Unable to understand what was going on, but very concerned for Bonnie's and Lucy's safety and wellbeing, she went to her doctor – the one she'd taken Bonnie and Lucy to when they'd first arrived. She explained her concerns and said that she wasn't sure what to do for the best. The doctor said that while confidentiality forbade him to discuss Bonnie and Lucy with Maggie, he would ask the health visitor attached to the practice to visit them. When he checked their contact details he found that they were still registered as temporary patients at Maggie's address, so Maggie gave him their new address, which he entered on the computer system. Two days later a health visitor called on Bonnie and Lucy and, having been allowed into the flat, subsequently alerted the social services.

Chapter Six

Neglect

Doris was in her late thirties and an experienced social worker with two children of her own. She had a good working relationship with Bonnie's health visitor, who was also a qualified nurse. Doris trusted her opinion, so that if she had concerns about a client and made a referral, it was acted on immediately. Doris had wanted to visit Bonnie and Lucy the day before, but with an emergency child-protection case conference in the morning and then having to place five siblings in foster homes in the afternoon, the day had disappeared. Now she was calling on Bonnie first thing the following morning. It was 9.30 a.m. when she rang the doorbell. Doris wasn't expecting Bonnie to be up and dressed – not many of her clients were at this time – so she rang the bell a second time.

A minute later the door to the flat next door opened and an elderly lady poked her head out. 'You the social?' she asked.

'Yes,' Doris said with a smile, wondering why it was so obvious.

'Good. That baby's been crying far too much for my liking, but the mother don't talk to me,' the neighbour said, and then disappeared back inside, closing the front door. Doris pressed the bell to Bonnie's flat again, more determined than ever to gain entry. If the mother didn't answer then she'd call back later, and if there was still no response she'd return with a court order and the police.

Giving the bell another push, Doris stooped so she was at eye-level with the letter box and peered in. Her view was blocked by a draught excluder, so she tried calling through the letter box: 'Bonnie, love, are you in? My name's Doris. I'm a social worker. Can we have a chat please, love? Nothing for you to worry about.' Doris knew from experience that you didn't go straight in talking about child-protection issues if you could help it. Sometimes it was unavoidable – if a child was in danger and had to be removed – but in cases like this it was likely that Bonnie could be helped with support and monitoring.

Straightening, Doris pressed the bell again and waited. A few moments later she heard the lock turn, and then the door opened. 'Hello, love,' she said, smiling. 'Are you Bonnie?'

The young woman nodded. Dressed in a crumpled T-shirt and shorts, with her hair dishevelled, she'd clearly just stumbled out of bed. 'What do you want?' she asked defensively.

'I'm a social worker. I'd just like to have a chat to make sure that you and your baby are OK, and that you're accessing every-thing you're entitled to. Your health visitor asked me to drop by. I work with her,' she added. The health visitor had told Doris that while there were no obvious signs that baby Lucy was being physically abused, the level of care she was receiving fell below an acceptable standard and was bordering on neglect – although Doris wouldn't be saying that yet.

'Can I come in?' Doris asked with another smile.

Clearly resenting the intrusion, the young mother stood aside and Doris stepped into the short hall, where a bag of rubbish was waiting to be taken out. She closed the front door behind her. She couldn't hear a baby crying, but there was a strong smell of soiled nappies.

'You can sit in there while I get her up,' Bonnie said grudgingly, nodding towards the door to the living room, while she opened the door to the bedroom.

'It's all right. I'll come with you,' Doris said brightly. 'We can talk while you see to your baby.' A less experienced social worker might have sat in the living room and waited for the mother to return, thereby missing the opportunity to see more of the client's home and how they related to their child or children.

As Doris followed Bonnie into the bedroom she took in the rumpled double bed with only one pillow, seeming to confirm what Bonnie had told the health visitor: that she had no partner or live-in boyfriend. Doris also saw the pile of dirty laundry in one corner, the overflowing clutter on the windowsill, which was being used as a shelf, and the cot against the wall where the baby sat in silence, holding onto the bars and staring out like a little caged animal.

'What a lovely baby,' Doris said, joining Bonnie at the cot and trying to put the mother at ease. She could feel Bonnie's hostility and it wouldn't help in building a relationship. 'Her name's Lucy, isn't it?'

Bonnie nodded, reached into the cot and lifted out her daughter. Doris noticed the toys in the cot – the infant activity centre and rattle. That was positive, she thought. But she also saw that the baby's sleep suit was saturated, as was the cot bedding, and there was a strong smell of faeces and ammonia, suggesting that Lucy had been in the same nappy for a long time. She watched as Bonnie laid Lucy on the bed and then, taking a roll of toilet paper from the windowsill, began removing Lucy's sleep suit. Doris saw the baby stiffen and brace herself, as though she was expecting pain. Having removed the wet and soiled nappy, Bonnie tore off a strip of toilet paper and began cleaning Lucy's red raw bottom. The baby cried out and

Doris looked at Bonnie expecting a reaction. There was none. The mother seemed impervious to her daughter's distress and continued cleaning Lucy's bottom with strips of dry toilet paper without trying to soothe her in any way.

'Don't you have any baby wipes or cream for her bottom?' Doris asked, as Bonnie reached for a clean nappy.

'No, I ran out.'

'You need to get some more, and a pot of antiseptic barrier cream from the chemist today. Or go to your doctor for a prescription. You're on benefit so the medication will be free. As soon as you can,' Doris added. 'Her little bottom's very sore and causing her a lot of distress.'

Bonnie gave a tight nod and picked up her daughter, who had now stopped crying. She carried her into the living room. Doris followed. She wasn't worried that Lucy was wearing only a vest and nappy as it was June and the flat was warm. However, she was concerned by the lack of interaction between mother and baby. At ten and a half months of age a baby would normally be seeking out its mother's attention, but Lucy didn't, and the most likely explanation was that she'd been ignored for so long that she'd given up trying to engage with her mother, and so far the mother had made no attempt to engage with her daughter. She held her, but didn't talk to her or make eye contact.

Doris noted that the living room was very bare considering a mother and child lived there. Two old chairs and a chipped coffee table were the only furniture, and there were no toys in this room apart from a heap of plastic building bricks in one corner. Clutter free and unlived in, it suggested to Doris that mother and daughter were either out a lot or lived mainly in the bedroom, possibly staying in bed for most of the day if the mother was very depressed, as the health visitor had thought.

Doris sat in one of the chairs and Bonnie sat in the other, setting Lucy on the floor. As soon as Lucy was down she went onto her hands and knees and began a slow and cumbersome crawl across the room towards Doris. Doris took some comfort from seeing this, for she hadn't crawled while the health visitor had been present, and babies who are severely neglected often fail to meet this developmental milestone, remaining like newborn infants from being left in their cot all day.

'She's doing well with her crawling,' Doris said encouragingly, taking a notepad and pen from her bag.

Bonnie nodded.

'You are a clever girl,' Doris said, smiling at Lucy. Lucy stared back, her large eyes unresponsive. 'Is she trying to pull herself up into a standing position yet?' Doris then asked Bonnie. This would be one of the next developmental milestones and was often achieved by babies of Lucy's age.

'No,' Bonnie said, fiddling with her hair.

'I expect she will soon,' Doris said positively, making a note. 'What does Lucy like to eat?'

'The health visitor asked me that,' Bonnie said resentfully. 'I told her – milk, yoghurt and porridge.'

Doris nodded. 'And I believe the health visitor suggested some new foods for Lucy to try?'

Bonnie nodded again.

'Good. We'll have a look in your kitchen later and you can show me what you're planning to eat today.'

'I haven't been shopping yet,' Bonnie said tersely. 'That health visitor was only here a few days ago.'

Three days, Doris thought; plenty of time to go shopping and to start implementing the health visitor's suggestions for feeding Lucy. She glanced down at Lucy who, having arrived at her chair, was sitting quietly at her feet like an attentive puppy.

Neglect

'Hello, love,' she said to Lucy, with a smile. But the look on Lucy's face was pretty much the same as her mother's – suspicious and watchful.

'It's very difficult bringing up a child on your own,' Doris said, returning her attention to Bonnie. 'Do you have any family living close by who can help you?' She was aware that this referral had come from a doctor after an aunt of Bonnie's had expressed concerns.

'No,' Bonnie said.

'You were living with an aunt?' Doris asked.

'For a while. But she has family of her own.'

'And your mother and father?'

'I don't see them.'

'Do they live locally?'

'No.'

Doris made notes as she talked, all the while wearing a smile and trying to put the mother at ease. However, although she was smiling, she was quickly forming the impression, as the health visitor had done, that all was far from well here; that the mother could be very depressed and, as a result, was neglecting her child.

'Have you been able to find Lucy's record book showing her checks and vaccinations?' Doris now asked, for when the health visitor had asked to see it Bonnie had said she wasn't sure where it was and that she'd try to find it. She'd also told the health visitor she couldn't remember if Lucy's development checks and vaccinations were up-to-date, which had added to the health visitor's concerns.

'No,' Bonnie said. 'I can't find the record book.'

'All right, don't worry. Your previous doctor will have a record of all of that. We'll arrange to have your notes transferred to your current doctor. This is your permanent address now?'

Bonnie nodded.

'So what was the name and address of your last doctor?' Doris now asked, pen poised to note this.

'I can't remember,' Bonnie said, biting her little nail.

'A street name and town will do. We can trace it from that.'

'I don't know,' Bonnie said again. 'I'll find out.'

Doris knew it was impossible not to know the name of the town that you'd lived in a few months previously, unless you had severe learning difficulties, which Bonnie did not. She wondered what it was that Bonnie was trying to hide or run away from.

'Do you know the name of the hospital where Lucy was born?' Doris now asked. 'They'll have details of your doctor.'

'St Mary's, I think,' Bonnie said.

'In which town?'

Bonnie shrugged and continued to nibble her little finger. St Mary's was the most common name for a hospital and Doris knew it would be impossible to trace the one where Lucy was born without knowing the town or at least the area. Bonnie was playing games with her.

'It can be very isolating living in a new town with a young baby,' Doris said evenly, changing direction. 'I understand the health visitor gave you some details of the mother and baby groups in this area.'

'Yes,' Bonnie said.

'Do you think these are somewhere you might go? It would be good for Lucy's development and will also give you a chance to meet other young mothers and make some friends.'

'Yes,' Bonnie said.

'And how do you feel in yourself?' Doris now asked.

'OK,' Bonnie said with a shrug.

'Are you sure? You seem a bit down to me.'

'I'm fine. I'm coping.'

Neglect

'Only coping?' Doris asked, hoping this might lead the way in, but Bonnie just looked back and nodded.

'Can you talk me through your average day, from when you get up in the morning?' Doris said.

Bonnie looked at her.

'Start with when you get up?' Doris prompted. 'What time is that usually?' She knew that those suffering from severe depression often stayed in bed for very long periods, sometimes most of the day.

'About now I guess,' Bonnie said.

'Then what happens? Do you shower and dress or go back to bed?'

'We have breakfast,' Bonnie said.

'Lovely,' Doris said, trying to give positive feedback wherever she could. 'What do you have?'

'Lucy has milk and I have a cup of tea.'

'Nothing else?'

'I give Lucy porridge as well.'

'Good. Has she had her porridge this morning?'

'No, only milk. You came before I had time to give her porridge,' Bonnie said.

Doris wrote and then smiled at Lucy.

'Then what do you do after breakfast?' she asked, looking at Bonnie.

Bonnie shrugged. 'Nothing really. We go out sometimes.'

'Where do you like to go?'

'To the shops sometimes, or the canal. I walk by the canal. I like it there, with the deep water.' Doris gave an involuntary shudder and made a note, for in her present state of mind it wouldn't take much, she thought, for this young mother who clearly wasn't coping to step into the canal with her daughter and end it all. She agreed with the health visitor that while there were no obvious signs that the mother was harming her child, the level of care was so low that this in itself was a form of abuse. Mother and baby needed help.

'What do you do for the rest of the day?' Doris now asked.

'We come home.'

'And?'

Bonnie shook her head.

'Why don't you see your aunt any more?' Doris asked. 'She's been worried about you.'

'I dunno. She has her own family.'

'But she'd still like to see you as well. Do you think you might be able to start seeing her again? Go round for dinner? She'd like you to.'

Bonnie nodded, but not very convincingly.

Doris glanced at Lucy, who was looking up at her, her large eyes round and imploring. 'Can I pick her up?' Doris asked. She knew better than to simply pick up a client's child, without asking the parent first. Social workers were often seen as the enemy and she wouldn't be the first social worker to be assaulted for touching a client's child.

Bonnie gave a stiff, indifferent nod and Doris bent down and lifted Lucy onto her lap. She was light, Doris thought, lighter than she should be for ten and a half months old. She hadn't had a bath and was wearing the same vest, so there was still a smell of ammonia coming from Lucy, which would probably transfer to her skirt, but she kept a change of clothes in the car for just such eventualities; that, and having drinks or worse thrown at her by angry parents.

'Who's a lovely girl then?' Doris said to Lucy.

Lucy looked at her but didn't smile.

'Is she smiling and trying to talk?' Doris asked, glancing at Bonnie.

'Yes,' Bonnie said. 'Sometimes,' although there'd been no evidence of either since Doris had been with her.

'Come on then,' Doris said cheerfully to them both, standing. 'Show me around your flat. Let's start with the kitchen.'

'There's nothing much to see,' Bonnie said, rising to her feet with a small sigh.

'Never mind. I just need to have a quick look round.'

It was clear that the nature of the social worker's visit had changed from 'a chat' to a scrutinizing assessment, and Doris could sense that Bonnie was trying to stifle her rising fear that she was about to lose her baby.

'I'm going shopping later,' Bonnie said, as they entered the small kitchen.

Doris opened the door of the fridge, revealing only a carton of milk and two yoghurts. She then opened the doors to the cupboards, but all they contained were some crockery and pans supplied by the landlord, and a packet of porridge, some biscuits and a few tea bags.

'What does Lucy drink from?' Doris asked. 'Can she use a trainer cup?'

'No. She has a bottle. It's in her cot,' Bonnie said.

Still carrying Lucy, Doris left the kitchen, had a quick look in the bathroom, which, while basic, was functional, and then returned to the living room. Doris passed Lucy to Bonnie and they returned to their chairs. Doris looked at Bonnie carefully.

'I have concerns, love,' she said evenly. 'I think Lucy isn't doing as well as she could, and I think you are finding things difficult too. I want to help you.' She paused and waited for Bonnie's reaction, but there was none. 'When I return to my office I'm going to arrange what's called a case conference so I can work out how best to support you and Lucy. Don't look so worried, I'm not going to take Lucy away. But you will need to make some changes, all right, love?'

Bonnie nodded. 'I know,' she said, though by now she sounded like she'd agree to anything just to get rid of Doris.

'One of the options might be for you and Lucy to live in a mother-and-baby unit for a while, where you will be shown parenting skills and monitored. Or – and I will need to discuss this with my manager – you could stay here with support. You'd be monitored and assessed and would need to attend parenting classes.'

Bonnie nodded. 'Yes,' she said.

'Good. I'll go now and I'll phone you later today, after I've discussed the options with my manager. Can I have your phone number please?'

Bonnie reeled off eleven digits as Doris wrote.

'Thanks,' Doris said with a reassuring smile. 'I'll leave the two of you to have your porridge now and we'll speak later.'

Bonnie nodded and, carrying Lucy, went with Doris to the front door and saw her out. As Doris left the building she was already calling her office. Although she wouldn't be taking Lucy into care today, the mother would need to start cooperating and making some changes, otherwise she'd have no alternative but to apply to the court for a care order. While this wasn't the worst case of neglect Doris had seen – far from it – she agreed with the health visitor that the warning signs were there, and without intervention she had little doubt Lucy's situation would deteriorate further.

Three hours later, having spoken with her manager, Doris phoned Bonnie to arrange a meeting. An automated voice message told her the number was unobtainable, so Doris concluded that Bonnie had either accidentally or deliberately

Neglect

given her the wrong number. As Bonnie and Lucy's case wasn't the most urgent she was responsible for, and her caseload was so heavy she had to prioritize, Doris set in motion the case conference and then put Bonnie's file to one side to concentrate on another, more pressing case. She decided to call in on Bonnie on her way home from work, check the phone number and advise her of the date of the meeting. It would also give her another chance to see how they were doing.

When Doris returned to Bonnie's flat at 5.45 p.m. and rang the bell there was no reply. She was about to call through the letter box when the door to the flat next door opened and the elderly lady Doris had seen that morning appeared.

'She's gone,' the woman said bluntly, as if it was Doris's fault. 'Packed her bags and left with the baby about an hour after you left this morning.'

'I don't suppose you know where they've gone?' Doris asked, her heart sinking.

'No. Like I said, she never spoke to me.' And, returning inside, she closed her front door.

Chapter Seven

No chance to say Goodbye

It may seem incredible in this age, when there is so much data stored on people, that someone could simply disappear. But on that fine June day when the sun was shining and the air was alive with birdsong, and Lucy was nearly eleven months old, that is what Bonnie did. Fearing Lucy would be taken away from her, she quickly packed her bags and vanished. Had Lucy been the subject of a court order the police would have been alerted, and a missing person bulletin put out. But there was no court order, only a concern of neglect, the level of which hadn't merited the measure of applying to the court for an emergency protection order. It's true that the social services could have applied for a court order after Bonnie had gone, but they didn't, presumably for the same reason one hadn't been applied for before: that though Lucy had been neglected she wasn't, as yet, at risk of significant harm – the threshold that needed to be reached before the social services applied for a care order. Had they done so, the police would have been alerted, resulting in a better chance of finding Bonnie and Lucy, and Lucy would have been taken into care.

With no court order and no verifiable details of Bonnie that might have helped trace her, it is likely their case stayed open at the social services for a few months – while Doris checked with

Maggie and local agencies to see if anyone had heard from Bonnie – before being filed away until such time as Bonnie and Lucy reappeared. It's on record that Maggie told Doris she'd telephoned her sister a couple of times during this period to see if she'd heard from Bonnie, but she hadn't, and Maggie said her sister was so immersed in her own problems that she had little interest in what her daughter and granddaughter were doing or even in whether they were safe.

With no evidence to go on, it's impossible to know of the life Bonnie and Lucy led during the next fourteen months while they were 'missing', but one can guess. Living 'underground', away from the attention of the authorities, relies on a hand-to-mouth existence, funded by cash-in-hand jobs if you are lucky, but more likely, borrowing, begging, stealing, prostitution and sleeping wherever you can: in doorways, under bridges, in squats, on someone's floor, in cheap bed and breakfasts, or in beds with no breakfast. It would have been even more difficult with a baby, but unregistered, unregulated and unscrupulous landlords can be found down the backstreets of any big city, their clientele hearing of their location by word of mouth. These 'landlords' cram as many mattresses into a room as it will hold and charge only a few pounds for the night. They are always full. Not only with runaways, but the short- and long-term homeless, drug addicts, alcoholics, those with mental-health problems and criminals wanted by the police – of all ages and both sexes. Such places are health hazards and are often responsible for passing on infections; for example, tuberculosis. With no fire escapes they can also be death traps. But if you are avoiding the authorities as Bonnie was, you are unable to obtain benefit money without risk of being discovered.

When Bonnie and Lucy reappeared, fourteen months later, it was in the Accident and Emergency department of a hospital two counties away. It was a Friday afternoon and they were both suffering from highly inflamed rashes that covered large areas of their bodies. They were diagnosed as having scabies. Scabies is caused by parasites burrowing under the skin and laying their eggs. It is most commonly found in those living in overcrowded conditions with poor hygiene. The irritation caused by the infestation is unbearable and most sufferers go to their doctor in the early stages of the disease. The doctor at the hospital noted that these cases were very severe, especially in the child, and had clearly been left untreated for some time, causing the child a lot of distress. The doctor prescribed a lotion, which had to be applied after a bath from the neck down to the toes, left on overnight and then washed off. He explained to Bonnie that a second treatment would be needed a week after the first and told her to go to her own doctor to get the prescription for it and also to have their condition checked. He was concerned that some of the child's sores were becoming infected, so he also prescribed an antibiotic cream. He explained that scabies was highly contagious and all clothing, bedding and towels used by them must be washed in very hot water and dried in a hot dryer to prevent another infestation. When registering at the hospital, Bonnie had given her address as the flat she'd lived in near her Aunt Maggie and her doctor as the one she'd seen when she'd first arrived at Maggie's. It is unknown if Bonnie took Lucy to a doctor for a follow-up appointment; she certainly didn't go to that doctor.

Bonnie and Lucy then disappeared again and reappeared when Lucy was nearly three years old. Bonnie was now living with a man in his thirties called Freddie – and using his surname for her and Lucy. She registered Lucy at a nursery so she could start just after her third birthday, and two nursery teachers made a home visit prior to Lucy starting. These home visits are normal practice in England; they are informal, last about half an hour and give the mother and child a chance to meet the nursery teachers and ask any questions. However, these two teachers were very worried by what they found, especially as their visit had been pre-arranged and was therefore expected. The one-bedroom flat was dirty, smelly and cluttered with bits of car engines, empty beer bottles, plastic fizzy-drink bottles, old pizza boxes and empty crisp packets, all of which Lucy was encouraged to play with in the absence of any children's toys. There were no beds: Lucy slept with her mother and Freddie under blankets on mattresses on the bedroom floor; none of the rooms in the flat had carpets or curtains. There was a used cat-litter tray in the kitchen, which was badly in need of emptying, and the kitchen and bathroom were filthy. The nursery teachers also later noted that the flat reeked of stale beer, cigarette smoke and a slightly sweet smell, which could have been cannabis.

During their conversation, Bonnie admitted that she was struggling to cope and, far from being supportive, Freddie – who wasn't present – spent most of his unemployment money on betting, so they never had enough to eat or pay the bills. They were behind with the rent and the landlord was threatening to evict them. Bonnie told the nursery teachers that she and Freddie often argued and he sometimes hit her – in front of Lucy. The teachers noted that Lucy was grubby, small for her age and afraid of strangers. They couldn't say much about her development from their visit as she hid behind the sofa all the time they were there. When one of them tried to coax her out, she screwed her eyes shut and screamed. Bonnie said they should just leave her there as she was scared of strangers because of some bad experiences they'd had, although she didn't say what these experiences were. Bonnie also said she hoped Lucy would learn to be less frightened of strangers when she went to nursery and 'met some nice people'.

The nursery teachers were with Bonnie for over an hour and when they returned to the nursery they immediately held a meeting with their head teacher to report their concerns. The head teacher contacted the social services and two days later a social worker telephoned Bonnie and made an appointment to visit her the following day. Although Bonnie knew in advance that the social worker was visiting (as she had with the nursery teachers), she made no attempt to clean the flat, so it was in much the same condition as the teachers had reported. Freddie was there when the social worker arrived but left straight away, pushing past her in the hall without saying hello.

Bonnie admitted to the social worker that she wasn't coping and said she felt very low and thought she was suffering from depression, although she hadn't been to a doctor. The social worker explained to Bonnie that there were concerns about Lucy and tried to persuade Bonnie to see a doctor for her depression. They then discussed various options with regard to Lucy's care. She was relieved that Bonnie was cooperative and quickly agreed that it would be best if Lucy went into care temporarily as an 'accommodated child' (under Section 20 of the Children Act). Often referred to as a 'Section 20', this is a voluntary arrangement between the social services and the parent(s) of a child who agree to the child living with a foster carer for a short time. The parent(s) retain full legal parental rights, which they wouldn't do under any other care order. Approximately a third of children in foster care are 'accommodated'. There is no court order and the arrangement should encourage a better working relationship between the social worker, the parent(s) and the foster carer. The parent(s) feel less

threatened as they retain legal control of their child, have regular and unsupervised contact and can remove the child from
foster care at any time. It is supposed to be a short-term measure
and should never be used when a child is in danger of being
abused; only when there is a good chance of the child being
rehabilitated back to live with the parent(s) within a reasonable
period.

Having gained Bonnie's consent, the social worker returned
to her office and set about finding a suitable foster carer for
Lucy. Annie was identified: she was married, with two young
girls of her own, and had been fostering for eighteen months.
Under a Section 20 the parents know where the foster carer lives
and can go with the social worker to the carer's home when the
child is placed, and so it was with Bonnie.

It was a hot day in late August when Bonnie and Lucy arrived
in the social worker's car. Bonnie carried Lucy into Annie's hall-
way. Lucy had her head buried in her mother's shoulder and
was wearing a little pink cotton dress and plastic jelly sandals
and was sucking on a grubby rag as a comforter. Bonnie, slightly
built, with her hair in a ponytail, was dressed in jeans, T-shirt
and badly worn plimsolls. She looked tired and very anxious.
Looped over her arm was a supermarket carrier bag containing
Lucy's clothes.

Straight away Annie set about making Bonnie and Lucy feel
welcome. She showed them into her living room, made them
cold drinks and introduced them to her children, who were off
school for the summer holiday. They talked for a while, with
her and the social worker doing most of the talking, and then
she showed them around the house. Bonnie marvelled at how
nice Annie's house was, and Annie felt sorry for her – she
formed the impression that Bonnie hadn't been in many decent

homes, as hers was average and no different from many others. All this time Lucy wouldn't be put down and when they returned to the living room she again sat on her mother's lap with her face buried in her chest. Annie asked Bonnie about Lucy's likes and dislikes and her routine, explaining that the more information she had about Lucy the easier it would be to settle her. Bonnie said that Lucy ate 'anything really' and went to bed and got up when she felt like it. Annie then asked if Lucy had a favourite toy – one she liked to take to bed – and Bonnie said, 'Just that,' referring to the frayed and dirty rag Lucy was sucking on.

Bonnie and the social worker stayed for an hour and during that time Lucy didn't say a word or leave her mother's lap. Despite a lot of encouragement from Annie and her two girls, Lucy sat facing her mother, refusing to look at anyone. Even when Annie's two girls suggested they could all play in the garden and maybe Lucy would like an ice cream, she didn't look at them. Bonnie told Annie, as she had the social worker and nursery teachers, that following 'some bad experiences' Lucy was afraid of strangers, although she didn't elaborate.

Eventually the social worker said they should leave so that Annie could settle Lucy. Annie said she'd phone Bonnie to reassure her that Lucy was all right. Bonnie gave Lucy a quick kiss on the top of her head and said: 'Mummy has to go.' Standing, she placed Lucy on Annie's lap and ran down the hall and out of the front door. Lucy immediately began screaming. Rigid with fear, she gripped Annie's blouse and buried her head in Annie's chest.

Concerned for Bonnie's safety and having promised to take her home in her car, the social worker said a quick goodbye and went after Bonnie. She later noted that Lucy's screaming was so loud it could be heard outside. There was no sign of Bonnie in the street, so she got into her car and returned to the office, intending to phone Bonnie later.

Inside the house, Annie was sitting on the sofa with her arms around Lucy, rocking her gently and quietly, talking to her, trying to reassure her as well as her own children, who were very worried at seeing a child so upset. It took half an hour to calm Lucy sufficiently so that Annie could persuade her to relax her grip a little and raise her head so Annie could wipe away her tears. As she did, Annie saw Lucy's face properly for the first time. With her petite features, porcelain skin, black silky hair and large dark eyes she was like a little doll; a truly beautiful child, but one who was clearly very scared. Annie also noticed what looked like a bruise on Lucy's cheek, just below her left eye, which she would mention in her log notes when she wrote them up later. All foster carers have to keep log notes. This is a daily record of the child or children they are looking after and includes appointments the child has, the child's health and well-being, significant events and any disclosures the child may make about their past. When the child leaves the foster carer, this record is placed on file at the social services and can be looked at by the child when they are an adult.

Lucy didn't speak at all that evening, refused all food and drink and cried so much at bedtime that Annie had to sleep on the floor in Lucy's room, holding her hand and continuously reassuring her. The following two days were little better; Lucy didn't speak or eat, cried incessantly and kept taking refuge behind the sofa, although after a lot of persuasion Annie did manage to get her to come out and drink some milk. Too frightened to tell anyone she needed the toilet, unsurprisingly Lucy kept soiling herself and Annie was constantly mopping up with a bucket of hot water and disinfectant, especially behind the sofa where Lucy would run and hide. When Annie telephoned Bonnie each evening, not wanting to worry her, she told her that Lucy missed her but was gradually settling in. It was difficult to know if Lucy was so upset because she was missing her mother. She didn't ask for her or say 'mummy'; she just seemed petrified of everyone and everything.

Annie wrote in her log notes that it was three days before Lucy ate anything, and then it was a yoghurt. She also stated that Lucy screamed hysterically when Annie's support social worker visited, when Annie's husband returned from work, when the postman rang the doorbell and when a friend of Annie's stopped by in the evening. It was clear (as Bonnie had said) that Lucy must indeed have had some bad experiences with strangers to make her so scared. As well as noting the bruise on Lucy's cheek in her log notes, Annie also mentioned it to the social worker. She subsequently asked Bonnie how Lucy had got the bruise and Bonnie replied that Lucy had tripped and fallen at the flat the day before. Perhaps she had. There was no way to know.

It soon became clear to Annie that Lucy wasn't used to a routine of any sort, so Annie began establishing one, explaining to Lucy why it was important that we wash, brush our teeth each morning and evening and eat regular meals. On day five Annie introduced bath time into Lucy's evening routine, and although Lucy shied away from the bath to begin with – as Annie turned on the taps and ran the water – after a lot of persuading and cajoling Lucy climbed in. Once she was in and felt the warm water lapping around her she began to relax and then actually enjoyed her bath, playing with the bath toys that Annie provided, while Annie washed her hair, which was very dirty. By the end of that first week Lucy had begun responding slightly more to Annie and her family, saying the odd word, pointing to what she wanted and answering their questions with a nod or a shake of her head, pretty much as a one-year-old child would.

Annie desperately needed to go shopping to buy clothes for Lucy as hardly anything in the carrier bag that Bonnie had brought with her was usable. Annie was dressing Lucy in the clothes she kept for emergency placements, but she wanted to buy new things so Lucy would have clothes of her own. However, she knew from her foster-carer training that, as a deprived child, Lucy shouldn't be subjected to too many new experiences all at once, as she would panic and it could set back her recovery. On day eight, just over a week after Lucy had arrived, when she was crying less and letting the girls take her by the hand and spend a little time playing in the back garden, Annie decided to risk taking her shopping. She explained to Lucy where they were going and why and Lucy nodded in response. But once in the shopping centre, Lucy was so scared of all the people, noise and lights that she wouldn't let Annie put her down and had to be carried everywhere. Annie kept their shopping trip short and just bought the essentials. Later Annie noted that Lucy's life seemed to have been so confined and limited that even a routine shopping trip scared her, and she wondered if Lucy had ever been shopping before.

Gradually, over the coming days, weeks and then months, Annie introduced Lucy to new experiences: playing in the park and feeding the ducks, for example; as well as slowly getting her used to meeting people – Annie's extended family, friends and other children. To begin with Lucy had no idea how to play or interact with other children, presumably because she'd never mixed. Any thoughts of nursery were put on hold as Lucy would never have coped, so Annie began taking her to a mother-and-toddler group two afternoons a week where Annie stayed while Lucy slowly found the confidence to leave her lap and tentatively play with the other children. Although the children were much younger than Lucy, Lucy was so far behind in her development that she could relate to them a little, rather than to children her own age.

Annie had registered Lucy at her doctor's and Lucy subsequently had a medical, and also a developmental check-up. Physically, Lucy was small for her age – probably as a result of poor nutrition – but equally worrying was that she had a vocabulary of only ten words, a milestone usually reached by a child at eighteen months. However, the good news was that the tests appeared to show Lucy had normal intelligence, so it was hoped that with a lot of help she would eventually be able to catch up with her peers. Speech therapy was suggested and Lucy was put on the waiting list. At home, Annie continued with the work she'd already begun to develop Lucy's skills, experiences and language – through play and by talking to her and encouraging her to talk back. It is to Annie's credit that Lucy improved as much as she did during the time she was with her.

Lucy's new doctor applied for Lucy's medical notes, but all that came back was the record of the visit Bonnie and Lucy had made to Maggie's doctor. Their visit to the Accident and Emergency department at the hospital didn't show up, presumably because of the way visits were logged and recorded at that time. Also, there was no record of Lucy having had any of her infant vaccinations, and when Bonnie was asked if she'd had them she said she couldn't remember. So, with Bonnie's consent, over the next six months Annie took Lucy to the clinic for the vaccinations she should have had as a baby.

Annie had been telephoning Bonnie every evening to reassure her that Lucy was all right, and if she didn't answer – which was often – she left a message for her. After a few weeks the social worker told Annie she should stop, as the emphasis was on Bonnie telephoning Annie to find out how her daughter was doing – it would be seen as an indication of her level of commitment and how serious she was in wanting her daughter back. Annie did as she was told and Bonnie fell into the pattern of phoning once a week and visiting Lucy about once every ten days. Bonnie usually stayed for a whole morning or afternoon and never wanted to take Lucy out, even when the weather was good. Bonnie seemed to enjoy the comforts of Annie's home and being looked after as much as Lucy. Annie formed the impression that Bonnie wasn't a vicious or uncaring mother, but had had such a bad start in life herself and now had so many problems of her own that she struggled to look after a child. Annie also noted that sometimes she thought she could smell cannabis on Bonnie's clothes when she came into the house, but obviously she didn't know if Bonnie was a user or not.

Lucy improved dramatically in the eight months she lived with Annie and her family. She gradually lost her fear of strangers, began playing and talking more, and was starting to catch up with her peer group. Annie took lots of photographs of Lucy during this time and some of the most poignant are of Lucy's third birthday and her first proper Christmas, where the look of astonishment and sheer joy on her face says it all. She was clearly overwhelmed, having never experienced anything like it before. Annie also took photographs of Bonnie and Lucy together, some of which she framed and put in Lucy's room, to keep the memory of her mother alive between visits. She gave Bonnie copies of the photographs and Bonnie thanked her profusely. She was really touched, having never had a photograph of her daughter before; she'd never been able to afford a camera. Lucy clearly became very secure and settled with Annie and began calling her mummy, although Annie always corrected her and said: 'I'm Annie. You'll be seeing mummy next Tuesday' – or whenever it was she would be seeing her, and pointed to Bonnie's photograph.

Although Annie and her family knew that Lucy's stay was likely to be temporary on a Section 20, and that once Bonnie had sorted out her life she would want her daughter back, Annie had reasonably assumed that the transition to return Lucy to her mother would be gradual. Bonnie would visit more often and then take her daughter home for short periods that would eventually include overnight stays and finally lead to a move home. This is how a planned move should be done for any child in care to minimize disruption and confusion for the child.

It therefore came as a great shock when, in the middle of one morning when Lucy had been with Annie for just over eight months, Annie answered the telephone to Bonnie who told her she would be coming to take Lucy that afternoon. Bonnie said she now had a new partner – Dave – who treated her right, and they wanted to be together as a family. Annie was shocked, upset and very concerned about the effect a sudden move would have on Lucy. She tried to persuade Bonnie that they should speak to the social worker and arrange a more gradual move – for Lucy's sake. But Bonnie was adamant and knew her rights. She said she'd already told the social worker that she and Dave would be coming for Lucy that afternoon, and asked Annie to have Lucy ready by one o'clock. As soon as Bonnie hung up Annie called the social worker, who confirmed that Bonnie had telephoned her and that, although she would have preferred a gradual reintroduction, as Lucy was placed under a Section 20 Bonnie was free to take Lucy whenever she wanted to. She added that Bonnie had given her their new address and she would be visiting them to make sure all was well. If she had any concerns, Lucy would be brought back into care – preferably with Bonnie's agreement, but if necessary with a court order. This reassured Annie a little, but not much.

With a very heavy heart, fighting back tears and trying to put on a brave face for Lucy's sake, Annie used the little time they had left together to try and prepare Lucy for going to live with her mother and Dave, as well as packing all Lucy's clothes and toys, of which there were now many. Lucy became very quiet and withdrawn, refused lunch and then asked Annie why she had to go. When Annie explained that her mummy loved her and she wanted her to live with her in her new home Lucy said: 'Can't Mummy come and live here with us?'

Clearly that wasn't possible and it was very difficult to try and explain this, and why she was suddenly having to leave, to a small child. Annie then spent the next hour cuddling Lucy on her lap and reading her stories to try to distract her until the doorbell rang at one o'clock. Lucy went with Annie to answer the door. Bonnie was in the porch, and parked outside was an old white van with its engine running and a man – presumably Dave – waiting in the driver's seat.

'Come and meet your new daddy,' Bonnie said, taking Lucy by the hand.

Giving Annie and Lucy no chance to say goodbye, Bonnie hurried Lucy down the path towards the van. She put Lucy in the front and slammed the door shut. She then returned for Lucy's belongings, which Annie had ready in bags and boxes in the hall. Without any thanks for all Annie had done or a promise to stay in touch and let Annie know how Lucy was, Bonnie began loading the van. Annie helped her. The rear of the van contained decorating materials, so Annie assumed Dave was a painter and decorator. He didn't turn or say hello.

Once all Lucy's belongings were in the van, Bonnie shut the rear door while Dave stayed in the van. Bonnie said a terse goodbye to Annie and climbed into the front of the van next to Lucy. Lucy was small, and, as she was sandwiched between the adults, Annie couldn't see her from the pavement, but she waved anyway. With Lucy now gone, there was no need for Annie to put on a brave face any longer and by the time she reached her front door she was crying openly. Not only for the uncertainty that Lucy faced, but for her own loss and that of her family, who would come home and find Lucy gone, having not been able to say goodbye.

Chapter Eight

A Good Friend

Mrs Bridges stood at the front of her class of six-year-olds and waited for them to finish packing away their worksheets before dismissing them for morning break. It was mid-September and two weeks into the new school term, before the coughs and colds had taken hold, so none of the children was absent. Thirty boys and girls, seated around five tables, were looking back at her and still smart in their new school uniforms. Some, though, looked smarter than others, for even behind the school uniforms it was obvious to Mrs Bridges – as it was to the other children in the class – who came from comfortably well-off, nurturing families and who did not. A second-hand uniform that accumulated a week's stains before it was washed; cheap plastic shoes that tore rather than scuffed; hair that was long, matted or unevenly short from a home cutting; and faces that were slightly grimy from missing the morning wash. But it wasn't only appearance that singled out a child from an impoverished home; it was the personality of the child too – either loud and attention-seeking or quiet and withdrawn. Mrs Bridges's gaze fell upon the table to her left and two of the children who sat there: Sammy and Lucy, who had joined the school last year within a week of each other and were now inseparable.

'Off you go then,' Mrs Bridges said, dismissing the class for morning break.

The usual clamour of excited voices rose as chairs scraped back and children jostled each other out of the classroom, eager to make the most of every moment in the playground. All the children except one, who having put his chair under the table remained standing behind it.

Mrs Bridges smiled at Sammy. 'I haven't got any jobs for you to do this morning,' she said kindly. 'Go and join your friends in the playground and get some fresh air. It's a nice day.'

Jabbing his hands into his trouser pockets, Sammy came out from behind the table and took a couple of steps towards his teacher. 'I will, Miss, but can I talk to you first please?'

Mrs Bridges paused from collecting the worksheets and looked at him. She always made time for Sammy. He was a thin lad with a shaved head, and as the eldest of five children in a one-parent family he had far more responsibility than he could cope with. His frustrations got the better of him sometimes, when he vented his anger in the classroom, but underneath he was a kind lad. The social services were involved with his family and had put in support to try and keep them together, but it wasn't looking very hopeful.

'Of course you can talk to me. How's your mum doing?' Mrs Bridges asked.

Sammy gave a small dismissive shrug. 'All right, I guess. But it's not me I want to talk about.'

'No?'

He perched on the edge of the table, his face fixed and serious. 'It's about Lucy, Miss.'

'Your friend Lucy, in this class?' Mrs Bridges clarified.

'Yes, Miss. She needs to tell you herself. I've told her she has to. But she can't, she's too shy.'

A Good Friend

'Tell me what?' Mrs Bridges said, setting aside the papers to give Sammy her full attention. As an experienced teacher she'd developed a sixth sense for knowing when a child was just telling tales or about to tell her something important.

'Lucy's being bullied, Miss. Some of the kids call her "smelly" and "nit head", but it ain't her fault. At her house she has to wash her clothes in cold water. And her aunt won't get her the stuff she needs to kill the nits 'cos it costs too much. I told her if she goes to the doctor you get it for nothing, like we do. But she won't. Can you tell her, please?'

Mrs Bridges looked at Sammy carefully, trying to identify which part of what he'd said had set alarm bells ringing. She knew Lucy often came to school smelling and wearing badly stained clothes, and that she was sometimes picked on by the other children. She kept a lookout for this and severely reprimanded anyone she caught name-calling – bullying was never tolerated. Mrs Bridges also thought Lucy probably had head lice; her long hair was unkempt and she often saw her scratching her head in class. In line with school practice, she'd sent a printed note home with each child asking the parents to check their child's hair and treat it if necessary. All this she knew, but what had set off alarm bells was Sammy's reference to Lucy's aunt and having to wash her clothes in cold water.

'I thought Lucy was living with her mother and stepfather?' Mrs Bridges now asked. Often the children who lived on the estate knew more about family arrangements than the school did.

Sammy shook his head. 'Nah, Miss. Not for a long time. Her mum went off with some bloke and her dad's got himself a new girlfriend.'

'And the girlfriend is the aunt you're talking about?'

'Yes, Miss. Lucy has to call her Aunt, and do all the washing. I told Lucy her bleedin' aunt should be doing the washing, not giving it to a six-year-old to do. Excuse me language, Miss.'

Mrs Bridges stifled a small smile. Despite Sammy's rough-and-ready nature, he was a real character and always polite. 'And Lucy told you this?'

'Yes, Miss.'

'Has she told you anything else about her home life you think I should know?'

The boy scratched his head thoughtfully, making Mrs Bridges wonder if he too had nits.

'Not really, Miss. Only that she hasn't seen her mum for ages and her aunt doesn't like her. You know Lucy, Miss, she don't say much. She keeps things bottled up. Not like me. I tell ya when things are bad at home. So I was thinking that as Lucy told me this it must be very bad, 'cos kids like her don't tell unless they really have to, do they, Miss?'

'No, you're right, Sammy. Thank you. I'll speak to Lucy later.'

In the hour and a half of lesson time between the end of morning break and lunchtime, as well as continuing with the class's project, Mrs Bridges gave the whole class a lecture on the unkindness of bullying. She said that everyone deserved to be treated with dignity and respect, and that anyone caught bullying would lose privileges for a whole week and their parents would be informed. As she spoke, she purposely kept her gaze away from Sammy and Lucy so the other children in the class wouldn't be alerted to the identity of those who'd sparked the lecture, as this could have led to more bullying and accusations of 'telling'.

A Good Friend

At 12.30 p.m. Mrs Bridges dismissed the class for lunch, but asked Lucy to wait behind for a moment. 'It's all right, love, you haven't done anything wrong,' she added, for Lucy always looked as though she expected to be told off. 'I just want to have a chat with you, that's all.'

She waited until the last child had left the classroom and then closed the classroom door so they wouldn't be overheard. 'Let's sit down,' she said, pulling out two children's chairs from under the table. She found that if she was sitting it helped the child relax and invited confidences.

Still looking very serious, Lucy sat on one of the chairs, while Mrs Bridges took the other. 'Sammy is a good friend of yours, isn't he?' she began.

Lucy gave a small nod, her large dark eyes growing rounder. She was an attractive child, though small for her age and, like Sammy, always looked as though she could do with a good wash and generally more nurturing.

'Did Sammy tell you he came to me this morning because he was worried about you?' Mrs Bridges asked.

Lucy nodded again.

'He says you're living with your stepfather and a lady you call Aunt? Is that right?'

She gave another small nod.

'Is everything all right at home?' Mrs Bridges now asked.

Lucy gave a little shrug and then said quietly, 'I guess so.'

'You don't sound very sure, love,' Mrs Bridges said.

Another shrug, and then Lucy shook her head, which was enough for Mrs Bridges to continue. 'Tell me what makes you happy and what makes you unhappy,' Mrs Bridges prompted. 'What do you like to do in the evenings and weekends?'

'I like to play, Miss,' Lucy said softly.

'What do you like to play?'

'I watch television, Miss, and sometimes I play outside with Sammy and his sisters, if I've been good.'

'That sounds fun. What do you have to do to be good?' Mrs Bridges now asked, for she couldn't imagine Lucy being anything but good, she was so quiet and conforming.

She gave another shrug and then said: 'I have to wash the dishes and clean the flat, then I can play out.'

'And how often do you do that?' Mrs Bridges asked, with a reassuring smile. Many children had chores to do, which was fine, as long as they weren't excessive.

'I don't know how often, Miss,' Lucy said, with a worried expression. 'Every day, I think.'

'All right, love. It's nothing to worry about. I'm just trying to get a picture of your life at home. Who makes the meals in your house?'

A pause, then: 'My aunt and Dad, I guess.'

'And who washes the clothes?'

There was a long pause as Lucy's gaze fell from Mrs Bridges and she concentrated on the floor. 'The same, I think. I don't know.'

Clearly the child was being very guarded in what she said, possibly fearing recrimination if she told and was found out.

'All right, don't worry. Have you seen your mum recently?'

Lucy shook her head. 'She sent me a card for my birthday, but I didn't see her.' Lucy had had a birthday the week before and as usual when a child in the class celebrated a birthday all the children had sung 'Happy Birthday'; what other celebrations had taken place that evening for Lucy at home Mrs Bridges didn't know. Most children told her, but Lucy hadn't.

'Did you have a nice birthday?'

Lucy shrugged.

A Good Friend

'Did you get some presents?'

'I think so.'

'But you're not sure?'

'No.'

Mrs Bridges continued to look at Lucy as she stared at the floor. All her senses screamed that there was a big problem at home and the child was too frightened to say. But she needed something concrete to take to the headmaster, which he could then act on. Lucy's evasiveness was making this difficult. Sammy was right when he'd said that Lucy didn't say much; she'd hardly spoken a word to Mrs Bridges all term, and it seemed she couldn't talk to her now.

'If you could change anything at home, what would it be?' Mrs Bridges asked, making one last attempt before Lucy had to go for her lunch. 'I know it's a difficult question, but can you think of anything you'd change? If I was asked, I'd say I'd like to see more of my sister.'

Lucy looked thoughtful for a moment and then, raising her eyes to meet Mrs Bridges's, she said: 'I'd like to live in Sammy's family, Miss.'

'Would you?' Mrs Bridges asked, surprised. Sammy's family was about as far removed from the ideal family as you could get. 'Why's that?'

Lucy took a moment before replying and then said: 'They've got a social worker. She helps Sammy. I would like a social worker to help me.'

'Can I have a word with you, please?' Mrs Bridges said, giving a perfunctory knock on the door to the headmaster's office as she entered. The head operated an 'open-door policy' – to staff and pupils – so that, to his credit, he was accessible most of the time, and also knew the names of all the children in his school.

'Have a seat,' he said, waving to the easy chair at the side of his desk. 'What can I do for you on this beautiful autumn day?'

Mrs Bridges smiled as she sat in the chair. Some of the staff found his effusive manner irritating, but she found it quite refreshing after the dourness of their previous head. And he had the children's best interests at heart.

'Lucy, in my class,' Mrs Bridges began. 'Her friend Sammy came to me this morning at break very worried about Lucy.'

'Oh, yes?' The head frowned and drew his fingertips together under his chin in a characteristic gesture.

'He said Lucy was being bullied, which I've dealt with, but he's also worried that the woman Lucy is living with – her step-father's girlfriend – isn't treating her well. I've spoken to Lucy. She's not saying much, but she did say that if she could change anything in her life she'd like to live with Sammy and have a social worker, which concerns me. I was wondering what we knew about Lucy's home life. Mum seems to have left a while back.'

'That's news to me,' the head said with another frown, lowering his hands. 'There were some concerns last year when Lucy first started at this school, but as far as I know the problems were sorted. Although I'm sure her mother was living there then. Who brings Lucy into school and collects her?'

'She comes with a neighbour and her child. She usually brings Sammy and his younger brother as well.'

'I see. So we haven't met the aunt?'

'No.'

The head looked thoughtful. 'Leave it with me. I'll check the records and get back to you. I take it Lucy's not in any immediate danger?'

'I don't think so. I've never seen any marks on her, although she's far too quiet for my liking.'

The head nodded. 'That was one of the comments raised by her teacher last year. Pity she's left – you could have had a chat with her. Anyway, give me a couple of hours and I'll look into it.'

Thanking the headmaster, Mrs Bridges left to eat a very quick sandwich before the class returned after lunch for the afternoon session.

All schools in England have a set procedure for reporting concerns about a child, and members of staff have to follow them. Mrs Bridges couldn't simply pick up the telephone and call the social services; she had to pass her concerns to her line manager, who in her school was the headmaster, and he would take the necessary action. Despite all his other responsibilities, the headmaster always prioritized any matter relating to a child's welfare, so by the end of that day he had checked their records, contacted the social services and updated Mrs Bridges. It seems that although there had been some concerns about Lucy's welfare the previous year they were around inadequate parenting rather than child abuse or neglect. A social worker had visited Lucy's mother and stepfather, Dave, and no further action had been taken, other than advising Lucy's mother and stepfather to enrol in some parenting classes to improve their parenting skills. Whether they had done this the school didn't know, nor if any follow-up visit had been made by the social services, but the file was closed at the time. Following the new concerns and the headmaster's phone call to the social services, the file was reopened and the head told Mrs Bridges that a social worker would be visiting Lucy's home within the next few days. In the interim, he asked Mrs Bridges to prepare a short report covering Lucy's educational and social development, as well as the concerns that had been raised.

* * *

Will You Love Me?

On the Monday morning of the following week, when Lucy came into school, Mrs Bridges noticed that she looked very downcast, more so than usual, so at morning break she asked Lucy if there was anything worrying her. Lucy shook her head and went out into the playground. Mrs Bridges tried again at lunch break, but Lucy said: 'No, Miss. Nothing's wrong. I'm fine,' and ran off to lunch.

Lucy looked anything but fine, and during the afternoon Mrs Bridges thought she was close to tears. At the end of the day, when she dismissed the class at home time, she asked Sammy if she could have a word with him. She asked him if Lucy was all right. Sammy, always willing to share his thoughts and worries, shook his head adamantly and said: 'No, Miss. Lucy certainly ain't all right. She's very upset. A social worker went to see her, Friday I think it was, Miss. After she'd gone, that wicked aunt and Dad yelled at Lucy for causing trouble. She's right scared. She won't be talking to you again, Miss.'

Chapter Nine

'I Hate You All!'

'It appears it was handled very insensitively,' the headmaster said, when Mrs Bridges told him what had happened. 'Do you think it would help if I talked to Lucy?'

'To be honest, I think it might make matters worse,' Mrs Bridges said. 'Lucy told Sammy that I mustn't say anything more about her to anyone, and to forget what she'd already said, or she'll run away.'

The head nodded. 'I'll be guided by you. I'll phone the social services and find out exactly what happened when the social worker visited, and also what steps they're taking to safeguard Lucy. Did she say anything else to Sammy about the visit?'

'If she did, he's not telling me.'

It was two days before the head managed to have a conversation with the social worker who'd visited Lucy, and afterwards he told Mrs Bridges what he'd learnt.

'The social worker said that Lucy's home was reasonably clean and her aunt and stepfather were cooperative and polite. In fact, she said that the aunt had been more cooperative and open to suggestions than Lucy's mother had been the year before. When the social worker explained what Lucy had told

Sammy and yourself,' the head continued, 'the aunt was shocked and said she had no idea Lucy felt that way or that she had head lice, and blamed herself for not noticing her scratching. She said she'd buy the lotion immediately. She showed the social worker around their house. Lucy has her own bedroom, where there were some toys and clothes in the wardrobe. There was also food in the fridge and a washing machine in the kitchen.'

'Just because there's a washing machine doesn't mean it's being used,' Mrs Bridges put in, unable to hide her frustration any longer.

'I know,' the head said. 'But I can only tell you what the social worker has reported. I can't tell her how to do her job.'

Mrs Bridges gave an apologetic nod and the head continued: 'The aunt said she does most of the cooking, although she admitted that Lucy doesn't have a very good appetite and sometimes prefers a sandwich to a cooked meal. The social worker said the aunt came over as genuine and caring of Lucy.'

'So why would Lucy make up these allegations and say she would rather live with Sammy if they're not true?'

'The aunt said it was very likely because Lucy resents her role as mother. Lucy obviously wants her own mother back, but that's not possible. She's cleared off and no one knows where she's gone. The stepfather said he was very grateful to his girl-friend for taking on the responsibility of looking after Lucy, because he couldn't have coped alone, so if she hadn't Lucy would have had to go into care.'

She might have been better off in care, Mrs Bridges thought but didn't say, and she didn't share the social worker's confidence that the aunt was acting in Lucy's best interest. A gut feeling said that Lucy wasn't being looked after and that the aunt was manipulative and possibly also a liar. 'So, what action are the social services taking to safeguard Lucy?' Mrs Bridges now asked the head.

'They're going to make a follow-up visit in a week or so, although there are no real concerns. The aunt said she thought it would take time for Lucy to accept her as a stepmother, which of course sounds reasonable.'

Mrs Bridges held the headmaster's gaze thoughtfully. 'I suppose it's possible that Lucy resents this new woman ...' she began. 'But ... Did the social worker speak to Lucy alone – separate from the aunt and stepfather?'

'I don't know,' the head said. 'But I think we have to accept the social services' findings, although I agree it could have been handled more sensitively. You'll keep an eye on Lucy, and if you have any more concerns we'll act on them straight away.'

Mrs Bridges nodded, thanked the headmaster and left him to attend to his other business. It was all they could do.

The following morning Lucy's aunt brought her into school. Lucy looked cleaner than she had done since the start of term: her hair was freshly washed and tied back neatly into a ponytail and her clothes were stain free. At the end of the day, Mrs Bridges stood in the playground dispensing children to the adults responsible for collecting them, and Lucy's aunt approached her.

'Nice to meet you at last,' she said, smiling. 'Sorry about the misunderstanding. Lucy and I have had a chat and we're getting along much better now.'

Mrs Bridges smiled and nodded, although, apart from looking cleaner, Lucy had been no less withdrawn that day and hadn't seemed much happier. Lucy's aunt was in her early thirties, with blonde hair, and was dressed in tight black leggings, knee-length boots and an imitation leather jacket.

'Let me know if I can help Lucy with her school work,' the aunt offered.

'You could hear her read each evening to help her catch up,' Mrs Bridges suggested. 'And also give her some help with her weekend homework.'

'Sure will,' the aunt said enthusiastically, and went to take Lucy's hand.

Mrs Bridges noticed that Lucy shied away and refused to take her aunt's hand, and then walked some distance behind her as they left the playground.

What impression Mrs Bridges formed of Lucy's aunt wasn't noted in the records. However, what *was* noted was that the improvement in Lucy's appearance lasted for a week and then quickly tailed off. Two weeks later Lucy was again coming into school looking unkempt and uncared for, and she remained quiet and withdrawn in class.

A month later – at the end of October – the class was preparing for Halloween. The children were cutting out silhouettes of ghouls and witches to stick on a wall frieze when Sammy casually remarked to Mrs Bridges: 'At least Lucy's witch has gone. Flown off on her broomstick. Hope she falls off.'

Mrs Bridges paused from cutting out to look at Sammy. 'Lucy's aunt has left?' she asked him quietly, so none of the other children could hear.

'Yes, Miss. Good riddance, I say.'

'So who's looking after Lucy now?'

'Her dad.'

'You mean her stepfather, Dave?'

'Yes, Miss. But he's no better than that aunt. Lucy hates him. Pity she can't live with me. I asked me mum but she said we

90

ain't got enough room, and Lucy needed to tell her social worker.'

'Lucy's aunt has gone, and Lucy told Sammy she hates her step-father and wants to live with Sammy,' Mrs Bridges said to the headmaster as soon as he was free. 'And I don't think it's appro-priate for a six-year-old girl to be in the sole care of a stepfather whom she doesn't even like.'

'But what real concerns are there?' the head asked. 'Is Lucy saying he's abusing her?'

'No, she's not saying anything, or if she is Sammy isn't telling me,' Mrs Bridges said a little tersely. 'It's not as though there haven't been concerns before.'

'But they were unproven,' the head said.

There was a pause as Mrs Bridges and the head looked at each other, both deep in thought. Mrs Bridges knew there wasn't enough evidence to action an investigation, but she couldn't just do nothing.

Fortunately, neither could the head. 'I'll speak to the social worker as soon as I have a free moment and explain that Lucy's home situation has changed. I'll suggest they make another home visit.'

'Thank you.'

Two weeks later the headmaster informed Mrs Bridges that a social worker had visited Lucy and her stepfather and that no further action would be taken. A note to this effect was placed on file at the school, and Mrs Bridges couldn't do any more, other than to keep an eye on Lucy as she continued in her role as class teacher; there were, after all, other children in the class apart from Lucy. Two months passed, Christmas came and went, and on the morning the children returned to school most of them were full of the wonderful time they'd had over the holiday and the presents they'd received. But Lucy, as usual, hardly said a word, and when Mrs Bridges asked her if she'd had a nice time at Christmas she replied with a small nod, which could have meant anything. Mrs Bridges knew better than to press Lucy and possibly embarrass her by asking what presents she'd had, for it might have been something very small or perhaps even nothing. However, Sammy, being Sammy, was more forthcoming.

'I got a brand-new bike!' he announced to the class. 'From me mum's new bloke. I've decided he's all right, so I've told me mum he can stay.' Even the class of six-year-olds appreciated Sammy's humour and laughed.

But later that morning, at break time, Sammy hung back as the children filed out of the classroom. 'Can I speak to you, Miss?' he asked. 'In private, please.'

Mrs Bridges waited until the last child had left the classroom and closed the door. She assumed the reason Sammy wanted to speak to her related to worries about his mother's new partner. There was an extrovert side to Sammy, which kept the class entertained, but there was also a much deeper, sensitive side that worried and fretted. He often confided his worries about his mother's new partners to Mrs Bridges. As usual she drew out two school chairs from under the table, and they sat down.

'It's about Lucy, Miss,' Sammy began, immediately serious. 'Don't tell her I told you, but she had a rotten Christmas. Dave brought home his new bird, and I don't mean the turkey sort. He and his woman spent all Christmas day in bed and left Lucy to play outside by herself. I couldn't play out with her, Miss. I was with me family. I mean, you have to spend Christmas with your family, don't ya, Miss?'

'Yes, indeed,' Mrs Bridges said, upset at the thought of Lucy alone and outside on Christmas day. 'It's not your fault, Sammy,' she added, for clearly Sammy felt guilty for not playing with her. 'But you understand that in order to help Lucy I'm going to have to share what you've told me with the headmaster, who will tell the social worker?'

'Yes, Miss, I know. I think you should. Lucy needs looking after. Even my mum says so.'

Mrs Bridges went to the head with what Sammy had told her and he duly contacted the social services, who said they would make a home visit. Following that home visit, it was felt that although the change in care provider – that is, Dave's new girl-friend (also referred to as Lucy's 'aunt') – was unsettling, at least the other caregiver – Dave – had remained constant, which gave Lucy some degree of stability. The decision to take a child into care is never taken lightly and has to be carefully weighed up, possibly leaving a child in a less-than-perfect home environ-ment, rather than placing them in a foster home where they would lose the family they knew and all that was familiar.

A second home visit was scheduled to take place a month later, but the records show that before this happened a fight broke out between Dave and his new girlfriend and the police were called. As soon as the police had gone, the new girlfriend packed her bags and moved out. Dave, a year behind with his rent and having ignored all demands and summons for payment, was then served with a court order giving him notice to leave the property. Dave took Lucy with him to live with his older sister, whose home was twenty miles away, which made it impossible for Lucy to continue to attend the same school. Without prior notice, and therefore giving the class no chance to say goodbye to Lucy, she vanished. The school informed the social services; they traced Dave's sister and a social worker visited. The social worker must have decided that the living arrangements were satisfactory, as no further action was taken at this time.

It was two years before Lucy came to the attention of the social services again. Now aged eight, she was living in the Midlands with her mother and her mother's new boyfriend. One night, a neighbour became so concerned by the adults arguing and throwing things next door that she called the police. When the police entered the flat they found the living-room floor littered with broken items that had been thrown and Lucy cowering under a blanket in a bedroom. The police calmed the adults and, once satisfied that they wouldn't resume their fighting, they left. However, concerned for the child, and following normal procedure, they reported the incident to the social services. Lucy had been using Dave's surname since she'd first been taken to live with him and her details came up on the social services computer system, together with the previous social services involvement. A social worker visited Bonnie and she admitted that she wasn't coping. Why she'd taken Lucy from Dave and his sister isn't known, but she told the social worker that Dave, whom she'd previously encouraged Lucy to look upon as a father and had happily left Lucy with, was a 'no-good piece of shit', and they wouldn't be having anything to do with him again. After some discussion, Bonnie agreed for Lucy to be taken into foster care – under a Section 20.

The foster carer Lucy was sent to live with already had two foster children, a brother and sister who'd been there for nearly three years. It's clear from the records that Lucy struggled to fit into this foster family right from the start. The carer commented that Lucy wasn't a sociable child; didn't make any effort to get along with the other two children; had low self-esteem; rarely smiled or laughed and was 'difficult' – hardly surprising given the momentous upheavals and anxieties that had beset Lucy throughout her short life. It can be hard in any case for a new child to fit into an established household such as this one, and the situation requires a lot of time and patience from the carer. But this carer seems to have labelled Lucy as sullen and uncooperative from the start, with every disagreement between the three children being put down to Lucy's bad temper and lack of cooperation. Whether Lucy was ill-tempered and obstinate or not, the carer's attitude meant that the placement was doomed to fail. Bonnie visited Lucy at the foster home once a week to begin with, then once a month, and then there was nothing for three months.

When Lucy had been with this foster carer for eleven months, the carer gave notice on the placement and asked for Lucy to be moved, citing the negative impact Lucy's presence was having on the other two children. Placement breakdowns, as they are known, happen; sometimes they are unavoidable and a move is in everyone's best interest. However, at other times, if support is given to the foster family, rather than just leaving the carer to get on with it, the placement can be saved and the child does not have to be moved. Whether support would have helped Lucy stay in this placement will never be known, but the result was that Lucy had to pack and leave. This meant another move, more insecurity and another rejection for Lucy in a lifetime of insecurity and rejections.

Lucy was now sent to live with a foster carer five miles away who was a single parent with a daughter the same age as Lucy. When Lucy first arrived the carer commented to her support social worker that Lucy was more like a child just coming into care (from a neglected home), rather than from another carer. She looked unkempt, had head lice and came with very few possessions. The hope is that all foster carers provide a high standard of care for all the children they look after, but sadly this is not always so. Although foster carers are trained and carefully monitored, the standard of care-giving can vary. When the previous carer was questioned by her support social worker, she said she washed Lucy's hair regularly, but Lucy insisted on taking out her plait at school, which made her prone to catching head lice. She also said that she'd bought Lucy lots of things, but when Lucy got angry she broke them. Maybe she did, or maybe she wasn't looked after as well as the other two children.

Lucy's new placement was quite different. Her carer put a lot of effort into making Lucy feel welcome and part of her family. Lucy got along well with the carer's daughter and finally began to smile and play as a child should. Sadly, this was a small oasis of security and happiness in an otherwise vast desert of change and anxiety. Three months later, Bonnie, having been notified of the change in carer (which the social services were obliged to do under a Section 20), said she wanted Lucy back. She was now living in a small rented flat, so she gave the social services her new address and, with a day's notice, took Lucy home with her. The carer said that Lucy hadn't wanted to go but didn't feel she had any choice. Bonnie promised to keep in touch with the carer and meet up, but she never heard from her again.

Bonnie hadn't been able to look after Lucy before and there was no reason to think she could do so now. Nothing had changed in her life apart from a different flat and a new boyfriend. The social services monitored the family for six months and as concerns grew, and the threshold for intervention was reached, Lucy was taken into care. This time it was with a court order and not under a Section 20, which gave the social services more power, and should have given Lucy more security.

The foster carers Lucy was now sent to live with were a married couple who had two teenage children and lived in a comfortable modern house on a new estate on the outskirts of the city. Unfortunately the mother didn't drive and the school Lucy had been attending for the previous six months – when she'd been living with her mother – was over an hour's bus journey away. It was felt that this was too far for a child Lucy's age to travel and that, in any case, Lucy might find it embarrassing to arrive at school with a foster carer when she had previously been seen with her mother. It was therefore decided that a fresh start at a new school would be beneficial, so Lucy was sent to the local primary school. By now, excluding nursery school, Lucy had attended at least six different primary schools in five years. Exactly how many different addresses Lucy had lived at by then is hard to ascertain, but a conservative estimate at the time put it in excess of thirty.

Although Lucy was nearly three years behind with her learning she began to make some progress at this school and also enjoyed a pleasant Christmas with her foster family. However, when Lucy had been living with these carers for five months, the family's fortunes abruptly changed: the factory where the foster father worked gave notice to all its employees that it was having to close. It made the offer that any employee who had been working at the company for over five years could relocate to their other factory – eighty miles north. With unemployment high and jobs scarce, the family understandably felt they should accept the offer to relocate, and they suggested to the social services that Lucy could go with them. Although Lucy was in care under a court order, it was an Interim Care Order, which meant that Lucy's mother still had a say in any decision-making about Lucy. Bonnie had seen Lucy twice during this five-month period, but now invoked her rights and objected to Lucy moving out of the area in case she wanted to see her more often, which would be difficult if Lucy was living so far away. As a result, the family moved and Lucy was moved to another foster home.

The only carer free in the area at that time was a baby carer – that is, she was approved to foster babies up to the age of two. Lucy was placed with her temporarily until a more suitable carer in the area became free. Repeated moves for children in care for reasons like these are all too common and the whole system needs a thorough overhaul to ensure that unnecessary moves are eliminated as much as possible.

Two months after being placed with this carer, Lucy, now eleven, began at the local secondary school – a big enough step in itself without the uncertainty of not knowing where she would be living in a few months' time. Six weeks later a more suitable carer became free in the area and Lucy arrived home from school one afternoon to be told that she would be moving at the weekend. Although Lucy had always known at the back of her mind that she'd have to move again one day, on top of just starting secondary school and the accumulated years of neglect, misery and continuous upheaval, it all became too much. As the carer began explaining to Lucy that her social worker would take her for a visit to meet her new foster carer, Cathy, and her two children, Lucy let out the most blood-curdling scream and then fled upstairs and locked herself in the bathroom – the only room in the house with a lock on the door.

The carer, frightened at the sudden outburst from a child who was usually very placid, quiet and obedient, ran upstairs after her. She then spent over half an hour outside the bathroom door trying to reason with Lucy and persuade her to come out.

'I Hate You All!'

Lucy's sobs grew louder and more disturbing. By the time the carer's husband came home from work, Lucy's hysterical shouts could be heard from outside: 'I hate you all! I'm not going anywhere! I'm going to kill myself!' she cried.

PART TWO

PART TWO

Chapter Ten

'A Family of My Own'

'It's a nightmare,' Jill, my support social worker, said over the phone. 'The carer's husband had to break down the bathroom door to get Lucy out, and she's *still* refusing to speak to anyone.'

'The poor child,' I said. 'You can't blame Lucy for being so upset. Her life has been a misery, more or less from day one. No wonder she's so angry and feels unwanted. No one *has* wanted her.'

'I know. You've read the referral?'

'Yes.' Because Lucy had been coming to me as a planned move, I'd had a chance to read the referral so that I could better understand Lucy and cater for her needs. As well as briefly describing Lucy's strengths and weaknesses, the referral gave a short history of her past. If a child came to me as an emergency foster placement I knew very little about the child, sometimes nothing. 'Yes, I've read the referral,' I said. 'I nearly cried. Lucy deserved so much better. She's been treated dreadfully.'

'Absolutely,' Jill said. 'But the fact remains, she still has to move and at present she's refusing to even visit you, or see her social worker. I'm sure she'd feel a bit better about the move if she could meet you, Adrian and Paula beforehand, see her bedroom and have a look around the house. But we can't force her.' And of course if Lucy was refusing even to meet me, how on earth were they going to move her?

Jill and I were both quiet for a moment and then I said: 'I wonder if Lucy would talk to me on the phone? It would be better than nothing. Is it worth a try?'

'Yes, it's a possibility, I suppose. I'll phone Lucy's social worker and see what she thinks, and then I'll get back to you. If you did phone it would have to be this evening – they're still planning on moving her tomorrow, although I'm not sure how.'

'I'm in all evening,' I confirmed. 'Speak later.'

We said goodbye and hung up. Jill had been my support social worker for the last six of the thirteen years I'd been foster-ing. We had a close working relationship and I respected her decisions and opinions. But as I walked away from the phone, visions of a screaming, struggling eleven-year-old girl being forcibly brought to my door flashed through my mind. I'd expe-rienced younger children being taken from their parents and handed to me in a very distressed state. I'd sat and cuddled them for as long as it took to calm them and until their sobbing eased. Rarely does a child willingly leave their parents – usually only in the worst cases of sexual abuse. But Lucy wasn't little and couldn't just be left in my arms. And also, she wasn't coming to me from her parents, but from a temporary foster placement. I thought it was an indication of all she'd been through that she'd become hysterical at having to move from a family she'd only been with for three months.

It was now 5.00 p.m., and a cold winter evening in February. My two children – Adrian, aged thirteen, and Paula, nine – were watching television while I was making the evening meal. Having grown up with fostering, they'd seen many chil-dren come and go, of all ages, of both sexes and from different ethnic backgrounds. They took any new addition to our family in their stride, and when I'd told them a couple of days ago that Lucy would be coming to stay for a while, Paula had predictably said, 'Oh good, a big girl to play with,' while Adrian, preferring a boy his own age for company, had pulled a face and sighed: 'Not another girl in the house!' Although, in truth, we all welcomed as family any child who came into our home.

Jill, efficient as usual, phoned back fifteen minutes later. 'The social worker was busy so I telephoned Pat, the foster carer,' she said. 'Lucy's still refusing to talk to her and she's certain she won't talk to you either, but Pat said she's happy for you to try. Also, and more worryingly, Lucy is refusing to eat – she hasn't eaten since all this blew up the day before yesterday. I'll give you Pat's number. I told her you'd phone at about seven o'clock. Is that all right?'

'Yes,' I said, now even more worried for Lucy. Picking up the pen I kept with the notepad by the phone, I wrote down the carer's telephone number and then read it back to check I had it right.

'Good luck,' Jill said. 'Pat and her husband were going to move Lucy tomorrow – Saturday – but if she's still not cooperating then they'll have to wait until Monday, when the social worker is back in the office and can sort it out.'

'And what will she do?' I asked.

'No idea. There doesn't appear to be a plan B,' Jill said, trying to lighten an otherwise dire situation.

'The whole thing is so tragic,' I said, my heart going out to Lucy.

'Yes, and the most tragic aspect of Lucy's case is that it needn't have happened,' Jill said. 'Lucy's life could have been so different if someone had made the decision to remove her early on. She could have been adopted. It's too late now. She's too old. The damage has been done.'

Adrian and Paula had been expecting to meet Lucy that Friday evening, just as I had, so once I'd finished speaking to Jill on the phone and before I served dinner, I returned to the living room and explained to Adrian and Paula that Lucy wouldn't be coming for a visit as she was too upset, but that I would phone her carer later and try to talk to Lucy.

'Why doesn't Lucy want to come?' Paula asked. 'Doesn't she like us?'

'She doesn't even know us,' Adrian put in quickly, always ready to correct his younger sister.

'I think she's just had all she can take,' I said. 'She's never had a proper home and she's been treated very badly.'

'Tell her it's OK for her to come here. We won't treat her badly. We'll be kind to her,' Paula said.

I smiled. 'That's nice, love.' If only it was that simple, I thought.

Once we'd eaten and I'd cleared away the dishes, and before I began Paula's bedtime routine, I left Adrian and Paula playing a board game in the living room while I went down the hall to phone Lucy's carers. I needed quiet in order to think what I would say to Lucy if I got the chance, and also I was nervous. Even after many years of fostering, I still get an attack of nerves just before the arrival of a new child, and it's always worse if the move doesn't go smoothly. But then, I thought, how much worse must Lucy be feeling, rejected and having to move in yet again with strangers?

'Is that Pat?' I asked, as the call connected and a woman's voice answered.

'Yes. Speaking.'

'It's Cathy Glass.'

'Oh, yes, Lucy's new carer. Hello.' I could hear relief in her voice. 'Jill said you'd phone.'

'So, how is Lucy now?' I asked.

'Still shut in her room and refusing to come out or speak to us. I don't know what to do. I feel awful, so does my husband. Lucy's blaming us for her having to move, but we're only approved to look after babies. To be honest, Cathy, I regret ever having agreed to take Lucy in the first place. It's so upsetting and we feel very guilty.'

'Don't,' I said. 'It's not your fault. The social services were desperate to place Lucy in the area after her mother complained, and you were the only carer available. It's not good practice, but it happens when the system is stretched to the limit. Have you been able to tell Lucy that I would be phoning?'

'Sort of. I called through her bedroom door and told her. She didn't answer, but I think she heard me.'

'How long ago was that?' I asked.

'About two hours.'

'All right. Could you go up now please and tell her I'm on the phone. I assume her bedroom door isn't locked?'

'No. We never put locks on the bedroom doors. We're not allowed to.' Pat was referring to the 'safer caring' recommendations for foster carers, which advise against locks being fitted to the child's bedroom door, as it could prevent the carer from entering in an emergency or if the child is distressed.

'Good,' I said. 'This is what I'd like you to do. Go up now, knock on Lucy's bedroom door and then poke your head round and say lightly: "There's a phone call for you. It's Cathy, your new carer. She's hoping she can have a little chat with you."'

'You think I should open her door and go in?' Pat asked, concerned. 'I thought she wanted to be alone.'

Not used to fostering older children, Pat had thought she was respecting Lucy's privacy in leaving her alone, but as an experienced carer of older children I knew that, once a child had had time to cool off, they usually wanted you to go to them and give them a cuddle. I would never have left a child alone in their room for any more than fifteen minutes if they were as upset as Lucy was.

'Yes, Pat. Open her bedroom door and go in a little,' I confirmed.

'All right, I'll do as you say.'

I heard the phone being set down and then Pat's footsteps receding upstairs. As I waited I could feel my heart thumping loudly in my chest. Adrian and Paula's distant voices floated through from the living room. I heard Pat knock on Lucy's bedroom door, then a slight creak as the door opened, followed by: 'Your new carer, Cathy, is on the phone for you. Can you come and talk to her?'

There was more silence and then I heard the bedroom door close. A few moments later Pat's voice came on the phone again. 'I told her, but she's still refusing to even look at me. She's just sitting there on the bed staring into space.'

My worries for Lucy rose.

'What should I do now?' Pat asked, anxiously. 'Shall I ask my husband to try to talk to her?'

'Does Lucy have a better relationship with him?' I asked.

'No, not really,' Pat said. 'She won't speak to him, either. Jill said that we might have to leave her until Monday, when her social worker is back at work.'

'Then Lucy has the whole weekend to brood over this,' I said. 'It will be worse. Let's try again to get her to the phone. I'm sure it will help if she hears I'm not an ogre.'

Pat gave a little snort of laughter. 'Jill said you were very good with older children.'

'That was sweet of her,' I said. 'Now, is your phone fixed or cordless?'

'Cordless.'

'Excellent. Take the handset up with you, knock on Lucy's bedroom door, go in and tell her again I would like to talk to her. But this time, leave the phone on her bed facing up so she can hear me, and then come out. I might end up talking to myself, but I'm used to that.'

Pat gave another snort of nervous laughter. 'Fingers crossed,' she said.

I heard Pat's footsteps going up the stairs again, followed by the knock on Lucy's bedroom door and the slight creak as it opened. Pat's voice trembled a little as she said: 'Cathy's still on the phone and she'd like to talk to you.'

There was a little muffled sound, presumably as Pat put the phone on Lucy's bed, and then I heard the bedroom door close. I was alone with Lucy. This was my chance to talk to her, to try and connect with her and reassure her. Maybe my only chance.

I took a deep breath and said gently: 'Hello, love. It's Cathy. Can you hear me, pet?'

I paused. Although I wasn't expecting a reply straight away, I wanted to give her the chance. I pictured the handset on the bed, presumably near enough for Lucy to hear. I wondered if she'd looked at the phone as my voice had come through.

'I know how dreadful this is for you,' I began, my voice gentle but hopefully loud enough for her to hear. 'I know how you must be feeling at having to move again. You've had so many moves, Lucy. I think you've coped remarkably well. I don't think I would have coped as well as you have.'

I paused again and listened for any response, but there was none, not even a sigh or a sob. For all I knew she might have stuffed the phone under her pillow so she didn't have to listen to me, but at least she hadn't severed the call; the line was still open.

'I'd like to tell you a bit about myself and my home,' I continued. 'So it won't seem so strange to you when you arrive. I live in a house about a twenty-minute drive from where you are now, so you'll be able to go to the same secondary school, which is good. You don't want to change schools again. I have two children: Adrian, who is thirteen, and Paula, who is nine. They are both looking forward to meeting you and having you stay. Paula is planning lots of games for you to play with her. There's just the three of us, as I'm divorced, so they'll be four of us in the family when you arrive. Five including our cat.' I paused again, but there was nothing.

'I've got your room ready,' I said. 'But I'm sure you'll want to change things around to suit you, which is fine. You'll be able to put posters and pictures on your bedroom walls to make it look nice. Just as you want it. As well as the bed, there's a wardrobe and drawers for your clothes, plenty of shelf space for your cuddlies and a toy box. There's also a small table, which you can work at if you need quiet for your homework, or you can do your homework downstairs if you wish. I'll always help you with your school work if you want me to, just like I help Adrian and Paula. We have quite a big garden with some swings. We like to go out in the garden when the weather is fine. We also like playing games. Adrian and Paula are playing a board game now. Do you like playing games, love?'

I stopped and waited, hoping for a reply, but none came. Was Lucy listening? Had I caught her attention? Or was she still in denial, refusing to acknowledge me, and perhaps sitting with her hands pressed to her ears not having heard a word I'd said. I waited a moment longer and then continued.

'So, Lucy, I'm wondering what else I can tell you? I'm sure you've got lots of questions. Our cat is called Toscha. You'll like her. She's very gentle and loves being stroked. The only time she ever scratched anyone was years ago when Adrian was little and he pulled her tail. Cats don't like having their tails pulled and Adrian learnt his lesson. He never did it again. Paula sometimes puts a doll's bonnet on Toscha and pushes her around the garden in her doll's pram. She does look funny.'

I stopped. I thought I'd heard a faint sound, possibly a movement. I waited, not daring to breathe, my pulse throbbing. Then I heard another noise and I stood perfectly still. I had the feeling Lucy had picked up the phone; I thought I heard the faintest sound of breathing. I waited a moment longer to see if she would speak, then, lowering my voice, I said softly: 'Hello, Lucy.'

A pause, and then an almost inaudible: 'Hello.'

Relief flooded through me. I could have wept. Her little voice sounded so very sad. 'Well done, love,' I said. 'You're being very brave. I know how difficult this is for you. Pat does, too. How are you feeling?'

Another pause, and then a very slight: 'OK, I guess.'

I swallowed the lump rising in my throat. I wished I could reach out and hug her.

'We're all looking forward to meeting you,' I said. 'Adrian, Paula, me and Toscha. Can you think of any questions you'd liked to ask?'

Silence; then her small voice again: 'What's the name of the game Adrian and Paula are playing?' So she had been listening.

'It's called draughts, love. Do you know the game?'

A very quiet: 'I think so.'

'You play it on a board with round pieces, and you take the other person's pieces by hopping over them. It's easy to play and good fun.'

'I don't know many games,' Lucy said quietly.

'We'll teach you. We have a cupboard full of games. When you arrive I'll show you where everything is and you can choose a game to play. Adrian and Paula are always playing games when they're not at school.'

'Do they watch television, too?' Lucy asked quietly.

'Oh yes, too much sometimes. Do you have a favourite television programme?'

A small pause, then a tiny: 'Not really. I watch what everyone else watches.'

'So, what do you like to eat?' I now asked. 'And I'll make sure I've got some of your favourite foods in ready for tomorrow.'

'I don't mind,' Lucy said, in the same small, self-effacing voice that made me want to cry. 'I don't really have any favourite food. I don't like eating much.'

Although I was pleased that Lucy was now talking to me, she seemed so sad and far too compliant – probably a result of having to continually fit in with other families. I was also concerned about her last comment in respect of not liking to eat, for the referral had said she was underweight and had raised the possibility of an eating disorder.

'What else can I tell you about us?' I now asked.

There was a pause, and then Lucy asked the one question I'd been dreading. 'If I come to you, will I have to move again?'

I took a breath. 'What did your social worker tell you?' I asked.

'She said my mum would have to go to court if she wanted me back, as there was a court order now.'

'That's right. You're in care now under what's called an Interim Care Order. Did your social worker explain what that was?'

'I think so, but I didn't really understand.'

'I know, love. There was too much going on. I'll try and explain. Until recently, when you were in care it was under what's called a Section 20, which is an agreement between your mum and the social services. It meant that your mum could take you out of care whenever she wanted to, which is one of the reasons you've had so many moves. That can't happen now there is a court order. The social services will be applying for a Full Care Order, when the judge will make the decision on where you should live permanently: if you can live with your mother or if you would be better off in foster care permanently. But we won't know the judge's decision for many months, possibly a year, as they have to read lots of reports to make sure it's the right decision.' I stopped. 'Does that make any sense to you, love?'

There was a long pause, which was hardly surprising; the workings of the care system are difficult enough for adults to grasp, let alone an eleven-year-old child.

When Lucy spoke again it brought tears to my eyes. 'I don't want to live with my mum,' she said. 'But I don't want to have to keep moving. Other kids have proper homes and families who love them. I just want a family of my own.'

Chapter Eleven

Lucy

I couldn't lie to Lucy. I couldn't tell her she would never have to move again, but I *could* tell her that eventually she would be found a permanent family of her own.

'Lucy, from what I know of your history I think it's highly unlikely the judge will decide you should live with your mother. So the social services will see if you have a relative who can look after you, and if not then they will find you a long-term foster family to suit you.' I didn't say 'one that will match your cultural heritage', although I knew that would be part of the criteria. Lucy was dual heritage, as her father was Thai, so the social services would want to find her a family that reflected this.

'But all that will take many months,' I said, 'maybe up to a year, and you won't have to move again during that time.' It was the best I could offer to reassure Lucy and, bless her, it was enough.

'So I won't have to move again for a whole year?' she said, her voice lightening a little.

'That's right, love. Only once the judge has made his or her decision will you move, and that will be to your forever family.'

'That's good,' she said. 'Will your cat be there when I come tomorrow?'

Lucy

'I'll make sure of it, love.'

We said goodbye, but Lucy didn't sever the call. I heard muffled sounds as she carried the handset downstairs and gave it to Pat, who I guessed was waiting for any news.

'Hello,' she said anxiously.

'Is half past eleven tomorrow morning all right for you and your husband to move Lucy?' I said.

'Oh, yes, of course,' Pat said, surprised. 'Has Lucy agreed to come then?'

'She has.'

'How did you manage that?'

'I think the cat did it,' I said, with a small laugh. 'So half past eleven is all right? I'd rather not leave it any later as the waiting will unsettle Lucy again.'

'Yes, we'll get going on the packing straight away.'

'Good. And you may not know this but, when an older child moves, it's usually best if the carers say goodbye and leave reasonably quickly, so I won't be offering you coffee. I know it's different when you move babies to permanency.'

'Yes, it is. Thanks for telling me.'

'You can phone Lucy in a week or so. That would be nice, and visit in a few weeks – once she's had a chance to settle in.'

'We will. See you tomorrow then. And thanks for all your help.'

'You're welcome. Enjoy your evening. You want to part on good terms.'

'Yes, we'll try.'

In truth, I hadn't really done much to persuade Lucy to move other than use my skills and experience from years of fostering. Pat and her husband were used to fostering babies and had been out of their depth looking after an older child, which is why carers are approved and trained to foster a specific age group. I returned to the living room where Adrian and Paula were just finishing their game of draughts and told them the good news: that I'd spoken to Lucy and she would be coming tomorrow. 'She's looking forward to playing with you both,' I added. 'And we need to make sure Toscha is in.'

'Why?' Adrian asked, glancing up from the board. 'What's the cat done?'

Ignoring his stab at humour, I said, 'Lucy's very keen to see her.'

He threw me an old-fashioned look, took the last of Paula's pieces from the board and, punching the air, shouted: 'Winner!'

'Well played,' I said.

Paula scowled.

'You played well too,' I said diplomatically.

They packed away the game and then Adrian went off to play on his Nintendo, while I took Paula up for her bath and to get her ready for bed. It was Friday, so both children were up later than on a school night. Paula can sometimes be a real little chatterbox, especially at bedtime, and tonight all she could talk about was Lucy.

'I'm very excited that Lucy's coming,' she said, flapping the water in the bath to make more bubbles. 'What does she like to play?'

'I'm not sure. You can ask her. I don't think she knows many games, so you can teach her some.'

'I will. And I'll show her my toys and let her play with them, even my new Christmas toys. And if it snows, we can go in the garden and build a snowman. I hope it snows. I'm going to like playing with Lucy.'

While Paula was happily planning all she was going to do with Lucy, I was also thinking about Lucy, and, among other things, about the school run on Monday. Like most foster carers, I had to juggle my children's commitments with the child or children I was fostering. Adrian, at thirteen, went to school with his friends, but I still took Paula, at age nine, to her primary school and collected her. Lucy's school was a twenty-minute bus journey away, and although most secondary-school children use buses I wasn't comfortable with her making an unfamiliar journey alone when she'd just moved in. Once I knew what time her school started, I was hoping I'd be able to work out something that would allow me to take both girls to school and collect them. When a new foster child first arrives, there's always a period of readjustment and then, once the new routine is established, the household runs smoothly again.

The following morning – Saturday – I was up, showered and dressed earlier than usual for the weekend, and with a mixture of excitement and apprehension I double-checked that Lucy's room was ready. Paula was up earlier than usual, too, and the first thing she said when she came downstairs was that she was looking forward to meeting Lucy. Adrian, true to form, only stumbled from his bed when he smelled bacon frying. We usually have a cooked breakfast at the weekend; it's the only two days in the week when we have time to enjoy it. By eleven o'clock Adrian was showered and dressed, too, and caught in the frisson of excited expectation that had enveloped the house. So, with half an hour to go before Lucy's arrival, we were all ready and waiting, except …

'Where's Toscha?' I asked, suddenly realizing she wasn't in her favourite spot on the chair by the window.

We looked around the obvious places and couldn't see her. Then the children helped me search the house from top to bottom: under the beds; in corners (especially by radiators); in and behind cupboards; even in the airing cupboard, where she'd once been found; but there was no sign of Toscha.

'I expect she's out,' Adrian said. 'I take it she is allowed to use the cat flap?'

'Very funny,' I said, unimpressed.

I peered out of the window but couldn't see Toscha in the garden. I slipped on my coat and, taking her bag of favourite cat biscuits with me, went into the garden. I shook the bag while calling her name, but no Toscha came running. It was now nearly 11.20, and apart from Lucy being disappointed when she arrived that there was no Toscha when I'd promised there would be, I was also growing concerned. Toscha was a creature of habit and didn't normally go outside and vanish in the middle of the morning, especially in winter.

Then I heard Adrian shout from inside the house: 'Mum! Come in. She was on the bed in Lucy's room! You shut her in!'

Relieved, I returned indoors, thinking she must have crept into Lucy's room without me seeing her when I'd checked it earlier. I'd closed Lucy's bedroom door as I'd come out, and her room had been the one room I hadn't thought to search. Fortunately, Adrian had.

'Well done, love,' I said, as he set Toscha on the sofa ready to receive our new arrival.

It wasn't a moment too soon, for as Toscha curled herself into a ball, comfortably resting her head on her front paws and unaware what all the fuss had been about, the doorbell rang. 'That'll be them,' I said.

Paula slipped her hand into mine and came with me down the hall to answer the door, while Adrian stayed on the sofa stroking Toscha. I felt a little rush of nervousness as I opened the door, and Paula squeezed my hand.

'Hello,' I smiled at the three of them.

Lucy

'Hi, Cathy,' Pat said brightly. 'This is my husband Terry, and this is Lucy.'

'Hi, Terry. Hello, love,' I said to Lucy. 'Come on in.'

Lucy's large dark eyes rounded as she looked at me. She was a petite, slender child with gorgeous long black silky hair, which hung loosely over her shoulders. She was wearing a smart winter coat, open at the front, with new jeans and a pink jumper underneath. I smiled at her again as she came in.

'I'll get the cases,' Terry said.

'Thanks. I'll leave the door on the latch,' I said, as he disappeared back down the path. Then to Lucy and Pat I said: 'This is Paula. Adrian and Toscha are in the living room – straight down the hall.'

'What a nice house,' Pat said encouragingly to Lucy as we went down the hall.

Lucy didn't reply; I didn't expect her to – even Paula was nervous and still had her hand in mine.

As we entered the living room, Adrian looked up from stroking Toscha and said, 'Hi.'

'Hi,' Pat said. 'Nice to meet you. This is Lucy.'

Adrian threw Lucy a small self-conscious smile. She was standing close to Pat, head slightly bowed and looking at the cat from under her fringe. 'Shall I take your coat, love?' I suggested. 'It's warm in here.'

Without speaking or looking at me, Lucy slipped out of her coat and handed it to me. The poor child looked so lost and ill at ease, it broke my heart. 'I'm sure Toscha would like a stroke from you, too,' I said, trying to make her feel at home.

Adrian looked at Lucy and threw her another smile. Then, very gingerly, almost cat-like herself, she lightly crossed the room and sat on the sofa on the other side of Toscha and began gently stroking her. Paula found the courage to let go of my hand and went over to join Lucy and Adrian, standing just in front of them to form a little semi-circle as they all stroked the cat. Toscha had never had so much attention and was purring loudly. Pat and I sat in the chairs watching them and made light conversation as Terry brought Lucy's bags into the hall. He closed the front door and then joined us in the living room, saying hello to Adrian. 'Nice garden,' he said, nodding at the view through the patio doors.

'Thank you,' I said. 'We make the most of it in the summer.'

There was a short awkward silence and then, turning to Pat, and following my advice about keeping their departure short, Terry said, 'Well, I suppose we'd better be off.'

Pat nodded. 'We'll phone you in a week,' she said to Lucy.

Lucy didn't reply or look up but concentrated on petting Toscha. Pat then went over and kissed the top of Lucy's head. I thought Lucy might have wanted a hug or, perhaps finding separating difficult, cry, but she didn't. She just gave a small nod and then said in a very quiet voice, without looking up: 'Goodbye.'

Lucy's face was emotionless, and I instinctively felt she was a child used to hiding her emotions, probably as a coping mechanism to stop her from being hurt again.

'Goodbye then, Lucy,' Terry called from across the room. 'Take care.'

Lucy gave another small nod and continued stroking Toscha.

I showed Pat and Terry to the front door. 'Don't worry, Lucy will be fine,' I reassured them. 'I'm sure she won't stay this quiet for long.'

They both looked at me a little oddly. 'She will,' Pat said. 'She's hardly said a word to us in the whole three months she's been with us. To be honest, we found her silence quite unnerving. The most she ever said was the other day when we told her she would be moving. Then she shouted and screamed. Perhaps she's schizophrenic?'

'More like traumatized,' I said, a little tersely, concerned that a serious medical condition could be assigned so loosely.

I reassured Pat and Terry again that Lucy would be fine and we said goodbye. Closing the front door, I returned down the hall, still thinking of Pat's comment. It wasn't the first time I'd heard an adult – carer, parent, teacher or even a social worker – resort to labelling a child for behaviour they didn't understand. Schizophrenia, ADHD, dyslexia, autism, etc. – these words should only be used after a medical diagnosis, because labels can stick. I hoped they hadn't said anything similar within earshot of Lucy.

In the living room, Adrian, Paula and Lucy were still grouped around Toscha, stroking her.

'I'll go and play in my room then, Mum, if that's OK?' Adrian said, standing, and eager to be on his Nintendo.

'Of course, love, and thanks for your help finding Toscha.'

'It's OK!' he called, disappearing out of the living room.

I went over to Lucy and Paula, who now slipped into the seat Adrian had vacated. Both girls were very quiet, still shy, so squatting on the floor in front of them I began making conversation. I was sure once they got talking they'd be fine.

'Before you arrived,' I said to Lucy, 'we had quite a scare, didn't we, Paula?' Paula nodded. 'We couldn't find Toscha anywhere. We looked all over the house and even in the garden. You'll never guess where we found her?' I paused, allowing time for Lucy to offer a suggestion or perhaps say, 'No? Where was she?' But she was too shy.

'She was on your bed! Fast asleep.' Paula said, supplying the answer. 'She's not really supposed to be on the beds.'

Lucy slowly raised her head and looked at me, her large dark eyes growing rounder with astonishment. Then, very quietly, she said: 'Was she really on my bed?'

'She was, love. I must have shut her in when I checked your room first thing this morning.'

The smallest, almost imperceptible smile now crossed Lucy's face. Then, in the same quiet voice, she said, 'I think if Toscha was on my bed it means she likes me, don't you?'

I felt my eyes brim. 'It does love. It most certainly does. We all like you.'

I hadn't planned any activities for the weekend. I'd kept it clear so that Lucy would have a chance to settle in and familiarize herself with us, her new home and routine, and hopefully start to relax a little. She came across as a very gentle child who could easily be taken advantage of; someone who needed protecting. I thought again how frightening it must be to come into yet another stranger's house, where you were expected to fit in. I also felt she was tense, on guard, almost in a permanent state of alert, as if at any moment she was ready to run. I knew from my previous fostering experience and training that this heightened anxiety wasn't unusual for a child who'd been severely neglected or abused; even a pin dropping can make them jump. I also knew it would take many weeks, if not months, and a lot of work before Lucy felt safe enough with us to lower her guard and completely relax.

Presently Paula tired of stroking Toscha and said to Lucy, 'Would you like to play a game now?'

Lucy gave a small nod.

'Or would you like to see your room first and then play a game?' Paula said.

'I don't mind,' Lucy said quietly, with a little self-conscious smile.

Lucy

'It's your decision,' I encouraged.

'Shall we see my room first?' Lucy asked Paula.

I was in no doubt that, had Paula said no, Lucy would have gone along with whatever Paula wanted to do.

'Yes. Let's see your room first,' Paula said. 'Then we can play a game.'

Both girls stood and we went out of the living room and upstairs, where I opened the door to Lucy's bedroom and we all went in.

'Do you like it?' Paula asked, crossing to the window. 'It's got a nice view.'

I smiled. The view was something I usually pointed out when I showed a new child and their social worker around the house, as the room overlooked the garden.

Lucy gave a small nod, but didn't go over to look out of the window.

'Your room will be better once you've got all your belongings in it,' I said. 'I'll bring up your bags shortly.'

She gave another small nod and then looked to Paula for direction.

'I'll show you the rest of the upstairs,' I said.

Leaving Lucy's room, we went to the next room, which was Adrian's. I tapped on his bedroom door. 'Can Lucy have a quick peek in your room, please?' I called.

'Yes, come in,' he returned.

'We always knock and wait to be asked into someone else's bedroom,' I explained to Lucy, taking the opportunity to mention one of our house rules. 'It keeps our rooms private and safe.'

Opening the door, I went in. Lucy took a little step in, just big enough for her to glance at the room, and then stepped out again.

'Thanks, love,' I said to Adrian, coming out. 'I'll give you a call when lunch is ready.'

Paula led the way along the landing to her room. 'I don't have to knock on my door,' she said with a mischievous grin, 'because it's my room and I'm not in it!'

I laughed. 'I've got a family of jokers,' I said to Lucy, and she managed a small smile.

'You can come all the way into my room,' Paula said, eager for Lucy to see her room, of which she was proud.

Lucy took a couple of steps in and gazed around. The theme in Paula's room was Disney's *Winnie the Pooh*, and images of the cartoon characters were on the duvet, pillowcase, wallpaper and curtains. Her shelves were brimming with soft toys and games that she'd been given for birthdays and Christmas. Paula's bedroom wasn't any more special than many girls' her age, but I could tell from Lucy's expression that it was to her.

'It's lovely,' she breathed after a moment. 'You are lucky.'

Paula smiled self-consciously, and I could see she felt a bit uncomfortable. Lucy wasn't the first child we'd fostered to be in awe of what we took for granted, and it was a timely reminder that not everyone was as lucky as we were.

We came out of Paula's room and I showed Lucy the bath-room and my bedroom. Then we went downstairs and I showed her the front room where the computer was, explaining that she could use it for homework. Then we went into the kitchen-cum-diner and I saw from the wall clock that it was nearly one o'clock.

'I thought we'd have some soup and a sandwich for lunch,' I said to both girls. 'We usually have our main meal in the early evening,' I added, for Lucy's sake.

Lucy glanced at Paula, and then said quietly to me, 'I'm not really hungry.'

'Did you have a big breakfast?' I asked.

She shook her head. 'I really don't like eating much.'

Lucy had said similar to me on the phone, but she couldn't afford to miss meals. I knew from the referral that she was underweight, and from what I could see of her frame – through her jumper and jeans – she was slender to the point of thin; plus, concerns had already been raised about her not eating. When she first came into care she would have had a medical, so when I saw her social worker I would ask about this. In the meantime, I needed to try and get Lucy in the habit of eating by establishing a regular pattern of mealtimes. Children from neglected backgrounds often swing between bingeing and then going without food altogether. I didn't know what the previous carers had done to address this and it was something else I would need to ask her social worker.

'While Mum makes lunch, shall we play?' Paula now asked Lucy.

Lucy gave a small nod.

'What would you like to play?' Paula asked.

Predictably, Lucy gave another small shrug and then said, 'I don't mind really.'

'Paula,' I said, 'why don't you show Lucy the cupboard where we keep the games, and then the two of you can choose something to play together?'

'I will,' Paula said, now feeling more at ease. And sensing that Lucy needed to be looked after as a much younger child would, Paula gently took her by the hand and led her out of the kitchen.

Chapter Twelve

No Appetite

Mealtimes in many family homes are often as important for their social interaction and family bonding as they are for eating food. In our house, as in many others, we eat our meals together whenever possible, seated on dining chairs around a table, talking between mouthfuls and sharing our news. Apart from in exceptional circumstances – birthdays, Christmas or when a child is upset and might want a cuddly toy with them – I don't normally allow toys, books, games consoles, mobile phones or any other distractions at the table while we're eating. I encourage the children in their table manners, as they not only ensure a pleasant meal for all, but will stand the children in good stead for later life, when much socializing and business takes place over a good meal. However, I realize that while my children are relaxed around the meal table, it could seem daunting for a newcomer: another new custom with its own rituals in a house of strangers. So I keep a watchful eye on the new child and do all I can to make them feel comfortable.

In the thirteen years I'd been fostering I'd seen all types of behaviour at the meal table, including shouting, screaming, tantrums, standing on the table, hiding under it, nose-picking, burping, farting, throwing food, grabbing food from others' plates and, very commonly, children who only ate with their fingers because they'd never used cutlery. But in all those years I'd never seen a child as anxious as Lucy was when she came to our table. I called her and Paula to come to lunch three times before they finally appeared. At first I thought it was because they wanted to finish their game, but when Paula drew Lucy by the hand into the kitchen I realized it was more than that.

'Lucy doesn't want anything to eat,' Paula said. 'She's not hungry.'

I looked at Lucy with a reassuring smile, but I could see how tense she was. 'Well, sit down, love, and just have a little,' I encouraged. 'You'll need something to eat; you didn't have breakfast and it's a long time until dinner.'

I drew out the chair next to Paula and smiled again at Lucy. 'We thought you'd like to sit here, next to Paula,' I said brightly.

'Yes, sit next to me,' Paula said. Adrian was already seated, opposite Lucy – he'd been the first to come when I'd called everyone for lunch.

Lucy hesitated, her brow creasing with worry. Then she slipped silently onto the chair next to Paula, and I helped her ease it closer to the table. I gave each of us a bowl of soup and set the platter of sandwiches, crisps, cherry tomatoes and sliced cucumber in the centre of the table ready for when we'd finished our soup. I sat down. Adrian and Paula were already tucking into their soup as I picked up my spoon, but Lucy sat stiffly upright, staring at her bowl. I didn't know how much of her anxiety was due to the intimacy of sitting and eating with strangers and how much of it was about the actual food. When I'd asked her if she liked tomato soup she'd said she did, but as I watched her out of the corner of my eye while I ate my soup she didn't make any attempt to start hers.

'Try a little,' I encouraged after a while. 'You must be hungry. You don't have to eat it all.'

Slowly, reluctantly almost, Lucy picked up her spoon and, dipping it into the bowl, took out the smallest amount possible and put it to her lips. I saw Adrian and Paula surreptitiously watching her and I motioned for them not to stare. Poor Lucy felt self-conscious enough already without having an audience. Lucy took a second and third spoonful as slowly and as measured as the first, then, when Adrian and Paula finished their soup, she put down her spoon, leaving over half a bowlful, and sat back in her chair.

'There's no rush,' I said, hoping she might have some more.

'I'm full,' she said quietly.

I finished the last of my soup, collected together the bowls, took them through to the kitchen and left them in the sink.

'Help yourselves,' I said, returning to the table and referring to the sandwiches, crisps and salad. 'Those sandwiches are ham and those are cheese,' I said, pointing. I'd previously checked with Lucy that she liked both.

Adrian and Paula began filling their plates with sandwiches, salad and crisps, while Lucy took one little sandwich. I'd cut them diagonally into quarters so that one sandwich amounted to half a slice of bread and a little bit of filling.

'Are you going to have some crisps and salad?' I suggested, offering Lucy the plates as she might not have liked to help herself, but she shook her head.

She ate the one sandwich slowly, taking small bites and chewing endlessly before swallowing. I made light conversation to try and help her feel at ease, and I also put on the radio in the background, but it didn't help. Lucy only had one sandwich and half a glass of water. It was her first meal with us and I didn't want to make her feel more self-conscious than she already did by encouraging her further. So once everyone else had finished and it was clear Lucy wasn't going to eat any more, I cleared away the dishes and hoped she'd make up for it at dinner time. As soon as Lucy left the table, she visibly relaxed and happily went with Paula to finish their game of dominoes.

Shortly after lunch, a friend of Adrian's who lived in the next street telephoned and asked if he'd like to go to his house for a few hours. Adrian asked me if it was all right and I said yes. I knew from experience that a new child would feel at home more quickly if we carried on with normal family life. I told Lucy that Adrian was going to a friend's house for a few hours and he called goodbye as he left. I then read a couple of pages of my book in the living room while the girls played snakes and ladders. In her playing and interaction Lucy was doing well, much better than Pat and Terry had led me to expect, so I was pleased.

Once the girls had tired of snakes and ladders, I suggested we unpack Lucy's bags, which I'd previously taken up to her room. I knew that once she had her possessions in her room and had arranged them to her liking she would start to feel more at home.

'We can both help you,' Paula said enthusiastically, jumping up and clapping her hands in excitement.

I saw that Lucy looked a bit uncomfortable. 'Is it all right if Paula and I help you with the unpacking?' I asked. For I wouldn't have expected an eleven-year-old child to unpack by herself.

Lucy gave a small nod and then said quietly, 'It's just that I've got some private things I don't want anyone to see.' She said it so sweetly and self-effacingly it was as though she daren't breathe for fear of upsetting others. I guessed these private things were small mementoes she was attached to. I'd seen children I'd fostered before arrive with all sorts of weird and wonderful objects they'd grown attached to and didn't want anyone to see, including one little boy who brought a clothes peg with him, which he said reminded him of his mother, and a girl who was inseparable from her father's (expensive) watch. I later found out he was in prison for breaking into a jeweller's shop!

'I understand, love,' I said to Lucy. 'We could help you unpack, and then when you take out your private things Paula and I will close our eyes. How does that sound?'

A small smile flickered across Lucy's face and I touched her arm reassuringly. 'You don't have to worry about upsetting me,' I said. 'I want you to feel relaxed and at home here. You must tell me what you want.'

She gave a small nod and then said to Paula: 'I can show you one of the private things, but not the other.'

'Great!' Paula exclaimed. Taking Lucy's hand, she drew her to her feet and then scampered off, with Lucy close behind.

Upstairs in Lucy's room, I asked Lucy which case we should unpack first and she pointed to the largest case, which contained her clothes. I began hanging and folding them into the wardrobe and drawers, showing Lucy where I was putting them, while Lucy began unpacking her bag of toys, with Paula's help. Lucy didn't have many possessions compared to the average eleven-year-old but, having been in foster care for a while, she had more than a child coming straight into care from a neglected home, who would often arrive with nothing.

'This is the private thing I can show you,' I heard Lucy say.

I glanced over from the wardrobe as she delved into a small pink rucksack and carefully drew out a soft toy rabbit. Clearly much loved and petted, it had chewed ears and a missing tail. Holding him against her chest, she hugged him hard.

'Why's he private?' Paula asked, voicing my thoughts.

'Because I don't usually show him to anyone,' Lucy said quietly. 'The children in one foster home were horrible to me, because he's old and has bits missing. So I don't let anyone see him. But I think you're kind. I know you won't laugh.'

I could see that, far from laughing, Paula was close to tears at the thought of children being unkind to Lucy because her favourite toy was old. I didn't know in which home this unkindness had taken place, but children can be cruel without anyone realizing it.

'What's his name?' Paula asked, as Lucy held the soft toy to her chest and stroked him protectively.

'He's called Mr Bunny,' Lucy said. 'Mr Bunny Rabbit if he's been naughty.' I smiled and thought that Lucy had a sense of humour buried beneath all her worry and anxiety.

'How old is he?' Paula asked, meaning: how long have you had him?

'I don't know,' Lucy said. 'He's always been with me, for as long as I can remember. My other toys got lost when I kept having to move, but Mr Bunny stayed with me. I used to take him out, but I don't any more. He's private.' And so saying, Lucy leant on the bed and tucked Mr Bunny under the duvet, so that only his ears were visible on the pillow. 'You can have a little sleep, Mr Bunny,' she said softly. 'You've had a busy day.'

I continued unpacking as Lucy and Paula explored Lucy's toys, slowly putting them into the toy box. Then I heard Paula ask: 'What's your other private thing?'

'No, Paula,' I cautioned lightly, turning from what I was doing to look at her. 'We said we'll close our eyes when Lucy unpacks her private things. She's already shown you Mr Bunny.'

Lucy gave a small nod. 'I can show you the cover, but no more. Not yet. Not for a long time, because it's very private.'

Before I looked away I saw her slide a large scrapbook from her bag. On the front of the book was a photograph of herself. I thought it might be her Life Story Book, started by a previous foster carer. Life Story Books are usually compiled by foster carers for children in long-term care. They contain photographs and some written history to support the child's memories. Children who are raised by their own families share collective memories, but foster children don't have this, and memories can become confused or even lost over time. If I was right and this was Lucy's Life Story Book, then it would be very personal to her and I could appreciate why she didn't want to share it with us yet.

'It's got some photographs in it and some writing about me,' Lucy said to Paula, as she hid the book under the bed.

'Why don't you put it safely in one of your drawers?' I suggested, pointing to the chest of drawers. 'No one comes into your bedroom without your permission, so it will be safe. No one will see.'

Lucy gave a small nod and reached under the bed to retrieve the book.

'Eyes closed,' I said to Paula.

Paula and I both screwed shut our eyes and I heard movements as Lucy placed the book in a drawer and closed it.

'You can look now,' she said.

At about the same time as the girls and I finished Lucy's unpacking, Adrian returned from his friend's house. He let himself in, called up, 'Hi, ladies!' and then went into the kitchen for a snack. Like most active thirteen-year-old boys, he was always hungry.

No Appetite

I stacked Lucy's empty suitcase and bags on the landing. 'I'll put them up in the loft later, out of the way,' I told Lucy, for I didn't want her to think that I'd just got rid of them.

As I went downstairs, with Lucy and Paula following, I heard Lucy tell Paula: 'I won't need my bags for a long time, maybe a year. Your mum said I can stay until the judge makes a decision.'

'I'm pleased,' Paula said. 'I like playing with you. I think we're going to be good friends.'

'That's nice,' Lucy said. 'I think I'm going to be happy living here with you and your family.'

You will, love, I thought. I'll make sure of it.

I served dinner at six o'clock, but far from making up at dinner what she hadn't eaten at lunch, Lucy looked just as uncomfortable, still had no appetite and picked at her food. I'd made cottage pie, a dish that is easily eaten with a fork or spoon, and a favourite with most children. When I'd asked Lucy before the meal if she liked cottage pie, she'd said yes. But the little she had she ate very slowly, almost as though she was scared of eating or didn't like the taste or feel of food in her mouth.

'Are you feeling all right, love?' I asked at length, wondering if perhaps she had a sore throat or was sickening for something.

Lucy nodded and continued slowly, eating a tiny bit at a time. Paula and I finished ours, and Adrian was already on seconds. Then Lucy looked up and said, 'I really can't eat any more.'

'All right, love, don't worry,' I said quickly. 'Just eat what you want and leave the rest.'

She set down her knife and fork; I guessed she'd eaten about four mouthfuls – not enough for a growing child, but I didn't say anything more. I served pudding – apple crumble and ice cream – and Lucy had one scoop of ice cream, but no crumble.

Had Lucy's poor eating not already been mentioned, I might have put it down to being in a new house – and that might well have been partly responsible – but I knew that if her appetite didn't start improving over the next few days then I would be raising the matter with her social worker and seeking advice.

After dinner we watched a film on television and when it finished I made everyone a hot milky drink, which Lucy had, and then I began the bath and bedtime routine. I usually put the children to bed in ascending order of age, so Paula first, then Lucy, and Adrian last. Adrian usually went up at about nine o'clock and read for a while in bed. So when Paula was snuggled in her bed, I called for Lucy to come up and together we collected her toothbrush, flannel, towel and pyjamas from her bedroom and took them into the bathroom. I showed her where everything was and ran her bath. I wouldn't normally bath an eleven-year-old unless they had learning difficulties and needed help, so once her bath was ready I checked that Lucy had everything she needed and then came out, telling her to call me if she needed anything. I'm always very cautious when a new child arrives, until I am sure what they can safely do and what they need help with, so I hovered on the landing while Lucy was in the bathroom. But fifteen minutes later she emerged, washed, dressed in her pyjamas and brushing her lovely long black shiny hair.

I showed her where the laundry basket was for her dirty clothes and then went with her to her bedroom. I asked her if she liked her curtains open or closed at night, and she said open a little. I also found out that she liked to sleep with the light off and the door slightly ajar.

'It's bound to be a bit strange at first,' I said, as she climbed into bed. 'Call me if you need me in the night. I'm a light sleeper, so I'll hear you.'

No Appetite

She gave a small smile and snuggled beneath the duvet. She looked very comfortable with Mr Bunny on the pillow beside her.

'All right then, love? Is there anything you need?'

She shook her head.

'Would you like a goodnight kiss?' I always ask a child when they first arrive if they want a kiss. Some do and some don't, and it's an invasion of their personal space to just assume they do and go ahead.

'Yes, I'd like a kiss,' Lucy said softly.

I leaned forward and kissed her forehead, and as I did she slid her arms around my neck. 'Can I have a hug too?' she asked quietly.

'Of course, love.' I looped my arms under her shoulders and gave her a hug. I could feel her smooth, warm cheek resting lightly against mine. It's unusual for a child to want this degree of physical contact on their first night and I thought that Lucy must either be a very tactile child, or she'd been starved of affection.

After a while I gently drew away and kissed her forehead. 'You get some sleep now, love. You must be exhausted. You've done very well for your first day.'

'Have I done well?' she asked, her dark eyes growing wider.

'Yes, you have. I'm very pleased with you. And you'll find it will be easier tomorrow, and the next day. Everything won't be so strange – well, apart from me!' I added, with a small laugh.

She smiled. Then her eyes flickered and began to close; the poor child was exhausted.

'Night, love,' I said, standing. 'Sleep tight, and see you in the morning.'

'Night,' she said. 'And thanks for having me.'

'There's no need to thank me, love. I'm glad you're here.'

That night Paula got her wish – it snowed. When I woke in the early hours to check on Lucy, who was asleep, I was aware the air outside seemed brighter and the sound muted. Returning to my bedroom I peered through the curtains to see a white blanket of snow. Not enough to cause travel chaos, but about two inches – enough to smooth the edges of reality so that everything had a magical, dreamlike softness to it. Yippee, I thought, we'll have fun tomorrow!

I returned to bed; it was only 3.30 a.m., but I couldn't sleep. Excited by the snow, I wanted the children to wake so they could see it too, but I was also thinking about Lucy. I find the early hours are a good time for worrying and fretting over the day's events, and I had plenty to worry about with Lucy. The referral had said very little and I hoped to learn more from the social worker. But when a child has been seriously neglected over a long period, as Lucy had – unprotected and living with a series of strangers – there's a strong possibility that at some point they've fallen victim to a predator paedophile and been sexually abused. There was no suggestion in the referral that Lucy had been sexually abused, and obviously this was a huge relief, but Lucy had spent so long living a hand-to-mouth existence with her itinerant mother that I knew she would have seen and experienced more than any child should have. Some children deal with their pain and anger by attention-seeking and aggressive behaviour, but Lucy seemed to be internalizing her pain. I knew at some point it would come out, just as it had at the previous carers' when she'd been told she would have to move again.

* * *

136

No Appetite

'Snow!' Adrian cried at 7.30 a.m., his voice reverberating around the house.

Within minutes Paula and Lucy were out of bed and at their bedroom windows, echoing: 'Snow! It's been snowing!' Paula then went into Lucy's room, remembering to knock on the door first, and joined her at her bedroom window. Still in my dressing gown, I joined Adrian at his bedroom window.

'Isn't it beautiful?' I called, loud enough for the girls to hear in Lucy's room.

'Yes! Can we play in it?' they replied.

'Of course!' Adrian shouted back.

As the four of us gazed out from the two bedroom windows over the back garden, the winter sun began to rise, a fiery glowing ball that cast a pink tinge over the white snow.

'It's magic,' Paula called.

And it truly was.

I'd never seen children dress so quickly (well, not since the last time we'd had snow the previous winter). Twenty minutes later, they were dressed, with coats, scarves and gloves on, and in the garden, making footprints in the virgin snow, throwing snowballs and generally having fun. I joined them in the garden for a while and then said I would go in and feed Toscha – who'd taken one look at the snow and dashed back inside – and also get some breakfast going. 'How does egg, bacon and beans sound?' I asked.

'Great,' they replied.

As I turned, a large snowball hit me on the back. 'You wait!' I called to Adrian. 'I'll get you!' But my feeble attempt fell far short of its target as Adrian ran for cover.

I hoped the fresh air and exercise would give Lucy an appetite, but when I called them in for breakfast she didn't want the cooked breakfast, just a bowl of cornflakes. I suggested she might like a piece of toast as well, but she shook her head. However, she did have milk and sugar on the cornflakes and ate them all, which was something. After breakfast the children returned to the garden, while Toscha and I stayed in the warm. The three of them played in the snow until their hands and feet were cold and their noses glowed red. When they came in I hung their wet gloves and coats on the radiators to dry and made them a hot chocolate, which Lucy enjoyed.

At about one o'clock I said I'd make a light lunch and I asked Lucy if she liked pasta. She said she did, but at the table she only ate about half a dozen pasta shapes and one thin slice of warm French bread. I didn't try to encourage her to eat more, as I didn't want to turn her eating into an issue, but Paula, who had a good appetite, said: 'Is that all you're having, Lucy?'

Lucy gave a small nod and I could see how self-conscious she felt.

'It's fine, just have what you want,' I said lightly, for pressuring her to eat wouldn't help.

As we neared the end of lunch the phone rang and Adrian, guessing it was his father, flew from the table and answered it in the living room. John, my ex-husband, usually saw the children every third or fourth Sunday and telephoned on the Sundays he didn't see them. Paula, hearing Adrian say 'Hi Dad', left the table and joined him on the sofa in the living room, waiting for her turn to speak to her father.

I explained to Lucy who John was. She had finished eating, but stayed at the table with me. 'Is he a nice man?' she asked.

Difficult question, I thought, considering he'd run off with a younger woman six years previously. 'Yes,' I said generously. 'He loves Adrian and Paula.'

No Appetite

There was a moment's pause and then Lucy said: 'My dad used to hit me. That wasn't nice, was it?'

Chapter Thirteen

'Do Our Best'

I looked at Lucy and for the first time since she'd arrived I caught a glimpse of the anger she must have been feeling about everything she'd been through, and then it was replaced with sadness.

'No, it certainly wasn't nice,' I said. 'Adults should never hit a child, not even if they are naughty, which I can't imagine you were.' As well as being concerned by what Lucy had just told me about her father, I was also puzzled, as it didn't tie up with what I'd read in the referral. 'Lucy,' I said, 'I might be wrong, but I didn't think you ever saw your father?'

She gave a small shrug and looked away. 'The social worker told me he was my stepfather, but I always had to call him Dad.'

'I understand,' I said. 'His name was Dave?'

'Yes. I lived with him for a long time.'

'You did,' I said, recalling this from the referral. 'Did you ever tell anyone Dave was hitting you?'

'I told Mum,' Lucy said in a small, tight voice. 'But she didn't believe me. He never hit me when she was there.'

'He doesn't sound like a nice person,' I said. 'Not like a father should be.' This may sound obvious, but it wasn't necessarily to Lucy, whose only experience of a father, as far as I knew, had been Dave.

'He was all I had,' Lucy said softly. 'He was the only one around when my mum wasn't there and my aunts left. So I tried not to upset him.'

'Your aunts?' I asked, again puzzled.

'Dad's girlfriends,' Lucy clarified. 'I had to call them Aunt. Dave said it was polite, because they looked after me sometimes.'

Not very polite of him to be hitting a young child, I thought.

'So where was your mother when these aunts were living with you and Dave?' I asked, trying to fill in some of the blanks and get a better understanding of Lucy's past.

'Mum used to go out and not come back for a long time. She wasn't there much. I don't see her often now.' I knew this from the referral, but hearing it on a child's lips made it all the more immediate and upsetting.

'Did you tell the social worker about Dave, and the aunts, and your mum not being there?' I now asked, wondering why Lucy hadn't been brought into long-term care sooner.

Lucy paused and I saw some of the anger flash across her eyes again, before it was replaced by hurt. 'It wouldn't have done any good,' she said despondently. 'He was nice when anyone came.' Then she quickly changed the subject and said: 'Is it all right if I go to my room until Paula's finished on the phone?'

'Yes, of course, love. You don't have to ask. This is your home. Do as you wish.'

Leaving the table, Lucy went upstairs. I felt so sorry for her. What an appalling, disruptive past she'd had, with her mother in and out of her life, Lucy in and out of care and a string of unrelated strangers looking after her. How much of what Lucy had told me was known to the social services I couldn't gauge from the referral, but with Lucy upstairs and Adrian and Paula still in the living room talking to their father, I took the opportunity to add what Lucy had said to my log notes. I'd already begun Lucy's folder with the referral and now I added what Lucy had told me about her stepfather. Sadly, from my past fostering experience, I knew that more disclosures were likely to follow and that they could get worse. Only when a child feels settled and secure do they find the courage to reveal what has happened to them, and often it's shocking.

On Sunday afternoon we went for a short walk to our local park, taking some bread to feed the ducks. We weren't out for long as it began to rain, which quickly turned the snow to slush. I was pleased the children had made the most of playing in the snow earlier, for if the rain continued the snow would be gone by morning. I now knew from Lucy that her school opened at 8.00 a.m., so on the way home from the park I told the girls that the following morning I planned to take Lucy to school first and then take Paula afterwards. Lucy said there was no need for me to take her as she could go on the bus, but I said she could go by bus the following week, once she was more familiar with the area and I'd shown her the route, and as long as her social worker agreed. For this week, I'd feel happier if I took and collected her in the car. I explained that it would also give me the opportunity to introduce myself at her school's office, check that they had my contact details and hopefully make an appointment to see her teacher.

'Why do you want to see my teacher?' Lucy asked, a little suspiciously, as she squished through the puddles of melting snow.

'To say hello and ask how I can help you with your school work. Is that OK?'

'Sure,' she said easily. 'It's just that no one ever did that before.'

Well, they should have done, I thought.

I made roast chicken for dinner that evening, with roast potatoes, peas and carrots, having checked with Lucy first that she liked these foods. However, I was quickly realizing that Lucy liking a food didn't mean she would eat it. At dinner she managed a few carefully chewed mouthfuls of chicken, one roast potato and a spoonful of peas; not enough to feed a gnat, as my mother would have said. I saw Paula and Adrian glance at Lucy's plate as she set down her cutlery, having left more than she'd eaten, but they didn't say anything and neither did I. Once the rest of us had finished, I simply asked Lucy if she'd had enough and when she nodded I took her plate away, hoping that when she felt more settled her appetite would grow. Toscha ate the chicken. Lucy didn't want any pudding, but did have a few grapes.

That evening I made sure all three school uniforms were laid out ready for the following morning, and then began the bath and bedtime routine. When it was Lucy's turn to go up, she said she didn't need a bath as she'd had one the night before. I said that we usually had a bath or a shower every day, but then she said she was too tired.

'Even for a quick shower?' I asked.

'Yes,' she said.

So I gave her the benefit of the doubt and didn't insist. So often in parenting we have to decide which issues to focus on and which we can reasonably let go. While good hygiene is important, as long as Lucy had a bath or shower the following day then little harm would be done. When she'd been with us longer, she'd fall into our routine of bathing or showering each day, just as she would take on other aspects of our family life and routines.

As I went to bed that night I was feeling quite positive. The weekend had gone far better than I'd expected, considering that on Friday evening, only forty-eight hours previously, Lucy had been shut in her bedroom at her previous foster carers' house, refusing to come out or even talk to anyone. Now, here she was, just two days later, talking and playing and making herself at home. I should have realized, with all my years of fostering, that this was the 'honeymoon' period, as we refer to it, and Lucy's behaviour would deteriorate.

The following morning I arrived at Lucy's school at 8.25 a.m. and parked in one of the visitor's bays. I knew I was short of time: Paula's school started at 8.55 and I had a return journey of twenty minutes. We'd left home later than I'd planned, as Lucy had forgotten one of her school books and we'd had to return to collect it.

'Reception is over there,' Lucy said helpfully, as we climbed out of the car and I pressed the key fob.

I hurried across the car park, a child on each side of me. Most of the other children arriving were without parents or carers, coming to school alone or with friends. I wondered if Lucy felt embarrassed having me here. 'I'll drop you off at the gates tomorrow,' I said, reassuring her. 'I'm just coming in for today.'

She nodded, but didn't say anything.

Inside the building, I introduced myself to the receptionist while Lucy and Paula sat on the chairs in the waiting area. I find that receptions in large secondary schools can sometimes be impersonal compared to those of smaller primary schools, where friendly office staff know all the children by name and welcome visitors. Having introduced myself, I explained that I was Lucy's new foster carer and asked the receptionist if my contact details were on file. She checked and found they weren't, so I gave her my address and telephone number, which she wrote on a piece of paper.

'Is this Lucy's permanent address?' she asked, glancing up.

'Yes, for the year.'

She made another note, although I couldn't see what it was.

'Also,' I said, 'I'd like to make an appointment to see Lucy's teacher, Miss Connor, please.'

'You'll need to arrange that with Miss Connor herself,' she replied – not terribly helpful.

'How do I do that?'

'Phone the school at lunchtime; she won't be teaching then.'

'Thank you,' I said, and turned to the girls. They stood ready to leave.

'Have a good day then, love,' I said to Lucy, as she swung her school bag over her shoulder.

She gave a small nod. 'Bye, Paula, see you later.'

'Bye,' Paula said, with a little wave.

We watched Lucy go through the swing doors that led into the main body of the school, and then Paula and I left the building and hurried to the car. Fortunately, most of the traffic was going in the opposite direction, so I arrived at Paula's school just as the bell was going. I gave her a big kiss, said a quick goodbye and drove home. I hadn't been in long when the phone rang and it was Jill, my support social worker, from the agency I fostered for.

'Well done,' she said, as soon as I answered. 'Pat tells me you performed a miracle and Lucy is with you now.'

'She is,' I said, appreciating the praise. 'I've just returned from taking her to school.'

'Excellent. So how's she doing? Settling in?'

'Yes, she's doing fine.'

'Has Lucy's social worker, Stevie, been in touch yet?'

'Not yet.'

'She'll be phoning you later to arrange a visit, and I need to see you and Lucy too. Can I come after school tomorrow?'

'Yes, half past four would be good. Give us a chance to have a drink and a snack first.' Both the child's social worker and the carer's support social worker have to visit as soon as possible after a child has moved in.

'I'll see you at half past four then,' Jill confirmed. 'Do you have any immediate concerns about Lucy?'

'Only her eating,' I said. 'But I'll discuss that with you tomorrow.'

'All right. See you tomorrow. And well done.'

'Thank you.'

I was smiling as I put down the phone. We all like praise – a verbal pat on the back – and foster carers are no exception. I really appreciated Jill's words, her recognition that I had done well to persuade Lucy to move in without a big scene, and I continued the day with renewed energy – even while doing the housework.

An hour later the landline rang again.

'Hello, it's Lucy's social worker, Stevie. I need to see Lucy, but my diary's full until Friday, so I'll come then at half past three.'

'Can we make it a bit later?' I said. 'We won't be home from school then. Half past four would be better.'

I thought I heard a small sigh before she said: 'Very well. See you at half past four.' And with no goodbye, she hung up.

'Do Our Best'

I excused Stevie's brusqueness on the grounds that, like most social workers, she undoubtedly carried a huge workload and did a very difficult job.

It was only as twelve noon approached that I realized I hadn't thought to ask the school's receptionist what time the school broke for lunch – the time I was supposed to phone Lucy's teacher – so I took a chance and telephoned at 12.30. I gave my name and said that I would like to speak to Miss Connor.

'She's at lunch,' the receptionist said.

'Yes, I know,' I said. 'I was asked to telephone at lunchtime to speak to her.'

'Hold the line and I'll see if she's in the staff room.'

The line went quiet and then a series of clicks followed before a male voice said: 'Hello, staff room.'

'Is it possible to speak to Miss Connor, please?' I asked, in my best speaking voice.

'Should be,' he said, sounding friendly and jovial. 'I'll ask her.' I heard him call across the staff room: 'Miss Connor, are you free?'

'Yes, she is,' he said. 'She's on her way.'

A moment later a young woman's voice answered. 'Hello?'

I gave my name again and said that I was Lucy's new foster carer and that I thought it would be a good idea if we could meet soon.

'Yes, absolutely, the sooner the better,' Miss Connor said enthusiastically. 'I'm pleased you've phoned. I knew Lucy was having to move again. I could see you after school this afternoon, if that suits you?'

'Yes, please. Although I'll have my younger daughter with me.'

'No problem. Come to my classroom when you arrive. It's E1; reception will direct you. I'll keep Lucy with me at the end of school.'

'Thank you.'

'I'll look forward to meeting you.'

'And you.'

Miss Connor came across as a very pleasant, well-organized and approachable lady. I was looking forward to meeting her and having the opportunity to discuss Lucy's progress and what help she might need with her learning.

That afternoon disappeared in a trip to the local shops for groceries, and then it was time to collect Paula. Paula knew she had to come out quickly this week and not lag behind chatting to her friends, as we would be collecting Lucy from school. Adrian had a front-door key and would let himself in as usual.

Paula came out on time and I drove to Lucy's school. The reception area was busy with other parents and it was a couple of minutes before I was seen. I explained that I had an appointment with Miss Connor and asked for directions to her classroom.

'E1 is through the swing doors, then turn right, down the corridor, up the staircase on your left, and Miss Connor's room is on your left,' the receptionist said.

I thanked her. 'Did you get all that?' I joked to Paula, as we went through the swing doors.

Paula grinned and pulled a face. But finding Miss Connor's classroom wasn't as complicated as it had sounded, and a couple of minutes later we were at the top of the stairs, standing outside classroom E1. Through the glass in the door I could see Lucy sitting at one of the tables near the front of the room, but there was no sign of her teacher. I knocked on the door and we went in.

Lucy looked up and smiled. 'That's my teacher, over there,' she said, pointing to the young woman working on the wall display at the rear of the classroom.

Miss Connor stopped what she was doing and came over. 'Lovely to meet you,' she said pleasantly.

'And you,' I said, shaking her hand.

'I thought the girls could wait in here while we have a chat,' Miss Connor said. 'We can use the English office next door.'

'You'll be all right in here, won't you?' I said to Paula. 'I'll be in the room next door.'

Paula nodded and, dropping my hand, went over and sat beside Lucy.

'Come and fetch us if you need us,' Miss Connor said to the girls, as we left.

'Yes, Miss,' Lucy said respectfully.

The door to the next room was labelled English Office, E2. 'We call it "The Cupboard",' Miss Connor said, as she opened the door and we went in. I could see why.

It was a small room that clearly doubled as the English department's stock cupboard as well as their office, and it was full. A small steel-framed table and three matching chairs stood in the centre of the room and the walls were lined with cupboards and shelves full of sets of English books. There was just enough room to draw out a chair either side of the table.

'I'm Lucy's English teacher as well as her form teacher,' Miss Connor explained as we sat down.

'Thank you for seeing me so quickly,' I said. 'I know Lucy's behind with her learning and I want to help her all I can.'

'That's great. Why did she have to move?' Miss Connor asked.

It was a question I'd been expecting and I explained that living with Pat and Terry had only been a temporary arrangement.

'She's had so many moves,' Miss Connor said. 'Will she be staying with you permanently now?'

It was another question I'd been expecting. 'Lucy will live with me until the final court hearing,' I said. 'Then the judge will make a decision on where she should live permanently. The whole process usually takes about a year.'

'But it's not likely Lucy will return to live with her mother, is it?' Miss Connor asked, concerned. 'I didn't think she ever saw her mother.' As her teacher, she would have some knowledge of Lucy's background from the school's records.

'Lucy doesn't see her mother often,' I said. 'And she'd have to complete a successful parenting assessment to convince the authorities that she is capable of looking after Lucy.'

'And if the judge decides Lucy shouldn't go to live with her mother, she'll stay with you?'

For those who don't know the workings of the social-care system, a child staying with their present foster carer often seems the most obvious solution.

'If the judge decides Lucy can't live with her mother, then the social services will try to find a relative to look after her,' I explained. 'That's always considered the next best option. If there is no suitable relative then the social services will find Lucy a long-term foster family to match her cultural needs. As you know, she's dual heritage – her father is Thai.'

There was a pause when Miss Connor looked concerned. 'And Lucy knows all this?'

'Yes. I've explained it to her and so has her social worker.'

'Poor kid. How very unsettling. It makes you grateful for your own family.'

'It does,' I said. Then steering Miss Connor back on track, I said, 'But while Lucy's with me I want to do my very best for her, and I hope to make a big difference in a year.'

'Yes, of course. Absolutely. We must do our best for Lucy. I'll start by telling you where she is with her learning.'

Chapter Fourteen

Control

Half an hour later I was driving home, mulling over everything Miss Connor had told me while the girls chatted in the rear of the car. I'd told Lucy that Miss Connor was pleased with her progress, although she still had some catching up to do, so Miss Connor and I would help her do that. I'd reassured Lucy that this wasn't her fault, but the result of all the times she'd been absent from primary schools. What I hadn't told Lucy was that Miss Connor was more concerned with Lucy's lack of friends than with her education, which she felt she could catch up on. 'Isolated', 'solitary', 'lacking in self-confidence', 'low self-esteem' and 'doesn't trust people' were some of the words and phrases Mrs Connor had used about Lucy. And while I knew, as Miss Connor did, the reasons why Lucy was like this, it was difficult to know what to do about it. Certainly telling Lucy she needed to make friends wouldn't help. I could support Lucy in her learning, help build her self-esteem through praise, but I couldn't make friends for her.

'Lucy, you know you can always invite friends home for tea,' I said, glancing at her in the interior mirror. 'I would take them home in the car afterwards,' I added, for Lucy's classmates lived in the catchment area of the school – about a twenty-minute drive from us.

Control

'Thanks,' Lucy said, and continued chatting to Paula.

I didn't know what else to say, but I was worried, as Miss Connor was, for social isolation can so easily lead to depression – in children as well as adults.

Adrian was already back when we arrived home. I set about making the dinner while the children unwound from their day at school. Once we'd eaten (with Lucy eating very little again), I explained to her that I liked everyone to do their homework before they watched any television.

'I haven't got much homework,' Lucy said.

'Nevertheless, I'd like you to do it first,' I said. I had to start as I meant to carry on.

A little reluctantly, Lucy fetched her school bag and brought it to the table, while Adrian, used to our routine, had already disappeared into the front room to research a piece of homework on the computer. He knew the sooner he completed his homework the sooner he could watch some television. Paula was playing, and I knew that on Mondays she just had reading homework to do, so I would hear her read once I'd seen to Lucy.

'We've got maths and science homework,' Lucy said with a sigh. 'I'm in the bottom group for maths.'

'Well, let's see if I can help you change that,' I said. 'Although maths was never my strong point at school.'

With another sigh, Lucy opened her maths exercise book where a worksheet had been stapled in. 'Fractions,' she said, and propped her head on her hand despondently.

I scanned the page and felt confident I could help her, for the sums were quite simple, although I could see that in the previous exercise she'd got quite a few wrong. 'Do you understand what a fraction is?' I asked, going back to basics.

'A part of a whole,' Lucy said.

'That's right. Well done. The number under the line is the whole number and the number above is the number of parts. So if you cut a cake in two and eat half, you are eating one part of two parts.'

'And the number below the line in a fraction is called the denominator,' Lucy said. 'And the number at the top is the numerator.'

'Excellent,' I said.

'I understand that,' Lucy said gloomily. 'It's when you have to add and take them away that I don't get it.'

'OK, let me talk you through the stages for adding and taking away one step at a time.' Starting with the first question, I went through the stages for adding fractions while Lucy did the maths involved. Although I was helping her, it was important she did the calculations herself so she would gain confidence and learn. I did the same with the second fraction, which was a subtraction, and she completed the third by herself, with me beside her to give help if necessary.

'Excellent,' I said. 'See, you *can* do it.'

She smiled, pleased with herself. 'You like helping kids, don't you?' she said, glancing at me before starting the next question.

'Yes, I suppose I do,' I said.

'Why?'

I was slightly taken aback. It seemed a strange question, and wasn't one I'd been asked before. I was surprised by the candidness of my reply. 'Well, we all feel better about ourselves when we do something right. I found some of my school work difficult. Not like some kids, who got everything right. I remember sitting in class and keeping my head down, hoping the teacher wouldn't ask me a question. I can also remember how relieved I was when my parents helped me with my homework and showed me what to do. Like you, I just needed it explained again, so I do the same for my children.'

'And while I'm here I'm one of your children?' she asked.

'Yes, of course, love.'

And I knew from Lucy's smile just how much that reassurance meant to her, and my heart ached.

As Lucy tackled the next question, I checked on Adrian to see if he needed any help, but he didn't. Then, telling Lucy to call me if she needed me, I went through to the living room to hear Paula read.

'Is Lucy's homework hard like Adrian's?' Paula asked.

'Yes,' I said, aware that Lucy could hear me. 'And she's doing very well.'

Lucy didn't need my assistance while I was hearing Paula read, so once we'd finished I went through to see how she was getting on.

'I've nearly finished,' she said. 'Can you check them?'

'Yes, of course, love.'

I looked down her answers and saw a couple of errors. 'Have another look at those two,' I said, pointing.

'They're wrong, aren't they?' she said, immediately losing confidence and becoming annoyed with herself.

'You've made a couple of small errors, that's all. The rest are fine.'

I waited while Lucy corrected them, and then she did the last sum.

'Well done,' I said. 'What's next?'

'Science,' she said with a groan.

She put away her maths book and took out her science book together with a rough notebook. 'We have to write up a science experiment,' she said, opening both books.

The previous piece of work in her science book was covered in the teacher's pencil corrections, and the notes Lucy had made in her rough notebook about the last experiment were littered with spelling mistakes and very poor grammar; I couldn't see a single full stop. Without making an issue of it, I picked up Lucy's pencil and began going through the rough draft of the experiment, correcting the spelling and grammar and explaining what was wrong.

'Thanks,' she said.

I left Lucy to copy the science experiment into her book under the various headings of 'Aim', 'Apparatus', 'Method' and 'Conclusion', while I played a game with Paula and then saw her up to bed. When I returned downstairs Lucy had finished her science homework and was packing away her books.

'All done?' I asked.

She nodded. 'Thanks for your help.'

I then mentioned to Lucy that Jill was coming to see us after school the following day. 'And Stevie is coming on Friday,' I said. 'I expect you're used to social workers visiting from living with your other foster carers.'

Lucy stopped what she was doing and her face set. 'You can talk to them, but I'm not. I hate fucking social workers!' Throwing her school bag on the floor, she stormed out of the room and upstairs, slamming her bedroom door behind her.

I was shocked by the sudden change in Lucy's behaviour and the vehemence of her outburst. I'd looked after children before who swore, sometimes at me – many children in care are angry because of the way they have been treated. But a second before Lucy had been sweetly thanking me for helping her with her homework, and now she'd just blown up, and over something quite small.

Control

I gave her a few moments to calm down, but not very long. Not as long as I would have given a child I'd been fostering for many months and therefore knew well and that they could be safely left alone. I was aware that Lucy had locked herself in the bathroom for hours at Pat and Terry's, and while she couldn't lock herself in any of the rooms in my house, as all the doors were fitted with safety locks that could be opened from the outside, I was worried she might do some something desperate – possibly barricade herself into her room or even harm herself in anger. As an experienced foster carer I'd dealt with all types of behaviour before and my instinct now told me that Lucy shouldn't be left alone for long and that I should go up to her.

At the top of the stairs I quickly looked into Paula's bedroom to see if she had been woken by Lucy's shouting, but she hadn't. I then knocked on Adrian's door, poked my head round and said, 'You OK?'

'What's the matter with Lucy?' he asked.

'She's upset. I'm going to her now. Don't worry.'

He nodded and, partly reassured, returned to the book he was reading.

Closing his door, I went to Lucy's room. It was quiet. 'Lucy?' I said, giving a small knock on the door. 'Can I come in?'

More silence, so giving another knock I slowly opened the door. The room was in darkness and it took a few seconds for my eyes to adjust after the brightness of the landing light. Lucy was lying face down on her bed with her face buried in the crook of her arm.

'Are you all right, love?' I asked gently, taking a couple of steps into her room.

'Go away,' she said, without raising her head. 'Leave me alone.' I could tell from her voice that she was crying.

I stayed where I was, a little way from her bed. 'I can't leave you alone while you're upset, love,' I said gently. I heard her sob. 'Can you try talking to me and telling me what's the matter?'

'I hate social workers,' she said. 'And I'm not seeing them.'

'All right. I won't force you to see them if you really don't want to. But they only want to help you. As you know, they have to visit regularly. Jill, to make sure I'm looking after you properly, and Stevie to make sure you're OK.'

'She doesn't care!' Lucy blurted from beneath her arm. 'No one does.'

Taking the couple of steps to her bed, I sat on the edge. 'I care,' I said.

'No, you don't,' she said vehemently. 'Fostering is a job to you.'

'It's far more than a job,' I said. 'Fostering is my life. I love looking after children and it hurts me when I see them upset.'

'Don't care,' Lucy said.

'I think you do care, or you wouldn't be crying.' I placed my hand gently on her shoulder. 'I know it's difficult, love. You've been through so much, but don't shut all the hurt inside you. It'll make it worse. Can you try and tell me what's really upsetting you? I'd like to help if I can.' For I felt sure this was more than just the visit of two social workers.

'No. You won't understand,' Lucy said, face down into her arm. 'You can't understand unless you've been there.'

'You could try and help me understand,' I said, my hand still lightly resting on her shoulder. 'I know you've had a lot of changes in your life. I know that some of the people who were supposed to look after you, didn't. I'm sure there's a lot more you can tell me.'

control

There was a long pause when I thought she might be summoning the courage to tell me, but then she said, 'Not now.'

'Sure? There's no rush. I can sit here all night if it helps.'

'No,' she said, and shook her head. I knew I shouldn't pursue it, as she clearly wasn't ready.

'All right, another time then,' I said. 'Now, let's dry those tears and get you into bed. Worries are always worse if you're tired, and you've got school again tomorrow.'

Lucy finally raised her head and, sitting up in bed, turned to face me. I wiped her cheeks with a tissue. 'There, that's better,' I said. 'You've got such a lovely face; I don't like to see you looking sad.'

She gave me the faintest of smiles, her anger gone now. 'Can I have a hug?' she asked, as she had the first night.

'Of course, love. I'm always ready for a hug.'

She slid her arms around me and buried her head in my neck. I held her close. 'Remember, love, when you're ready to share your worries with me, I'll be here ready to listen. It doesn't matter how busy I am; you say, "Cathy, I have something to tell you and I need to talk." And I'll listen. OK?'

'I'll remember that,' she said, and hugged me tighter.

'So the honeymoon period is well and truly over,' Jill said, with a knowing laugh, as I finished updating her the following day. 'That was quick.'

As Lucy had threatened, she'd refused to see Jill and had stormed up to her room when she'd arrived, shouting as she went that she wouldn't come down until Jill had gone.

'You could say that,' I said, returning Jill's smile. 'Lucy's anger is very fierce but short-lived. She recovers quickly, although I think there's plenty more to come out.'

'Absolutely,' Jill agreed. 'And the longer Lucy's here, the more secure she'll feel, so the easier it will be for her anger to come out.'

'Thanks, Jill,' I said. 'But on the positive side, she is sleeping well; she's made friends with Paula and Adrian, she's talking to us and I've seen her teacher and we're giving her some extra help to catch up. Lucy was happy for me to help her with her homework.'

'Excellent. It's good she wants to learn,' Jill said. 'I've updated Stevie about the allegations Lucy made against her stepfather and she'll be talking to Lucy about that on Friday, assuming Lucy will see her.'

'I'll try to persuade her,' I said. 'I'll explain that it's important.'

'Good. Now the paperwork,' Jill said. 'Have you received it?'

'No.' Usually the placement and essential information forms came with the social worker when the child first arrived, but because Pat and Terry had brought Lucy this hadn't happened.

'I'll speak to Stevie,' Jill said, taking out her notepad and making a note. 'You need those forms. She can post them or bring them with her on Friday.'

'Thank you.'

'And Lucy's eating? How's that going?' Jill now asked.

I frowned, concerned. 'Well, as I said on the phone, she's eating, but not nearly enough. Lucy's very slim. She can't afford to lose weight. I haven't weighed her because I don't want to draw attention to it, and anyway it wouldn't help – not knowing what she weighed before, I won't know if she's losing weight. She's very anxious at the meal table and doesn't seem to get any pleasure from eating. I always ask her if she likes the food I'm planning to cook. She says she does, but then hardly eats anything.'

control

'Does she have school dinners?'

'Yes, but I've no idea if she's eating them.'

'No, and at secondary school the staff won't encourage the children to eat as they do in primary school. I'll speak to Stevie and see what she knows about Lucy's eating.' Jill made another note. 'I believe concerns were raised about Lucy's eating by her previous carers,' Jill said. 'And Stevie will have a copy of Lucy's medical. We may need to seek medical help if Lucy's eating doesn't improve, and we'll also need to raise it at her review.'

Jill was referring to the regular reviews that all children in care have. At these meetings, issues such as the child's health, education and general wellbeing are discussed to make sure everything that needs to be done is being done to help the child.

'And in the meantime I'll continue as I have been doing?' I now asked Jill. 'I'm giving Lucy a variety of foods in manageable portions and letting her eat what she wants. I haven't been overtly encouraging her to eat, as I didn't want to make her feel more self-conscious than she already does.'

'No, that's right,' Jill said, and looked thoughtful. 'It's possible Lucy is suffering from an eating disorder, like anorexia or bulimia. I take it she's not going to the toilet straight after a meal and making herself sick?'

'No!' I said, shocked. 'I'd have noticed, although I'll obviously keep an eye on her.'

Jill made another note. 'It might be that, once she feels more settled here, her appetite will improve, but we can't rule out anorexia, which is more about control than food. Given how little control Lucy has had in her life, you could see how she might use food to gain control. You've attended training on eating disorders, haven't you?'

'Yes, a while back. I think I need to read up on the subject.'

'Good idea. Make sure you give Lucy as much control over her food as is practical for an eleven-year-old. Let her help with the preparation and cooking of the food when possible, and allow her to serve herself rather than plate it up for her. If she feels she has control over her food, she's likely to feel less anxious and may eat more.'

'Thanks, Jill,' I said, grateful for her advice. 'I'll do that. But isn't eleven very young to be suffering from an eating disorder? I thought it was teenagers who had the condition.'

'It's more prevalent in teenagers – boys and girls – but it's becoming increasingly common in children, even those under ten. I blame the girly magazines and media, which portray thin girls as beautiful.'

I nodded. I agreed with Jill, for I'd often felt glossy women's magazines showed unrealistic body shapes as the ideal. Certainly I could never look like those models.

Jill concluded her visit, as she usually did, by reading and then signing my log notes, and I then saw her to the front door.

'Goodbye, Lucy, Adrian and Paula!' she called from the hall.

'Goodbye!' Adrian and Paula returned from upstairs, but there was nothing from Lucy.

'No worries,' Jill said. 'Tell her I said goodbye and I look forward to meeting her next time.'

I went upstairs and relayed Jill's message to Lucy, who was now playing with Paula in her room, and she just shrugged. A quarter of an hour later I called everyone downstairs for dinner. Following Jill's advice, instead of serving the meal onto plates as I usually did, I set the casserole dish in the centre of the table and, warning them that the dish was very hot, I told everyone to help themselves. The result was a very messy tablecloth. Adrian, Paula and I ate our usual-sized portions, and Lucy, who took a very small amount, finished with a clean plate. Whether this was progress or not I didn't know, but one thing I did know was that the following day, when everyone was at school, I would go online and research eating disorders.

Chapter Fifteen

'I Don't Want Her Help!'

Twenty per cent of those who develop anorexia will die from their illness, I read. I read the words twice. What I was reading was shocking and I was having difficulty taking it all in. I'd been on the computer reading and scrolling for nearly an hour and I was shaken to the core. All I needed to know about anorexia and other dreadful eating disorders was online. Gruesome photographs of emaciated young people accompanied agonizing testimonials from devoted parents who'd battled for years to try to help their child overcome an eating disorder. Some families had won the battle and were now giving support and advice to other families facing the same illness, while others had lost the battle and their child had died. It was heartbreaking, and more than once my eyes welled as I read the painful accounts of young lives ruined and even ended by these horrendous illnesses.

Jill had been right when she'd said that children under ten were being diagnosed with eating disorders – some were as young as five or six. There was mention of the media being partly to blame by using very thin models, and also discussion about various therapies for discovering the underlying problems of the sufferer. It seemed that anorexia and other eating disorders were never only about eating food, but the manifestation of a deeper unhappiness, which often needed to be addressed by the whole family going into therapy.

As well as parents sharing their experiences, there were blogs and forums run by sufferers or those who had recovered, and they described in candid detail the horrors of being at the mercy of a severe eating disorder. One of the most harrowing I read was by a woman, aged twenty-two, who'd suffered from anorexia since the age of sixteen. Her blog stopped abruptly one day, and then her best friend had added a 'Rest in Peace' message, stating that her friend had died the day before, having literally starved herself to death. One of the most heartening posts was from a mother who'd twice brought her daughter back from the brink of death and she had now made a full recovery. The mother was sharing what she'd learnt to try and help other parents, and her advice made good sense and fitted in with what Jill had said: give the young person as much control over their food as possible, for eating disorders are tied up with a feeling of helplessness and being at the mercy of others. I also learnt that weighing scales should be put away, as someone with anorexia will often weigh themselves repeatedly – upwards of ten times a day – and if they gain an ounce they purge themselves with laxatives. While I didn't think Lucy was doing this, as soon as I'd finished on the computer I went upstairs and took the scales out of the bathroom and put them at the back of my wardrobe. We didn't need them.

What I'd read played on my mind. While Lucy's eating problems seemed relatively mild compared to the accounts I'd read online, I felt a huge responsibility to make sure she didn't develop full-blown anorexia, which she could easily do, given her past.

* * *

In line with what I'd read, I decided not to do a big supermarket shop during the week as I usually did, but to wait until Saturday when Lucy would be home from school and could come with me to help choose our food. In the same mode, I left the preparation of the ingredients for the fish pie I was planning for the evening meal until the girls were home from school. Adrian had an after-school activity and wouldn't be home until later.

'Would you both like to help me make the fish pie?' I asked the girls enthusiastically, once they'd taken off their coats and had a drink.

Paula looked at me a bit oddly. 'Fish pie? I like helping make cakes, but making fish pie doesn't sound much fun.'

Lucy said, 'Do we have to? I wanted to watch television before dinner.'

'No, you don't have to,' I said, for it seemed counterproductive to insist. 'I just thought you might like to help, and it wouldn't take long.'

The girls looked at each other and then at me. 'We'd rather watch television,' they chorused.

'OK. Another time then.'

When dinner was ready I called everyone to the table (Adrian was home by then). As I had done the previous evening, I placed the dish containing the main course in the centre of the table with a serving spoon and, with a warning that the dish was very hot, told everyone to help themselves. The result was the same: Adrian, Paula and I ate heartily, and Lucy took the tiniest of amounts, but ate it all. She also had a glass of milk, which would be good for her. She didn't go to the toilet straight after the meal, so I assumed she wasn't making herself sick. I therefore remained hopeful that with lots of TLC, and by encouraging her to talk about her problems, her issues surrounding food and eating would gradually disappear.

That first week Lucy was with us, I'd taken her to and collected her from school, and on Friday, when we arrived home, Lucy reminded me: 'Don't forget to ask my social worker if I can go by bus next week.'

'Or you could ask her yourself?' I suggested. 'She'll be here soon.'

'No, thank you. I'll be in my room,' Lucy said, and flounced off upstairs.

'I'll be in my room too,' Paula said, following Lucy upstairs.

Adrian wasn't home yet, so when Stevie arrived fifteen minutes later there was just Toscha and me to greet her. I opened the front door and Stevie took one look at the cat and cried out: 'I hate cats! They make me sneeze. Can you put it out?'

Toscha didn't need putting out. Stevie's cry had startled her so much that she'd shot out right past her, which just left me to welcome Lucy's social worker.

'Nice to meet you,' I said. 'Shall I take your coat?'

'No. I'll keep it on, thanks.'

I showed Stevie through to the living room and then offered her a drink.

'Water, please,' she said.

I poured the glass of water and when I returned to the living room Stevie was still standing.

'Do sit down,' I said.

'Where? Which chair does the cat sit on? I can't sit where the cat does or I won't stop sneezing.' So I guessed she had a bad allergy to cat's fur.

'She sits over there,' I said, pointing to Toscha's favourite seat by the window. 'Although I do vacuum the cushions regularly.'

Stevie sat on the sofa furthest from Toscha's favourite seat and set her briefcase on the floor beside her. 'Where's Lucy?' she asked, quite brusquely.

'In her room,' I said. 'I'll try to persuade her to come down later. I'm afraid she's still a bit anti social workers at the moment. She wouldn't see Jill, either.'

'I'll need to see her at some point,' Stevie said bluntly.

'Yes, I appreciate that,' I said. 'I can always take you up to her room, if she really won't come down.' For I knew it was a requirement that the social worker had to actually see the child when he or she visited. The same wasn't so for my support social worker.

Stevie opened her briefcase and took out a wodge of papers. 'Here's the paperwork you need,' she said, handing me the placement and essential information forms. 'You can look at those later.'

'Thank you,' I said, setting them beside me on the sofa.

'So, how is she?' Stevie asked, taking a pen and notepad from her briefcase. 'Jill tells me you've got some problems.'

'Not so much problems,' I said. 'Lucy is settling in well. More worries.'

'Go on then,' she said, with her pen poised. I was finding her manner rather abrupt and I wondered if this was the reason why Lucy had found it difficult relating to her.

'Well, her eating,' I began. And I explained my concerns about how little Lucy ate, her anxiety around food and that she was thin. I then asked about the medical.

'Lucy had a medical,' Stevie said defensively. 'You can't have a copy, it's confidential. But I can tell you she's in good health.'

'I Don't Want Her Help!'

'So nothing was said about her eating or weight?'

'Her weight's low. At the very bottom of normal. The last carer thought she could be anorexic, but it wasn't confirmed. We'll start Lucy in therapy once she's with her permanent family – after the final court hearing.'

'But that's a year away,' I said, concerned.

'Yes. But we don't usually start therapy until the child is settled, and she won't be staying here. As an experienced foster carer I'm sure you know the reason – therapy is long-term and it releases all sorts of emotions, behaviour and pain which are best dealt with in a settled environment. If you've still got concerns in a few months, we'll send her for another medical. But too many medicals are a form of abuse. You wouldn't like to keep having to take off your clothes in front of strangers, would you?'

I thought this was a strange comment. We were after all talking about a doctor and a possible life-threatening condition. But I didn't comment.

'Was there anything else?' Stevie asked.

'The allegations Lucy made about her stepfather, Dave ...' I said.

'Yes. Jill told me. The matter's already on file. It was investigated at the time and there was no evidence.'

'I see,' I said thoughtfully, meeting Stevie's gaze. I was expecting her to give me a little more detail and clarification, but she just looked back, waiting for me to move on to whatever else I had to raise.

'I've seen Lucy's teacher,' I said. 'As you know, Lucy is behind with her education so I'll be helping her at home to catch up.'

'Don't put the child under pressure,' Stevie said bluntly. 'There's enough going on in her life.'

'Of course I won't put her under pressure,' I said. 'Lucy's happy for me to help her. She was so pleased when she got all her maths homework right. You could see her confidence grow.'

'So what are you doing to meet her cultural needs?' Stevie now asked. Before I had a chance to answer she'd added: 'I wanted a foster family to match her ethnicity, but we didn't have one.' And I felt she could have added, 'So you'll have to do.'

I wondered if this was the reason for the sharpness in Stevie's attitude towards me. She was dual heritage, although not of the same racial origins as Lucy, so possibly meeting Lucy's cultural needs was a sensitive issue for her, and higher on her agenda than it might otherwise have been. However, like most foster carers, I was used to looking after children from different ethnic backgrounds and prided myself on meeting their needs, although many, like Lucy, had been born in the UK and saw themselves as British.

'I'm right in saying Lucy was born in this country and her mother is English?' I asked.

'Yes, and her father is Thai, which seems to have been forgotten,' Stevie said. 'Lucy has been raised mainly by white English people. I'll try and trace her father and arrange some contact, but you need to start engendering a positive cultural identity in her. Talk to her about Thailand, cook some Thai food and hang the Thai flag on one of the walls in her bedroom along with some pictures from her country.'

I knew better than to say that England was Lucy's country, so I just nodded agreeably. I heard the front door open and close as Adrian returned home from school. 'That's my son,' I said to Stevie, and Adrian called 'Hi' from the hall as he went through to the kitchen.

'I'll be trying to set up some contact with Lucy's mother too,' Stevie continued. 'Lucy hasn't seen her mother in over six months and only twice the year before that. At present I don't have her current contact details, but as soon as I do I'll arrange for Lucy to see her. I think that's everything,' Stevie concluded.

'Is there anything else you can tell me about Lucy's background that will help me look after her?' I asked.

'Everything you need to know is in those papers,' she said, nodding to the placement and essential information forms beside me on the sofa. I doubted it. These forms usually provided basic information on the child, but gave little more background information than the referral. It wouldn't give me a clearer understanding of Lucy's past. Foster carers rely on the social worker for that; some are forthcoming and others are not.

'Lucy doesn't have any other relatives apart from her mother, does she?' I asked.

'Yes, she does,' Stevie said, quite curtly. 'There's her father, although we're not sure if he's in this country. And Lucy has two uncles on her mother's side, although she doesn't see them. She also has a maternal grandmother and a distant aunt on her mother's side. Lucy stayed with the aunt for a short time when she was a baby.'

'So Lucy has a grandmother?' I asked, slightly surprised that Lucy hadn't mentioned her when we'd talked about my parents, whom she would meet soon.

'As far as we know, Lucy has never seen her grandmother,' Stevie said. 'Bonnie is estranged from her family. She's had a hard life too.'

I nodded sadly. 'Well, at least Lucy has been saved from further suffering,' I said, trying to focus on the positive.

'The care plan for Lucy is a Full Care Order,' Stevie said, oblivious to my sentiment. 'Then for a relative to look after her long-term, if there is one, or, if not, a long-term foster placement to match her cultural needs.'

I nodded. 'Lucy would like to use the bus to go to school from next week,' I said. 'Is that all right with you?'

'Yes. Why shouldn't it be? She's not likely to run away. She hasn't got anywhere to run to.'

'I just wanted to check with you first.'

'Well, if that's everything, can you take me up to see her now?' Stevie said, putting her pen and notepad into her briefcase.

I stood and led the way out of the living room and upstairs to Lucy's room, where I knocked on her bedroom door. 'Lucy, Stevie wants to see you,' I said, and opened her door a little. 'Can she come in?'

'No!' Lucy said loudly. 'She can't!'

I glanced at Stevie, but opened the door slightly wider so I could see in. Lucy was sitting on her bed cuddling Mr Bunny. 'She needs to see you, love,' I said. 'To make sure you're OK.'

'Tell her I'm OK,' Lucy said rudely.

'And I need to talk to you,' Stevie added, over my shoulder.

'Go away. I'm not talking to you,' Lucy said.

'Don't be rude, love,' I said. 'Stevie only wants to help.'

'I don't want her help,' Lucy said.

'Suit yourself,' Stevie retorted with a shrug. I think it was supposed to be a joke to defuse the atmosphere, but it didn't work.

'Bugger off!' Lucy shouted.

'Lucy!' I cautioned. I felt embarrassed by her rudeness and, as her foster carer, responsible for her behaviour.

'If you don't want me to come in, you can come to the door,' Stevie said.

'No.' Lucy said. 'I'm not moving.'

Lucy could be very determined when she wanted to be, and I thought of her previous carers, Pat and Terry, who'd spent hours trying to talk her out of the bathroom and had then had to break down the door. It was clear that Lucy wasn't going to come out or even come to the door, so I moved aside so that Stevie could see into the room and see Lucy.

'Is there anything you need?' Stevie asked from the open door.

'No!' Lucy said.

'I'm trying to arrange contact for you to see your mother,' Stevie said. Lucy didn't reply. 'I'm also trying to trace your father and your uncles to see if they can offer you a permanent home.'

While all this was correct social-work practice, I thought that mentioning another move now, when Lucy had only been with me a week, could be very unsettling for her.

'Don't care!' Lucy said. 'Do what you want. You will anyway.'

Again, I felt embarrassed by Lucy's behaviour, although I appreciated that she was angry and frustrated. 'Lucy, you're a big girl,' I tried from where I stood. 'Try talking to Stevie properly.'

There was no reply. Then Stevie said, 'All right, I've seen you. I'll be in touch. Take care.'

She closed Lucy's door, went along the landing and headed downstairs. I followed her down, but as we neared the bottom a loud crash came from Lucy's room. I shot back upstairs while Stevie went to fetch her briefcase from the living room. I gave a perfunctory knock on Lucy's door and went in. Lucy was sitting on the bed with Mr Bunny clutched to her chest, having over-turned the table. Her expression was one of anger, but her eyes glistened as though she was about to cry. 'I'll be with you in a second,' I said.

I quickly went to the top of the stairs. Stevie had fetched her briefcase from the living room and was ready to leave. 'Lucy's upset. Can you let yourself out?' I asked.

'Will do,' Stevie said. Then without any trace of irony she added, 'Have a good weekend,' and let herself out.

Chapter Sixteen

Testing the Boundaries

Adrian and Paula appeared on the landing, wondering what the noise was. 'It's all right. Lucy's table fell over,' I said. 'I'm going to have a chat with her now and then I'll make us some dinner.' We'd been fostering long enough for them to know that a loud noise coming from the child's bedroom and a chat meant that the child was upset and angry and needed me. They both returned to their bedrooms and I returned to Lucy's room. The light was on and I sat on her bed, close, but not quite touching. She was now holding Mr Bunny in a sitting position on her lap facing her, as though she'd been talking to him. Neither of us spoke for a few moments, and then I said, 'Stevie says you can start going to school by bus next week, so that's good news.'

Lucy shrugged, as though it no longer mattered.

There was silence again and then I said, 'You know, it's all right to be angry and upset sometimes, but it's better to talk if you can. I think there's a lot going on in your thoughts that needs to come out. Have you tried talking to your social workers?'

'There's no point,' Lucy said firmly, her expression hard. 'They don't listen.'

'I'm sure the social workers do listen,' I said, 'although they may not always be able to do as you would like them to.' Many children in care want to go home and blame their social workers for not making this happen, although I didn't think this was the reason for Lucy's hostility.

Lucy shrugged dismissively. 'Mr Bunny thinks the same as me, don't you?' she said, looking at him. 'He doesn't talk to social workers, either. He's always with me when they visit. He was before. He knows they don't help me.'

'Mr Bunny has been with you a long time,' I said. Lucy nodded. 'So what do you think Mr Bunny would tell me if he could?' I asked. Children can sometimes share their worries by using a favourite doll or toy as a mouthpiece – to say what they can't.

Lucy sat very still for some moments, her eyes still glistening with unshed tears as she concentrated on Mr Bunny. 'Do you think there's something he'd like to tell me?' I prompted.

There was more silence and then, still looking at Mr Bunny, Lucy said: 'He'd tell you that social workers came to see me lots of times, but they didn't help me. He would say I was often hungry and cold, and I had to do all the washing in cold water. He'd say my aunts and stepdad were horrible to me, and that I wanted to live with Sammy, or someone else, but they didn't talk to me. He'd say they talked to my aunts and stepdad, but not to me. I was so unhappy I wanted to die.'

A cold shiver ran down my spine at Lucy's last words. This is when it would have helped to have known more of Lucy's past. 'You must have been very unhappy,' I said gently. 'Who is Sammy?'

'He was my friend at school,' Lucy said, concentrating on Mr Bunny. 'Sammy lived near me. He had social workers who helped him. I wanted them to help me. But when they came to my house they believed my stepdad and his girlfriend. They were good liars. Mr Bunny knows, don't you?' She gave Mr

Testing the Boundaries

Bunny a little jerk so he nodded his head. It was pitiful and touching. I moved a little closer to Lucy and slipped my arm around her waist.

'Does Mr Bunny know how old you were when this happened?' I asked, trying to fit this into the jigsaw of Lucy's past.

'I was six,' Lucy said with conviction. 'I know because I was so bad that year I didn't get any Christmas presents. I didn't have any birthday presents either, because I was bad.'

'You weren't bad,' I said, horrified by this cruel treatment.

'I was,' Lucy said. 'My aunt said Father Christmas wouldn't come because I'd been telling lies about her at school. But I didn't. Mr Bunny knows I didn't. I told Sammy because I was so unhappy and he told my teacher. It wasn't my fault. The social worker came and told my aunt to get some lotion for my nits. She was so angry when the social worker went. But then she took me to school and was friends with my teacher. I thought they were ganging up on me, so I didn't tell anyone again. And because I told, we had to move and I lost my only friend, Sammy. There were more social workers after that, but no one helped me, so I don't talk to them any more. There's no point.'

What a shocking indictment of our child-protection services, I thought. All that social services involvement, on and off for much of Lucy's life, while she waited for someone to rescue her – and no one had.

'Didn't any of the social workers speak to you by yourself, away from your aunt or stepdad?' I asked.

'No. I would have asked them to take me away if they had. I knew I couldn't live with my mum, but she wasn't horrible to me. She just couldn't look after me. I thought that when I came into care it would be better, but it's not, is it Mr Bunny?'

'Isn't it?' I asked, shocked. 'It should be. What's wrong?'

Lucy gave a little shrug and I held her closer.

'If you can tell me what's wrong, I'll try to put it right,' I said.

She gave another shrug. 'I know foster carers have hot water and they do my washing. And I have nice clothes and no nits, but I still keep having to move. It's like no one wants me. I don't have a family of my own, and no one loves me.'

My eyes welled. I felt so sorry for her, but pity wouldn't help her. 'You will have your own family one day,' I said positively. 'Stevie is going to find you one. Do you remember I explained that when the judge makes his or her decision – in about a year – you will go to live with your forever family? I know it will mean another move, but it will be the last one.'

'I guess,' Lucy said despondently. Then, addressing Mr Bunny, she said: 'At least I'll always have you to love me, won't I?' She gave the soft toy another little shake so he nodded his head. The scene was so tragic I could have wept.

There wasn't much more I could say to Lucy, other than reassure her as I had been doing and also concentrate on the present. I suggested she come downstairs to help me with dinner. I didn't want her sitting alone in her room while she was feeling so low, and also I was trying to involve her in the preparation of her meals and hopefully improve her eating. Lucy did come down with me and helped – peeling and chopping vegetables and then laying the table – but she didn't eat any more. In fact, she ate less. I thought this might be due to the previous upset, as she was subdued for most of the evening. At bedtime I asked her if there was anything else she or Mr Bunny wanted to tell me, but she said no. I tucked her into bed, kissed her goodnight and went downstairs where I sat in the living room and wrote up my log notes. When I'd finished, I looked through the paperwork Stevie had left.

Testing the Boundaries

The placement forms were as I'd expected and included, among other things, the form that gave me the legal right to foster Lucy on behalf of the local authority. The essential information forms, which Stevie said would give me what I needed to know, were a disappointment, with many of the information boxes left blank. Lucy's full name and date of birth were given, together with her mother's name, date of birth and ethnicity as white British, but there was no other information. The box for Lucy's father's details was even barer, without so much as a name, but it did give his ethnicity as Thai. Under the 'Other Relatives' section it stated that Lucy had two uncles who were in their thirties and a great-aunt, but that they weren't known to Lucy, and there were no names, dates of birth or contact details. Lucy's doctor was given as her last – when she was at her previous carers' – and I'd register her with my doctor soon.

I read that Lucy had had a medical nine months previously, the test results of which were normal, although she was in the bottom percentile for her height and weight, and it was noted that she had a poor appetite. There were no details of her birth, and under 'Education' it gave the contact details of her present secondary school and stated that Lucy had missed a lot of primary schooling and was therefore three years behind with her learning. All of which I knew. The next box was headed: 'Does the child have any behavioural issues?' and the answer inserted was 'Yes'. It then stated that a foster carer had noted that Lucy had difficulty expressing her emotions in an acceptable way, and could easily become angry and aggressive. It didn't say which carer had made this observation and it didn't matter. From what I'd seen so far, I thought that the second part of this statement might have some truth in it – Lucy could fly off the handle – but the first part certainly wasn't true. Lucy had just spent half an hour talking to me, so she could express her emotions in an acceptable way given time and encouragement.

The care plan was included in these forms and was as I expected: the social services would apply to the court for a Full Care Order, and then a suitable relative or foster carer would look after Lucy permanently. What was most striking in these essential information forms was the condensed bullet-pointed history it gave of the social services' involvement. It began when concerns had first been raised, when Lucy was six months old, and continued to the present and her placement with me. I couldn't remember ever having fostered a child before where there'd been so much social services involvement, with so little result. I knew it wouldn't be the fault of any one person, but I felt the social services held a collective responsibility for monitoring a case, rather than intervening.

I finished reading and closed the folder with a heartfelt sigh. The poor kid, I thought. Little wonder Lucy felt no one cared for her or loved her; no one had.

On Saturday morning, with no school, we had a more leisurely start to the day, and as usual I made a cooked breakfast, although Lucy only wanted one rasher of bacon and half a slice of toast. I then helped Lucy with her homework – there was no pressure; she'd asked for my help – while Adrian did his homework. After which Lucy, Paula and I went supermarket shopping while Adrian went to his friend's to work on a school project. At the supermarket the girls decided I should push the trolley and call out the items from my list and they would load the trolley. I also told Lucy to select anything she fancied from the shelves. I wouldn't normally have given this invitation to the children I fostered, as we'd have ended up with a trolley full of sweets, biscuits and ice cream and no fruit and vegetables. But I wanted Lucy to have as much say in what she ate as possible, and I was pleased when she selected a bagel from the fresh-bread counter and also a packet of honeycomb cereal. It was a start.

Halfway round the supermarket we came to the aisles dedicated to foods from around the world – shelves of labels from exotic countries: Indian spices, poppadoms, naan and ready-made curry sauces; Chinese noodles, egg-fried rice and sweet-and-sour sauce; Mexican fajitas, tortillas and tacos; and then we came to an assortment of Thai foods.

'Let's make some Thai food for dinner tonight,' I suggested, hoping it didn't sound too contrived. I didn't want to make Lucy feel self-conscious by stating why I was suggesting we ate Thai food. I didn't have to!

'My social worker's been talking to you,' Lucy said easily, with a theatrical sigh. 'She told my last carer I needed to know more about Thailand.' Then turning to Paula she explained: 'My dad is from Thailand, but I don't know him or anything about his country, and my social worker says I should.' She rolled her eyes upwards in exasperation and both girls giggled. So much for political correctness, I thought.

'We'll discover Thai food together,' I said enthusiastically. 'It'll be fun. I've eaten in Thai restaurants, but I've never cooked Thai. We'll make something easy to begin with.'

'Isn't it very spicy?' Paula asked, not a great fan of highly spiced food.

'It needn't be,' I said.

The girls stood either side of me as we surveyed the bewildering assortment of packets, tins and jars. Then I spotted a holder containing leaflets with recipes for Thai food, with a sign beneath telling customers to help themselves. The girls and I began flicking through the recipe leaflets until we came to a

Thai stir-fry. 'I've got a wok,' I said. 'A stir-fry is easy and fun to make.'

'Yes, I like stir-fry,' Paula said.

'So do I,' Lucy agreed.

Holding the leaflet between us, we gathered together the ingredients needed and then completed the rest of our shopping. That evening, all four of us, including Adrian, made the stir-fry, and working together as one family was fun and rewarding in itself. I would like to say that Lucy ate heartily that night, having chosen and cooked the food, but she didn't. While she'd been happy preparing the food, as before, when it came to eating it her anxieties returned and she ate very little. I knew from my research that this behaviour was typical of many who suffered from eating disorders – they are happy to prepare and cook the food, but not eat it. I was worried, and decided that if Lucy's eating didn't improve soon I'd put it to Stevie that we should seek medical advice sooner than she'd suggested.

That evening, Pat, Lucy's previous foster carer, telephoned as promised, but Lucy refused to come to the phone.

'Are you sure you won't speak to Pat?' I asked Lucy.

'Yes.'

'Don't take it personally,' I explained to Pat. 'Lucy's had a lot of changes in her life and is feeling a bit rejected right now.'

'Not by us, I hope,' Pat said defensively. 'It wasn't our fault she had to move.'

'I know, and I've explained that to Lucy. She doesn't blame you.' But of course, deep down, as far as Lucy was concerned, having to move from Pat and Terry's was just another rejection.

Lucy was in the living room and out of earshot, so I took the opportunity to see if I could find out more information about Lucy that might help me look after her better. 'Pat, I know Lucy didn't talk to you much,' I said, 'but I understand you raised concerns about her eating. Stevie mentioned it to me, as I have concerns too.'

'Yes, I took Lucy to my doctor,' Pat said. 'But when I told Stevie she went on at me something awful. Apparently I should have got her permission first.'

'What did the doctor say?'

'That Lucy might be borderline anorexic, and that we should try to talk to her about her feelings. But Lucy didn't want to talk to us. How do you get on with Stevie?'

'I've only met her once,' I said, not wanting to be drawn into a conversation about Lucy's social worker. 'Can you tell me anything else about Lucy or what the doctor said?'

'Not really. Would Lucy see Stevie?' Pat now asked.

'No.'

'She wouldn't see her here either,' Pat said. 'Stevie made me feel it was my fault, but when Lucy decides she's not doing something there's no changing her mind.' I didn't respond. 'Oh, well, best be off then,' Pat said. 'Give Lucy our best wishes.'

'I will,' I said. 'And thanks for everything.' For I doubted we'd hear from Pat again.

When I told Lucy that Pat sent her best wishes, she gave one of her dismissive shrugs. However, I was now realizing that shrugging, far from being a sign that Lucy didn't care, was an indication of just how much she did care and was hurting; not wanting to be hurt again, she pretended it didn't matter.

Sunday was bitterly cold (though it didn't snow again), so I suggested a trip to the cinema. Lucy had been to the cinema a couple of times before with a previous foster carer and was eager to go again. The four of us had a lovely afternoon laughing at the cartoon and eating popcorn. Little outings such as this help bond a family and create a sense of family unity. Interestingly, in the dark and with her mind on the film, Lucy forgot her anxiety about eating and absent-mindedly ate a large hotdog. However, that evening she ate very little at dinner – just a couple of mouthfuls – which she didn't enjoy. Ignoring her eating habits any longer seemed like ignoring the elephant in the room, and later, when I went to say goodnight to her, I said, 'Love, I am concerned that you're not eating enough. You won't get fat, you know.' My research had mentioned that those suffering with eating disorders often obsessed about putting on weight.

'It's not that,' Lucy said, a little tersely, as though something similar might have been said to her before. 'I'm just not hungry. I didn't have meals before.'

'Before you came into care you mean?'

'Yes.'

I nodded. 'I think you need to try to get into the habit of eating. Will you try to eat just a little bit more? I'm sure Mr Bunny would want you to.'

She smiled. 'OK. I'll try, for Mr Bunny.'

'Good girl.'

I kissed her goodnight and came out.

On Monday Lucy began taking the bus to and from school. I gave her the bus fare, checked she had the school books she needed and then waved her off at the door. When I returned from taking Paula to school I phoned the office at Lucy's school to let them know that Lucy would be using the bus in future. Most schools like to know their pupils' means of transport to and from school as a safety precaution, in case they don't arrive, and also to try and reduce the instances of truanting. The school receptionist made a note in their records.

Testing the Boundaries

The week went well and I thought I saw a slight improvement in Lucy's appetite, so I crossed my fingers, hoped for the best and quietly thanked Mr Bunny. On Sunday, my parents came for dinner and met Lucy for the first time. All the children I foster love my parents, and Adrian and Paula adore their nana and grandpa. They are the archetypal grandparents: kind and very generous. My father often tells silly jokes and loves to play board games, and my mother has endless patience for reading the children stories and listening to their news. As my mother and I cleared away the dinner things, my mother commented that Lucy seemed a lovely child, but what a sad life she'd led. While confidentiality had prohibited me from telling my mother about Lucy's past, Lucy had easily confided in her that she'd had to move lots of times and had lived with some horrible people, and that she didn't have a proper mummy or daddy. 'She gets on very well with Paula,' my mother added.

'She does,' I agreed. 'And Adrian, although at his age he tends to be out with his friends more.'

That evening, after my parents had left, I overheard Lucy telling Paula that she was very lucky to have a nice gran and grandpa, as she didn't have any.

'I know,' Paula said. 'And while you're here they are your gran and grandpa too.'

'That's good,' Lucy said. 'I like them nearly as much as I like you.'

Now we were in a weekday routine, the weeks slipped by and very soon Lucy had been with us for over a month. It was March and spring was just around the corner. On many levels, Lucy had fitted easily and successfully into my family, and I knew Adrian and Paula felt that too. However, the more relaxed and at home Lucy felt, the more easily she let go of her anger and

185

frustration. While it was positive that she was able to express herself, what wasn't so positive was her mode of expression: objects hurled across her bedroom and often broken in temper. Triggers that caused her to flare up included any mention of her social worker, an unkind word or a snub from a pupil at school, a lengthy or difficult piece of homework, general frustration, and sometimes there was no obvious reason at all – she'd just arrive home from school, bursting with anger and pent-up frustration, go upstairs and trash her room.

I spent hours talking to Lucy about her feelings, reassured her that hurting was to be expected and made some suggestions for managing her anger. Then, when her behaviour didn't improve, I stopped some of her privileges, and some of her pocket money to pay for breakages (with the social worker's permission). And finally, exasperated, I told her I was very disappointed in her behaviour and that she needed to find other ways to express her anger.

'Don't care!' Lucy shouted. But of course she *did* care and, when she'd calmed down, she was always very sorry.

I showed Lucy how to take out her frustration and anger by pummelling a pillow, rather than breaking objects, which she tried. She pummelled the pillow on her bed and then trashed her room. I knew Lucy had some control over her actions, because while most of the objects in her room had at some time all been thrown, Mr Bunny had escaped.

'I'm sure Mr Bunny isn't impressed by your behaviour, Lucy,' I said, when yet again the contents of her shelves lay strewn across her room.

'Yes, he is!' she retorted. 'He's on my side.'

And sometimes it felt like we were on warring sides – opposing armies in a battle of wills.

* * *

Testing the Boundaries

'You know why Lucy's behaving like this and testing the boundaries?' Jill said, when I updated her yet again.

'To see if I really care or if I will reject her like everyone else has,' I replied.

'Exactly. She's making you prove that you care by pushing you to the limit.'

'I know, Jill, and I've told her I care many, many times. Don't worry, we'll work through this. We have to.'

Seeing my resolve strengthen, Lucy upped the testing and became the most obnoxious, argumentative child I'd come across in a long time. Teenagers can be confrontational and challenging, but Lucy, aged eleven, perfected the art, and I now appreciated where some of the comments from her previous carers had come from. Cooperation had vanished and Lucy questioned everything I did or asked of her, often refusing to do even the simplest of tasks, like getting up in the morning or having a wash and cleaning her teeth at bedtime. When she refused to have a bath for three nights in a row, I stopped her watching television, and when she refused to do her homework I stopped her from going on the PlayStation, which of course led to accusations that I hated her, and she stamped off upstairs and trashed her room. Gone was the quiet, undemanding and convivial child who'd first arrived. Lucy constantly looked for new ways to provoke me. 'Don't like your smelly house!' she said one day. 'Don't like you or your children.' Which I ignored.

'Why is Lucy being horrible to us?' Paula asked one bedtime. 'I don't like it. I want the old Lucy back.'

'Lucy's angry, love,' I said. 'She's had a difficult life and now she feels settled she's letting go of her anger. Try not to worry. She's not angry with you.' And indeed, when Lucy wasn't in a bad mood she played nicely with Paula, and Adrian too.

But Paula did worry, and not for the first time since I'd begun fostering I was concerned about the impact this was having on my children. Adrian, that bit older, seemed able to ignore Lucy's outbursts and unkind words and rise above them as I did, but Paula – two years younger than Lucy – looked up to her and was hurt. I hoped that at some point Lucy's behaviour would peak and then we'd turn a corner. In the meantime, I continued with my strategy of always making time to talk to and listen to Lucy, rewarding her good behaviour and sanctioning her bad behaviour. At the end of March we celebrated Adrian's birthday and then, at the beginning of April, it was Paula's birthday. Lucy was pleasant on both occasions, but once our visitors had left she reverted to her obnoxious behaviour, and I wondered how much longer this could go on. Then something happened, something unplanned that completely changed everything, almost overnight.

Chapter Seventeen

Progress

'I wouldn't ask but we're desperate,' Jill said. 'I know we agreed you'd wait until Lucy had been with you for longer and had calmed down before you fostered another child, but Lucy's taking her time to calm down, and none of our other carers are free. It would only be for two weeks' respite and David's very sweet. It's just while his mother is in hospital.'

'I really don't know, Jill,' I said again, wishing she hadn't asked. Although I had the space in my house to foster another child, I had my hands full with Lucy, and David was sure to be upset at being separated from his mother. 'Will I have to take him to visit his mother in hospital as well?' I asked, feeling this would be impossible with everything else that was going on.

'No, his aunt will take him,' Jill said. 'She can't look after him during the day because she works full time, but she can take him to the hospital in the evenings and at the weekend. David won't give you any trouble,' Jill added. 'And we'd be very grateful.'

'When do you need to know by?' I asked.

'Now, please. His mother would need to bring him to you tomorrow morning, before she goes into hospital.'

'And there really is no one else?'

'No.'

'All right, I'll do it,' I said. 'Although I have big reservations.'

'You'll be fine,' Jill said, with a confidence I didn't feel. 'And you never know, it might do Lucy some good. Give her someone else to focus on for a change, rather than herself.' Although Jill was highly sympathetic to Lucy, as I was, I think she was starting to lose patience and felt that maybe Lucy was revelling in all the attention her outbursts evoked. 'Thanks, Cathy.'

We said goodbye and I went straight upstairs to the spare bedroom and made up the bed with a fresh duvet cover and pillowcase. That evening over dinner, I explained to Adrian, Paula and Lucy that David would be coming the following day to stay for two weeks while his mother was in hospital. Adrian and Paula were very enthusiastic, probably because a well-behaved three-year-old would be light relief after Lucy's recent tantrums. Lucy looked at me, amazed by the news, shocked even, and then became confrontational.

'You're fostering another child as well as me?' she asked disparagingly.

'That's right, love. Just for two weeks.'

'Are you allowed to?'

'Yes, of course. I'm approved to foster two children or a sibling group of up to three. Don't worry. It won't affect my care of you.'

Lucy scowled, while Paula and Adrian wanted to know more about David. 'Why's his mother having to stay in hospital?' Paula asked, concerned.

'She's got to have an operation, and she'll need time to recover afterwards,' I said. Jill had told me that Beth, David's mother, was having a hysterectomy, but Paula didn't need to know that.

'Hasn't David got a gran and grandpa to look after him?' Adrian asked, which is what would have happened to Adrian and Paula had I had to stay in hospital.

190

Progress

'Unfortunately not,' I said. 'David's grandparents are dead.'

'That's sad,' Paula said.

Then Lucy asked, or rather demanded, 'What about his dad? Hasn't he got a dad who can look after him?'

'No, he died last year,' I said. 'He wasn't very old.'

And just for a moment I saw on Lucy's face the briefest acknowledgement that there could be at least one other child in the world who'd had a sad and difficult life just as she had, albeit in a different way. Paula looked close to tears, so I changed the subject and talked about the games we could play with a three-year-old.

That evening, when I went to say goodnight to Lucy, it was obvious she'd been thinking about David, for she had some questions about him. 'Does David still miss his daddy?' she said quietly.

'I'm sure he does,' I said.

'Will he miss his mummy and cry at night?'

'Very likely, but I'll look after him. Then, when you come home from school, you can help me if you like.'

But Lucy had lowered her guard enough for one evening and retorted with a sharp, 'No. That's your job.'

Ignoring her ill humour, I said goodnight, kissed her forehead and came out.

Beth arrived with David at 9.30 the following morning, just after I'd returned from taking Paula to school. Beth was a lovely lady in her thirties, although she was anxious at the thought of the operation she was about to have, and also about leaving David, whom she'd never left with anyone before. She brought with her a suitcase containing David's clothes, a toy box of his favourite toys and books and a cuddly toy, which she told me he took to bed with him at night – all of which would help him settle with me. Although Beth was worried about leaving David, as we talked, David – not fully appreciating what was about to happen – was happy to chase Toscha and then play with the toys I'd put out in the living room. Beth had written down David's routine, which would be useful for me to follow, and had also included his likes and dislikes in food, which again would be very helpful.

'Jen, my sister, will collect David after work tonight,' Beth said, 'at about half past five, and bring him to the hospital. She'll have him back to you by seven – that's the time he normally goes to bed. I won't see him tomorrow as it's the day of my operation, so Jen will collect him again the day after.'

I reassured Beth that David would be fine and then I showed them around the house, with David holding his mother's hand. When we went into David's room, Beth explained to him that he would be sleeping here for two weeks while she was in hospital and then he would come home again, but I doubted that at his age he really understood. Beth left shortly after, as she had to be at the hospital for 10.30. David and I waved her off and then, once I'd closed the door and his mother had gone, he began to cry. I picked him up, took him through to the living room where I sat with him on my lap and cuddled him, explaining that he would see Mummy later. Then I distracted him with toys and games, which I played with him for most of the day. Every so often he would ask, 'Where's Mummy gone?' I said, 'To the hospital. You will see her later, after dinner.' Soon he began repeating very sweetly, 'Mummy gone to the hospital, see her later after dinner.' He was so cute. I cuddled him a lot.

When it was time to collect Paula from school, I helped David into the car seat in the rear of my car and he asked: 'Going to see Mummy in hospital now?' Bless him.

Progress

'No, love, later,' I said. 'Auntie Jen is taking you after dinner.'
But of course at three years of age these arrangements must have
seemed very confusing to him.

Paula treated little David like a large doll and he revelled in
the attention. She played with him while I began making an
early dinner, as Jen would be collecting David at 5.30. Soon I
could hear chuckling coming from the living room as Paula
made him laugh. David's chuckle was very infectious and was
lovely to hear. However, when Lucy arrived home from school,
I knew as soon as I opened the door she was looking for
trouble.

'My friend says it's wrong of you to foster another child when
you have me, and you're only doing it for the money.'

While I was pleased to hear that Lucy had a friend, I knew
that telling me this was obviously designed to provoke me.

'I don't expect your friend knows much about fostering,' I
said lightly, as Lucy glared at me antagonistically. 'Perhaps she'd
like to come here for tea so she can see what really goes on.
Come and meet David.'

'No!' Lucy said, and stormed off up to her room where she
stayed sulking until I called her down for dinner.

Adrian and Paula kept David amused at dinner while I made
sure he ate something. I don't think he'd ever had so much
attention and I could tell from Lucy's expression that she didn't
like it and may well have been jealous. Each time he chuckled
she scowled at him and then finally said to me: 'Tell him to be
quiet. He's making too much noise. It's doing my head in.'

'No. I'm pleased he's happy,' I said. 'And he's eating.'

Lucy glowered at me and carried on picking at her food, but
even she wasn't immune to David's sweet, smiling face and
infectious laugh, despite missing his mother. I saw her snatching
glances at him, and gradually during the meal her expression

193

lost its resentment and finally she allowed herself to smile. By the end of the meal she was laughing with the rest of us each time David chucked.

After dinner Lucy came with Paula and me into the living room where we played with David until Jen arrived at 5.30 to take him to the hospital. David was very pleased to see his aunt's familiar face and threw himself into her arms and gave her a big kiss. Jen picked him up and hugged him, thanked me for looking after him and then confirmed that she'd have him back by seven o'clock. I think she felt a bit guilty for not having him to stay with her, but she had to work.

While David was out, I took the opportunity to unpack his suitcase and take some of his toys up to his room so he felt more at home. The rest of his toys would stay downstairs for him to play with in the living room. Lucy was in her bedroom and must have heard me moving around in David's room, for presently she appeared at his bedroom door. She stood watching me for a few moments and then said, 'I'm sorry I was horrible about David coming. I like him really.'

'I know,' I said. 'That's good.' But Lucy was often sorry after the event, and I was used to hearing her apologize. However, she then said something I hadn't heard her say before: 'I don't know why you still want to look after me. The others didn't.'

I paused from unpacking and looked up at her. 'Because I like looking after you,' I said. 'I like you, and I understand why you're hurting.'

She looked away. 'There's a lot you don't understand,' she said quietly. 'Things you don't know about me. Some horrible things that make me behave badly.'

I smiled sadly. 'You're not the first child I've looked after who's had secrets. I hope one day you may be able to tell me, or when you start therapy you can tell your therapist. But one thing

I do know, Lucy, is that whatever happened to you wasn't your fault. No matter what you were told. All right, love?'

She gave a small shrug. 'I guess.' Then, with a small puzzled frown, she asked, 'How did you know I was told it was my fault?'

'Because that's what bad adults tell the children they hurt. So the children will feel guilty and won't tell anyone else.'

She held my gaze for a moment and then looked away. 'I won't be horrible while David is here.'

'Good. He's going to enjoy playing with you.'

For the next two weeks, while David was with us, Lucy's behaviour did indeed improve. We didn't have any angry outbursts, so I didn't feel I was continually on a knife edge waiting for her to explode. Lucy became polite and cooperative and went out of her way to help me look after David. She'd always been nice to Adrian and Paula and my parents; it was me she'd directed her anger towards. Maybe Jill had been right when she'd said that Lucy had been receiving too much attention and that having David to stay would give us another focal point, or perhaps Lucy realized that there were other children in the world who'd had sadness in their lives as she had, but could still laugh. I didn't know. But whatever the reason, I was grateful for the change in Lucy – the atmosphere in the house improved tremendously. I also noticed that her eating improved; not hugely, but since David had arrived she was more relaxed at the dinner table and was eating a little more.

Stevie paid us one of her scheduled visits during the second week that David was with us. It was 4.30 p.m. and Lucy was downstairs playing with David and Paula when Stevie arrived. Lucy blanked Stevie when she said hello, and then went up to her bedroom. I apologized to Stevie, but didn't go up and try to persuade Lucy to come down; Stevie didn't expect me to. Stevie stayed for half an hour, and while I updated her on Lucy Paula kept David amused. Among other things, Stevie asked what I was doing to meet Lucy's cultural needs. I told her about the Thai meals we were cooking and that I talked to Lucy about Thailand whenever the opportunity arose.

'Have you got her a Thai flag for her room?' she asked.

'No, but I will,' I said, making a mental note to do so, as I'd previously forgotten.

I told Stevie that, while I still had concerns about Lucy's eating, it had improved since David had been with us. Stevie made a note and said she was still trying to trace Lucy's family – her parents and uncles. Stevie then said that, although she'd seen Lucy briefly, she still needed to have a quick look into her bedroom (it was a requirement of the social worker's visit). So I took her up, knocked on Lucy's bedroom door and opened it. Lucy still refused to speak to Stevie, but Stevie had seen enough to be able to include it in her report. As we returned downstairs, Toscha suddenly appeared from Lucy's room. Stevie turned and shrieked.

'I'm sorry,' I said, rushing to pick up the cat, who was look-ing pretty scared. 'I put her out earlier. I didn't know she was up here.'

I heard Lucy laugh.

Later, after Stevie had gone, I reminded everyone that Toscha had to be kept out while Stevie was here, as she was allergic to cats.

Lucy grinned. 'Toscha wanted to say hello to Stevie,' she said.

Adrian exploded into laughter.

'Well, please don't do it again,' I said. 'You know Stevie's got an allergy to cats.'

Progress

Of course Lucy knew, that's why she'd done it – to cause Stevie discomfort.

After David had returned home, Lucy's behaviour didn't immediately deteriorate as I was half expecting it to: she'd been on her best behaviour for David's sake, after all, and now there was no need to be any more. I wouldn't say she was an angel, but the improvement in her behaviour continued, and she was also still eating a little more.

'You'll have to help us out with respite more often,' Jill said, when I updated her.

I nodded. 'Although not for a while,' I said. 'I need time to recover.' I'm not always sure social workers appreciate just how tiring it is looking after children.

Spring gave way to summer and Lucy continued to make progress at home and school. When I saw her teacher, Miss Connor, for the end-of-term consultation, she said she was very pleased with Lucy's academic improvement. She thanked me for all I was doing at home to help her, but said that Lucy was still struggling to make friends. She said she felt Lucy had erected a protective barrier around herself to stop others getting close. Lucy talked to other children, but didn't form meaningful friendships as most children of her age did. Miss Connor had partnered Lucy with a new girl in the class to be her buddy: to show her around the school, be with her at lunchtime and generally help her settle in. Lucy had done what was required, but hadn't developed the friendship as Miss Connor had hoped. When Miss Connor suggested to Lucy that she might like to be friends with the girl and take her home for tea, Lucy replied it wasn't worth making friends, as she'd lose them when she moved in a year. This had upset Miss Connor, as it did me when

I heard, although we both recognized the truth in what Lucy had said. When the court made its decision Lucy's forever family would almost certainly live out of the area, which would mean a change of school.

'I just hope the court hurries up, so Lucy can get on with the rest of her life,' Miss Connor said.

But I knew from experience that the wheels of the law turn slowly.

By July, when Lucy had been with us for five months, I was feeling quietly confident that she was over the worst of her behaviour. She got annoyed and frustrated sometimes, but then so do most children. The only time Lucy really grew angry now was when there was any talk of her social worker or when she visited us, which she had to do. It wasn't so much that Lucy didn't like Stevie, more that she was anti social workers per se, because they had failed to protect her when she was younger. Telling Lucy it wasn't Stevie's fault didn't help, and each time Stevie visited Toscha appeared. While I could see the humour in this, I was concerned by Lucy's blatant disregard for Stevie's welfare, so I told Lucy that if it happened again I'd stop her television.

'Don't care,' Lucy said. 'Do what you want.'

Later, she apologized to me for being rude.

Stevie telephoned me the day before the schools broke up for the summer holiday and very excitedly told me she'd managed to trace Lucy's mother, Bonnie, and had set up contact for the following week. While I knew that Stevie had been looking for Lucy's family, and that this was correct social-work practice, I wondered what effect this would have on Lucy, who'd come to terms with not seeing her mother. Also, if everything went to plan, Lucy would be with her permanent foster family in about eight months, and she would be expected to bond with them as her own family. I therefore wasn't sure about the benefits of reintroducing her natural mother to her now.

'I hope it doesn't unsettle Lucy,' I said.

'Why should it?' Stevie asked, quite sharply. 'It's the child's mother, for goodness' sake.'

'It might give Lucy mixed messages,' I said. 'She might think there's a chance of her returning home.'

'I doubt it,' Stevie said. 'But if you're worried, explain to her again what's happening with the court and so on. She won't see me, so I can't.' Stevie sounded extremely put out and I wondered if she'd expected me to congratulate her on tracing Lucy's mother.

'I will,' I said. 'Also, I'd like to take Lucy on holiday with us at the end of August. Do I have your permission?'

'I should think so. Send me the details, and we'll need Lucy's mother's permission as well, as she still has parental rights. You can mention it to her when you meet her at contact.'

'Will do,' I said.

When I told Lucy that Stevie had traced her mother and had set up contact, she shrugged as if she didn't care.

'It's for an hour,' I added. 'At the contact centre. I'll take and collect you. It will be nice for me to meet your mother.'

'Will it?' Lucy said blankly.

'Yes,' I said, trying to be positive. 'And I'll be able to talk to her about you coming on holiday with us. Reassure her that you'll be safe by the sea.' I'd already told Lucy I was hoping to take her on holiday.

'She won't care where I go,' Lucy said, and changed the subject.

* * *

Will You Love Me?

I thought that as Stevie was on a mission to trace Lucy's family, and had already succeeded in tracing her mother, then she might succeed with Lucy's other relatives, specifically her father. I talked to Lucy about this and the Thai culture and put renewed effort into acquiring a Thai flag, which wasn't proving easy. I knew what the Thai flag looked like – it was horizontally striped in red, white and blue, but it wasn't easy to find one to buy in England. I phoned various shops and department stores, and even our local Thai restaurant to see if they knew where I could buy one, but without any success. Then I went online, which is what I should have done to begin with. The Flag Store sold flags from all around the world, in various sizes and made from different materials. I could have bought a thirty-foot bunting, but I thought that was a bit over the top, especially as Lucy wasn't even keen on the idea of having a flag. The smallest flag I could order was three feet by two feet. I put in my card details and the flag arrived three days later. I handed the parcel to Lucy and said, 'I'll help you hang it in your bedroom later.'

She shook out the flag and a look of disdain crossed her face. 'I'm not having that in my bedroom!' she said.

'Perhaps I could trim it to make it smaller,' I suggested.

'No. I want to keep my posters.' Lucy's bedroom walls were covered with pictures of cuddly animals and cuttings from her favourite magazines.

'You can keep those as well,' I said. 'The flag will only take up part of one wall, and it will make Stevie happy.'

'No,' Lucy said, her face setting.

'We could pin it on your bedroom door?' I suggested.

'No,' Lucy said.

'What about on the outside of the door, so you can't see it?'

'No,' Lucy said.

Progress

'Or we could use it as a throw-over on your bed? Flags make popular bedspreads, especially with football supporters.'

Lucy glared at me and pushed the flag into my arms. 'No, Cathy. I'm sorry, you've wasted your money. I don't want it.'

Which I accepted. I put the flag away. At least I'd tried, and I could understand why a young girl would rather have pictures on her wall than a flag. There were other, more important issues to concentrate on, like preparing Lucy for seeing her mother, which I did over the coming week.

Chapter Eighteen

'I'd Rather Have You'

I'd arranged for Adrian and Paula to spend the afternoon at their friends' houses, rather than having to sit in a hot car while I took Lucy to contact and then wait while she saw her mother. As the contact was only for an hour, it wasn't worth me returning home, so once I'd seen Lucy into the centre and met her mother, I planned to go for a walk in the local park until it was time to collect her. When I'd talked to Lucy about seeing her mother, she'd seemed quite unfazed by the prospect; she hadn't had any questions to ask me and said she remembered the contact centre from when she'd seen her mother there the year before. However, now we were in the car and on our way she'd fallen very quiet, and I appreciated how unsettled and anxious she was probably feeling, although she was keeping a tight lid on her emotions. I felt nervous. Lucy hadn't seen her mother for over six months, and I was imagining a very emotional reunion where they fell into each other's arms and cried openly.

'Stevie said if it all goes well today she'll set up regular contact,' I said to Lucy, as I pulled into the car park at the centre. 'She's thinking of making it once a week.'

'Mum won't be around long enough for that,' Lucy replied.

I thought Stevie wouldn't have suggested it if she wasn't sure it was feasible, but I didn't say so. 'Where does your mother go when she disappears?' I asked. 'Do you know?'

'No,' Lucy said bluntly. 'She never told me. She just went.'

I thought I'd said enough. Lucy clearly resented my question and now she'd withdrawn into her shell. 'No worries,' I said. I parked and cut the engine.

I turned in my seat to face Lucy. 'It's bound to be strange for you both,' I said, trying to reassure her. 'But if you have any worries, tell the contact supervisor. Sometimes parents don't know what to say in contact and can say the wrong thing when they don't mean to.' They often talk about their home lives, which can be very upsetting for a child in care.

Lucy shrugged.

'Come on then,' I said, with a cheerful smile. 'Let's go in. We're a bit early, but we can wait inside, rather than in the hot car.'

I got out of the car and went round to open Lucy's door, which was child-locked. She clambered out and I pressed the fob to lock the doors. As we went up the path leading to the main entrance, Lucy slipped her hand into mine and I gave it a reassuring squeeze. She hadn't held my hand before and I thought it was an indication of how vulnerable she must be feeling that she needed this extra reassurance. Arriving at the door to the centre, I pressed the security buzzer and the door clicked open. Inside, I said hello to the receptionist, who was seated behind the open sliding-glass window of the office. She knew me a little from my previous visits to the centre with other children I'd fostered.

'This is Lucy,' I said. 'She's seeing her mother, Bonnie, at three o'clock.'

The receptionist smiled. 'Bonnie isn't here yet, so if you'd like to sign in, you can have a seat in the waiting area.'

Lucy and I signed the visitors' book and then went round the corner to the waiting area, which was tucked away from the main reception area and had a few books and games to keep children occupied while they waited for their parents. Once the parents arrived, they went into one of the contact rooms with a contact supervisor. There were six contact rooms in the centre and they were cosily furnished, like living rooms, with carpet, curtains, a sofa, a television and lots of books and games. Although it obviously wasn't home, it was made to look home-like so that the children relaxed as much as possible and enjoyed the short time they had with their parents.

We were the only ones in the waiting area, but I assumed other children with different contact times were in the rooms with their parents. It was now one minute before three o'clock and I hoped Bonnie wouldn't be late. One of the most upsetting things for a child in care is being kept waiting by a parent at contact, or worse, the parent not arriving at all. It's stressful enough for the child to be separated from their family and then reunited briefly at contact, without being kept waiting or let down. For this reason, the contact rules are very firm: if a parent doesn't phone to say they have been delayed, or if they don't arrive within fifteen minutes of the scheduled time, then the contact is terminated and the foster carer takes the child home. Although this is upsetting for the child, it is less upsetting than if they are left waiting endlessly, only to be disappointed yet again.

I tried to interest Lucy in a book or a game of cards while we waited, but she preferred to just sit and wait. Upright on her chair and with her hands folded loosely in her lap, I thought I was more nervous than she appeared to be. She was dressed smartly in new summer clothes I'd bought for her, and her hair was shining and tied in a loose plait. I always make sure the child or children I foster look nice when they see their parents. It reassures the parents that their child is being well looked after, and also gives the meeting a sense of occasion – which it is, a very special occasion.

At 3.05 we heard the security buzzer sound, followed by the outer door clicking open. Then we heard the receptionist say to the person who'd just arrived: 'They're here.' So I thought she must be referring to us, as we were the only ones in the waiting area.

I felt my heart start to race at little, but Lucy remained outwardly calm. We heard footsteps coming along the corridor, and then two women appeared from around the corner; one I recognized as a contact supervisor, and the other I assumed to be Bonnie. She looked at Lucy and smiled.

I stood, so too did Lucy. 'Hello,' Bonnie said to her daughter. 'How are you?'

'I'm well, thank you,' Lucy said politely. 'How are you?'

'I'm good, thanks.'

Formal and distant, they made no move to hug or kiss each other, which fell far short of the emotional scene I'd envisaged. There was silence, so I stepped forward and offered Bonnie my hand for shaking. 'I'm Cathy,' I said, 'Lucy's foster carer.'

Bonnie didn't shake my hand, but gave a small nervous laugh. 'Nice to meet you, Cathy. I hope Lucy hasn't been giving you any trouble.'

'Not at all,' I smiled. 'She's an absolute treasure and a delight to look after.' But my enthusiasm seemed strangely out of place in this emotional void, as Bonnie and Lucy continued to look at each other from a distance, not embarrassed, but just not connecting; more like distant acquaintances than mother and daughter.

'Shall we go into the contact room now?' the supervisor suggested, then turning to me she said, 'You and Bonnie could have a chat later when you come to collect Lucy.'

'Yes, that's fine with me,' I said.

The three of them turned and the supervisor led the way down the corridor towards the contact rooms. Before they disappeared through the double doors I heard Bonnie ask Lucy: 'So, what have you been doing?'

'Going to school and other things,' Lucy replied flatly.

Outside, I left my car in the car park and crossed the road to the park to go for a walk. It was a lovely summer's day and the play area was full of children running and shouting excitedly under their parents' watchful gaze. I followed the path that ran around the perimeter of the park, under some trees and beside a small lake. I breathed in the beautiful scent of summer flowers, fresh from a recent watering by the gardeners. I knew from the original referral that Bonnie was thirty-six, but having met her she looked a lot older. There had been a suggestion in the referral that she'd been drink and drug dependent at various times in her life, and this could explain her premature ageing. I'd met parents of other children I'd fostered who'd looked old before their time from drug and alcohol abuse; many far worse than Bonnie. Some had been skeletally thin with missing teeth, a hacking cough and little or no hair. Apart from looking older than she should have done, Bonnie appeared well nourished and was smartly dressed in fashionable jeans and a T-shirt. I'd noticed that, while Lucy had inherited her father's dark eyes and black hair, there was a strong family likeness between her and her mother. Although their initial meeting had been awkward, I assumed that as the hour passed and they got to know each other again they'd relax and feel more comfortable, so that when I arrived to collect Lucy they'd be laughing, chatting and playing games.

I completed the circuit of the park and stopped off at the cafeteria to buy a bottle of water, which I drank on the way back. It was exactly four o'clock when I arrived at the contact centre.

'You can go through and collect Lucy,' the receptionist said. 'They're in Blue Room.' Sometimes the carer collects the child from the contact room and at other times the supervisor brings the child into reception once they've said goodbye to their parents in the room.

Each of the contact rooms was named after the colour it was decorated in. I went down the corridor, through the double doors and arrived outside Blue Room. I knocked on the door. Through the glass at the top of the door I could see the contact supervisor sitting at a table, writing. She looked up and waved for me to go in.

Inside, Lucy was sitting on the sofa next to her mother, close, but not touching. Usually at the end of contact the child is very excited – often over-excited – and has to be persuaded to pack away the games they've been playing and say goodbye to their parents. But there were no games out and apparently no excitement. The room was eerily quiet.

Bonnie and Lucy looked over at me as I entered, and I smiled.

'It's time for you to go,' Bonnie said evenly to Lucy.

'Yes,' Lucy said, and stood.

'Have you had a nice time?' I asked.

Bonnie glanced at her daughter. 'It was good to see her again,' she said, in a tone devoid of emotion. Lucy looked sombre and subdued. Then Bonnie said to me: 'Thank you for bringing Lucy. We might meet again some time.'

I hesitated, not sure what to make of this comment. I took a couple of steps further into the room. The supervisor was busy writing. If I was feeling confused, then surely Lucy was too?

'I believe Lucy's social worker is going to set up regular contact,' I said to Bonnie. 'She was talking about once a week.'

Bonnie gave another tense little laugh and looked slightly embarrassed. Then, glancing at her daughter, she said, 'Oh, no, Lucy won't be expecting that, will you? She knows what I'm like. I'm sure I'll see her again some time, though.'

'So you won't be seeing her regularly?' I asked, unable to believe what I was hearing.

'No, that's not possible,' Bonnie said. 'It's nice of you to look after her, though; she seems happy with you.'

I smiled weakly and looked at Lucy. Her face was emotionless. She appeared to be taking this in her stride; perhaps she'd been expecting this reaction from her mother.

'Well, goodbye,' Bonnie now said to me, ready to go. 'I understand I have to wait in this room until you two have left the building.'

'Yes,' I said. 'That's what usually happens.' Then: 'There's something I need to ask you before we go.'

'If it's anything to do with Lucy, ask her,' Bonnie said. 'She knows more about herself than I do.' She gave yet another nervous laugh.

'No, it's nothing like that,' I said. 'I know Lucy quite well now. It's that I need your permission to take Lucy on holiday. I think Stevie was going to mention it to you?'

'Oh, yes, she did,' Bonnie said nonchalantly, waving the question away with her hand. 'It's fine with me. I hope you have a nice time.'

'Thank you,' I said. I had planned to give Bonnie the details of our holiday – where we were going and when – but she didn't seem interested. She was now slipping her bag over her shoulder, getting ready to go after we had left the centre. 'Goodbye then,' she said.

I said goodbye and then waited to one side while she said goodbye to Lucy. I was anticipating that she would give her daughter a hug or goodbye kiss – even friends do that – but she didn't. Standing a little in front of Lucy, she said, 'Goodbye, love. Look after yourself.'

'Goodbye,' Lucy said, not expecting any more. It was one of the saddest goodbyes I've ever witnessed.

Without saying anything further, Lucy came over to me and slipped her hand into mine.

'Be good,' Bonnie called, as we turned to leave.

'She always is,' I said.

We walked down the corridor and through the double doors. My immediate impression of Bonnie was that she wasn't callous or uncaring, but just completely detached from her daughter. There appeared to be no bond between them, other than the genetic link. I was shocked, and sad for Lucy, but it did explain a lot of what I knew about her. I was so preoccupied and choked up by what I'd just seen that I walked straight past the visitors' book.

'Hey, Cathy!' Lucy said, drawing me to a halt. 'You've forgotten to sign out.'

We returned to the visitors' book and both signed our names and wrote our time of departure. Then outside we walked in silence. Lucy had her hand in mine again and a couple of times I glanced at her, feeling I should say something, but not knowing what. She clearly knew her mother better than I did, and had known what to expect, while I'd had a completely different set of expectations, based on how I would feel at being reunited with my daughter after six months' separation. Quite clearly

Stevie had had different expectations too – unrealistic expectations. If she phoned I'd tell her what had happened, or she'd
read the supervisor's report in a couple of days. Either way,
regular contact wasn't going to happen, and for reasons I really
didn't understand.

In the car I turned in my seat to face Lucy, who was fastening
her seatbelt. 'Are you all right, love?' I asked gently. 'How are
you feeling?'

'I'm all right,' she said quietly. 'Mum's like that because she
was hurt badly when she was little. She can't let people close to
her, not even me, because of the horrible things some people did
to her.'

I looked at Lucy, shocked, and my heart ached – not only for
Lucy, but for Bonnie too. How easily Lucy's life could have
followed that of her mother's had she not been brought into
care.

'It's not her fault she's like she is,' Lucy added. 'I don't blame
her any more.'

'No, it's not her fault,' I said sadly.

Lucy had previously told me things about her mother and
her life before coming into care – usually on the Sundays when
Adrian and Paula were out with their father and it was just the
two of us – but she hadn't told me this before. 'I think your
mother had a very difficult life,' I said, still turned in my seat
facing her. 'I think she gets by as best she can. It's such a pity
someone didn't help her, like you're being helped now. I'm
pleased you've forgiven her.' For so often when children are
failed by their parents they become consumed by anger, which
can easily blight the rest of their lives.

* * *

'I'd Rather Have You'

That night I gave Lucy an extra-big hug. Mr Bunny was tucked in beside her on the pillow, and sometimes, like tonight, she asked me to kiss him goodnight. Although Lucy must have been affected by seeing her mother and all the emotions, memories, hopes and disappointments it no doubt resurrected, she wasn't showing it. I wondered what was really going on in her thoughts.

'Is there anything you want to talk about?' I asked gently, as I sat on the bed.

Lucy shook her head. 'Not really. Mum will be fine. She can look after herself,' she said, as though reassuring us both.

'I'm sure she can,' I said. 'And when she feels up to it, she'll get in touch with Stevie and arrange to see you again.'

Lucy looked thoughtful and then frowned. 'I think I'll have left you by then.'

'Yes, if it's in six months' time or more, you'll probably be with your forever family, but they'll take you to contact.'

Lucy frowned again and then said, 'I wish I could stay here with you.'

'Oh, love,' I said, stroking her forehead. 'I know how unsettling this must be for you.'

'Mum asked me if I was staying with you and I told her I couldn't. But why can't I stay, Cathy?'

This was so difficult. Lucy knew the care plan, as Bonnie would, and I wondered what they'd said about this in contact. 'Do you remember I explained that Stevie was trying to find your relatives to see if one of them could look after you?' I said. Lucy nodded. 'And if there isn't anyone suitable, Stevie's going to find a permanent foster family for you, where one of the parents is Thai or Asian, so you'll fit in.'

'But I fit in here, don't I?' Lucy said.

'Yes, of course you do, love. I think the world of you, so do Adrian and Paula, but it's not my decision. Social workers like children to be with families that have the same ethnic background. Do you remember I explained what that meant?'

Lucy nodded solemnly. 'What if I let you put that flag up in my bedroom? Could I stay then?'

'Oh, love,' I said again, a lump rising in my throat. 'I wish it was that simple.'

Lucy then gave a small mischievous smile. 'If Stevie lets me stay, I'll stop letting Toscha in when she visits.'

I laughed. 'You need to stop letting her in now,' I said playfully. 'Stevie's coming next week for your review, and I don't want her sneezing the whole time.'

'I'm not coming to my review,' Lucy said matter-of-factly.

'I know, and no one is going to make you. But if you feel able, you could come in for a few minutes. We're having it here, so you can stay for as long or as short a time as you like.' Lucy shook her head. The social workers usually expected a child of her age to be present for part of their review, unless there was a good reason why they shouldn't or couldn't attend.

'No, not going at all,' Lucy said, her face setting. 'I hate social workers.'

'All right, I hear you,' I said. 'But now I want you to forget about hating and think of some nice things so you can get off to sleep. We're going on holiday in a few weeks and then in September it's your birthday. You'll have to tell me what you want to do for your birthday treat, and what presents you'd like.'

A smile replaced Lucy's frown. 'That's better,' I said.

'I'm looking forward to going on holiday, and my birthday,' Lucy said, snuggling her face against Mr Bunny. 'Will you take lots of photographs of me, so I can remember the nice time I had after I've gone?'

'I'd Rather Have You'

'Yes, of course, love. You'll have lots of happy memories to take with you.'

'I'd rather have you,' Lucy said, and I could have wept.

Chapter Nineteen
Happy Holiday

Lucy's review began at eleven o'clock the following Tuesday. Stevie, Jill, Peter (the reviewing officer) and myself were seated in my living room with coffee and biscuits. The children were amusing themselves upstairs, and I'd said that Lucy didn't want to attend her review. Lucy's mother would have been invited to the review, but she'd disappeared again, without leaving a forwarding address. Lucy's teacher, Miss Connor, had been invited, but because it was the school holidays she was away, so she had sent in her report, which the reviewing officer had just finished reading out. The gist of her report was that Lucy was making steady progress, but still found it difficult to make friends, which I knew from the consultation evening. Miss Connor had included some test results and finished by stating that she was grateful for the help I'd given Lucy at home and that Lucy wouldn't have made the progress she had without it, which was kind of her. Having finished Miss Connor's report, the reviewing officer, Peter, now turned to me: 'Cathy, would you like to tell us how Lucy is doing, please?'

I glanced at my notes, ready to begin, but as I did all eyes went from me to the living-room door, which was now slowly opening. I thought it must be one of the children having come down from upstairs for something, perhaps even Lucy feeling brave enough to attend her review. However, once the gap was wide enough, Toscha sauntered in with a loud meow. Stevie shrieked, and I was immediately on my feet going after Toscha who, frightened by the noise, had fled into the kitchen. I let her out the back door and returned to the living room.

'Sorry,' I said to Stevie, as I sat down. 'I'm sure I put her out earlier.'

Jill, who knew as well as I did how Toscha had got in, threw me a knowing look and we both stifled a smile. Fortunately, Toscha hadn't been in the room long enough to trigger a sneezing fit in Stevie, and Peter was looking rather bemused by her hysterical reaction. Once Stevie had finished explaining why she hated cats so much and how she was allergic to them, Peter looked to me to give my report. He made notes as I spoke and I began by saying how well Lucy had settled into my family and that she had a very good relationship with my children, my parents and me. I said I was pleased with her progress at school and that she wanted to do a bit extra at home. I described her routine and what she liked to do in her spare time. I said that while I was encouraging Lucy to bring friends home she hadn't done so yet, and I mentioned Lucy's comment to Miss Connor about it not being worth her making friends as she would be leaving the school in under a year.

'That's a great pity,' Peter said, as he wrote.

'She could still make friends,' Stevie said. 'And keep in touch with them after she's left.'

I nodded, and continued with my report, saying that Lucy was much better at managing her anger now, and that her eating had improved, although I still had concerns as her eating fluctuated and she wasn't eating as much as she should for a child her age. I then said that Lucy had seen her mother the week before and that I didn't think it had been a great success.

'Perhaps we could leave contact for now and discuss that when Stevie gives her report?' Peter said.

'Yes, of course,' I said. I finished my report by saying that Lucy was looking forward to our holiday and her birthday and that she was a delight to look after.

'Thank you,' Peter said. Then turning to Jill: 'As Cathy's support social worker, do you have anything to add?'

'Not really,' Jill said. 'Because of all the upheaval and Lucy's early life experiences, she struggled to begin with, but she's settled down now. I'm sure Lucy will benefit from therapy when she goes to permanency, which should address her issues with eating as well.'

'Are there plans for Lucy to have another medical?' Peter now asked Stevie. 'I remember the previous carer raised the same concerns as Cathy and took Lucy to her doctor.' Peter had been the reviewing officer at previous reviews so was aware of Lucy's history.

'Lucy will have another medical before she goes to permanency,' Stevie said. 'If necessary, we can bring that forward, but I don't think it's necessary yet.' She looked to Jill and me for confirmation and we nodded. Peter made a note.

Jill didn't have anything further to say, so Peter asked Stevie for her report. She began by outlining the care plan: that the social services would apply for a Full Care Order and then Lucy would go to a suitable relative or a long-term foster placement.

Peter asked, 'So how is the search going for a suitable relative? You were looking into that at the last review.'

'I haven't been able to trace Lucy's father,' Stevie said.

'And he's hardly a suitable relative,' Peter put in. 'He's never featured in Lucy's life. He hasn't seen her since she was a baby, and as far as we know he's not even in this country. Does his name appear on her birth certificate?'

'No,' Stevie said.

'So I think we can rule him out,' Peter said. 'Unless he suddenly materializes and applies to look after Lucy, which is highly unlikely.' Stevie nodded. 'What about the other relatives?' Peter now asked Stevie. 'We need to get this moving so that Lucy is settled. She's had enough uncertainty in her life. At the last review you were looking for two uncles, an aunt and a grandmother?' Peter said, checking back in his notes. 'Where are they?'

'Lucy's maternal grandmother lives in Scotland,' Stevie said. 'She has had her own problems and Bonnie is adamant that she doesn't want Lucy to go and live with her. I agree; because of her lifestyle, it's not an option. Bonnie doesn't know where her brothers are – there's been no contact for many years – and Lucy has never met them, so I've ruled them out too.'

'And the aunt?' Peter said, checking back in his paperwork. 'This was the lady who gave Bonnie and Lucy a home when Lucy was a baby. We thought that sounded hopeful.'

Stevie shook her head. 'I've spoken to Maggie on the phone. She's a lovely lady, but she can't offer Lucy a home as she is in poor health herself.'

'So that leaves us with a long-term foster family for Lucy?' Peter said.

'Yes,' Stevie confirmed. 'The family-finding team are looking for a good match.'

'Well, I hope they don't take too long,' Peter said quite forcefully. He finished writing and then said to Stevie: 'Perhaps you could now tell us about the contact Lucy had with her mother last week?'

Stevie sighed. 'It wasn't good. The contact supervisor's report shows that both Bonnie and Lucy found the meeting very difficult.'

'How long was the contact?' Peter asked.

'One hour.'

He made a note, and Stevie continued: 'Bonnie and Lucy didn't engage with each other at all. They struggled to make conversation and weren't able to communicate at any meaningful level. There were long, awkward silences and they were awkward with each other, and not at all tactile.'

'You mean they didn't hug or kiss each other?' Peter asked.

'That's right. Not even when they met or said goodbye.' Which of course I'd also noticed.

'According to the supervisor's report,' Stevie continued, 'Lucy suggested that they play some games together – draughts, dominoes and Scrabble – but Bonnie said she didn't know how to play any of these games. Lucy offered to teach her and said that Cathy had been teaching her, but Bonnie said it was better she played them with Cathy, who knew how to play the games. In fact, Lucy talked a lot about Cathy and her family and the things they do together.'

'Did Bonnie resent this?' Peter asked.

'Surprisingly, no,' Stevie said. 'In fact, Bonnie told Lucy she was pleased she was happy with Cathy. Cathy met Bonnie at the start and end of contact.'

'How did that go?' Peter asked, turning to me.

'All right,' I said. 'I only met Bonnie for a couple of minutes, but she was polite to me.'

'And how was Lucy after contact?' Peter asked me.

'Lucy wasn't upset; she seemed to take it in her stride,' I said. 'I formed the impression that she hadn't expected much more from her mother. Lucy told me that she didn't expect to see her mother regularly and that her mother couldn't help being the way she is, because she'd been abused as a child.'

'How very sad,' Peter said as he wrote. Then he looked at Stevie. 'You were hoping to set up regular contact between Lucy and her mother; I take it that's not going to happen now?'

'No,' Stevie said. 'It's not practical.'

'Is Bonnie going to contest the case in court?' Peter now asked Stevie.

'No. Bonnie recognizes she can't look after Lucy.'

'It took her long enough,' Peter commented dryly. 'So, we're just waiting for your family-finding team to come up with a good match for Lucy?'

'Yes,' Stevie confirmed.

Then turning to me, Peter said, 'And while the social services are finding a suitable family for Lucy, she can stay with you?'

'Oh, yes,' I said. 'For as long as it takes to find a family. The night she had contact, we were talking and she told me she would like to stay with us permanently. I've explained why that's not possible.'

Peter looked at Stevie. 'And as Lucy's social worker you've explained all this to Lucy?' he asked.

'As much as I can,' Stevie said. 'Lucy won't have anything to do with me at present.'

'Well, someone needs to explain the recent developments to Lucy,' Peter said. 'That none of her extended family has come forward to look after her, so she'll be going to a long-term foster family. I take it she's too old to be adopted?'

'Yes,' Stevie said.

'I think Lucy understands most of this already,' I said. 'But I can have another chat with her if you like and tell her, as she won't see Stevie?'

'Yes, please,' Peter said. 'It's a pity Lucy didn't feel able to join us for her review.' I felt I was receiving a little smack on the legs. 'And her Life Story Book?' Peter now asked Stevie.

'She should have it here,' Stevie said to me.

'It's in a drawer in her bedroom,' I said. 'She's very protective of it and hasn't let any of us see it. I'm taking lots of photographs that can be added to it.'

'Good,' Peter said, making a note. 'Now, is there anything else?' He looked around the room, but no one had anything to add. 'In that case, we'll set a date for her next review and I'll close the meeting.'

We took out our diaries and a date was set in January, in five months' time. Peter thanked us all for attending, which is customary, and he and Stevie left while Jill waited behind.

'That went reasonably well,' Jill said, once they'd gone.

'Yes, although it's a pity Lucy wouldn't come down.'

'She did once,' Jill said with a smile. 'To let the cat in.'

'I know!'

'Hopefully she'll come to her next review. It will be very close to her going to permanency so it will be an important one.' I nodded. 'Cathy, how do you feel about doing another short respite?' Jill said, changing the subject. 'Just for next week.'

'I don't see why not,' I said. 'Everyone was happy about David staying.'

'Thanks. His name is Toby. He's twelve and has been with his foster family for a year. His carers had booked to take him on holiday, but the social services didn't get him a passport in time, so rather than have the whole family cancel their holiday, I've said we'll arrange a week's respite.'

'That's all right with me,' I said. 'Although it's a pity Toby couldn't go on holiday.' The dilemma that faced Toby's family highlighted an ongoing problem experienced by many foster families: that the child or children they are looking after don't have passports, and the application to acquire one can only be

Happy Holiday

made by the social services, not the foster carer. While this might not seem a high priority, it often resulted in either the foster family not having a holiday (sometimes for years), having to cancel a pre-booked holiday and losing their money or the foster child being left behind in respite care.

Jill called goodbye to the children upstairs as she left, and once she'd gone I went up and told them that we were going to look after Toby from Friday evening for a week. Adrian was delighted to have a boy of a similar age to himself for company, and Lucy and Paula were happy for Toby to stay too. We made the best of the good weather that week and were outside most days, either in the garden or the local parks.

When Toby's foster father, Sid, brought Toby on Friday evening, he and Adrian immediately went off to play. Sid was still angry that he couldn't take Toby on holiday with them and, out of earshot of the children, he said to me: 'My wife told the social services ten months ago that we were booking this holiday. We had permission to take him abroad. You'd have thought they could have got him a passport! How long do they need?' I sympathized, for had I wanted to take my family abroad I could have been in the same position; Lucy didn't have a passport and she'd been in care for three years!

I reassured Sid that I would give Toby a good week with lots of outings, which is what I did. We went out every day and I included a day at the zoo and a day trip to the coast. While Toby enjoyed all of this, it wasn't as good as a holiday abroad, which Toby had clearly been looking forward to – it would have been his first time on a plane. Apart from missing out on this experience, he also missed his foster family, as I was sure they were missing him. When Sid returned to collect Toby, they hugged each other hard and I thought they were close to tears. While

Toby went up to his room to collect his bag, I asked Sid if he and his family had had a nice time. He shrugged and said, 'We made the best of it, but to be honest we all felt guilty about leaving Toby behind. I think we should have cancelled and lost the money.' I felt sorry for him and thought: all this, for the sake of some paperwork!

It was now halfway through August and our thoughts turned to our own holiday, which was in a week's time. Adrian, Lucy and Paula were all very excited and were planning all the fun things they were going to do: build sandcastles, paddle and swim in the sea, eat loads of ice creams, watch the Punch and Judy show on the beach, stay up very late and lots, lots more. They'd been saving up their pocket money so they could go on plenty of rides at the funfair, and when the time came to pack their cases they were more than happy to help. It was a five-hour drive to the coast, but we left home at 6.00 a.m., stopped at the services on the motorway for breakfast and arrived at twelve. We dropped off our cases at the self-catering bungalow we were staying in and were on the beach by early afternoon. We stayed on the beach until the sun began to drop and then we returned to the bungalow, unpacked our cases and went out to eat in a family restaurant overlooking the sea. It was a lovely start to the holiday, and that evening three tired but very excited children climbed into bed and were asleep as soon as their heads touched their pillows.

We made the most of every day of our holiday; on the beach, in the sea, visiting local attractions. The resort was popular with families and, like all the other happy families around us, we had a great time. Lucy was ecstatic and kept thanking me and telling me what a fantastic time she was having – over and over again.

Happy Holiday

'It's OK, love,' I said. 'You don't have to keep thanking me. I'm pleased you're having a good time.'

'I am! Thanks, Cathy. It's the best holiday I've ever had.'

As far as I knew, it was the *only* holiday she'd ever had.

As I sat on the beach watching Adrian, Lucy and Paula playing in the sea, I thought more than once how much of a family unit we really were. Perhaps it was because Lucy had no proper family of her own that she'd bonded with us so quickly, and us with her. She'd fitted in so easily, and I often felt she was my daughter, and the three children were so natural together that they could easily have been siblings by birth. True, Lucy's hair was darker than Adrian's and Paula's, and she had some of her father's Thai features, but the differences were so negligible that she didn't stand out as different. Many families are now comprised of children with different fathers, and I might have been married more than once for all anyone else knew. Stevie was looking for a good ethnic match for Lucy, but I knew such a family would be difficult to find. How long would she and the family-finding team leave Lucy in uncertainty while they looked? And how much did it really matter that a perfect ethnic match was found? Surely a stable, loving family should be the first priority?

I ran through these questions in my mind quite a few times during the holiday, and by the end of the week there was something pressing I needed to ask Jill as soon as we returned.

Chapter Twenty
'Will You Love Me?'

'Jill, would you back me if I were to apply to look after Lucy permanently?' I asked, my heart pounding nervously in my chest. 'I haven't said anything to Lucy, Adrian or Paula yet; I wanted to discuss it with you first.'

It was 5 September, the day after the schools returned from the summer holiday, so there was just Jill, Toscha and me in the house. Jill was looking at me carefully, clearly deep in thought.

I continued, 'I appreciate that Stevie is looking for a long-term foster family with the right ethnic mix for Lucy,' I said. 'But is finding such a family realistic? And how long will it take? Lucy sees herself as British. She doesn't have issues with her cultural identity, and I'm doing all I can to promote her dual heritage. She's had such a rough life, with so many moves and so much uncertainty. She's settled here with us. Adrian, Paula and I think the world of her and I know she does us. More than once she's asked if she can stay, and we want her to.' I'd spoken passionately, straight from my heart. Jill was still looking at me intently. 'Well? What do you think, Jill?'

'Do you love Lucy?' Jill asked after a moment.

'Yes, I do,' I said, without hesitation. 'She's like a daughter to me, and a sister to Adrian and Paula. I know they feel the same as I do. At present they understand that Lucy will leave us one day, just as all the other children we've fostered have. That's something you have to accept when you foster, but I know they would be over the moon if Lucy could stay.'

Jill gave a small thoughtful nod and then her face broke into a smile. 'Yes, I'll back you,' she said. 'I'd be pleased to. I can see how settled and happy Lucy is with you. She's integrated perfectly into your family.'

'Oh, thank you!' I cried, clasping my hands together. 'Thank you so much!' I stood and, crossing the room, gave Jill a big hug. 'You're a star!'

Jill laughed. 'You're welcome. Now, the first thing I need to do is to approach Stevie. As Lucy's social worker, her view will be paramount in this.'

In all my excitement I'd almost forgotten Stevie's role in this. 'Do you think she'll support my application?' I asked, immediately growing concerned.

'Yes, I'm sure she will,' Jill said. 'No social worker wants to move a child unnecessarily. And Stevie will know that the chances of finding a perfect match for Lucy are very remote. If I was Stevie, I'd be on my knees thanking you for giving Lucy a permanent home. I'll phone her as soon as I return to my office.'

I was grinning from ear to ear. 'So how long do you think the process will take? Can you talk me through it?'

'Sure. Now, let me see. The final care hearing is set for December, but the deadline for submitting the paperwork to court will be next month. Included in that paperwork will be a copy of the care plan. Stevie will need to revise that before she submits it, to show that Lucy will be staying here as a long-term foster placement. Then, after the final court case in December, when the social services will have been granted the Full Care Order, your application to keep Lucy will go before the permanency panel. More paperwork, I'm afraid, and that will need to be in a month before the panel meets. It meets once a month, so if your application misses the January deadline then it will be included in February. You'll have to attend the permanency panel, but not the care proceedings.' I gave a small gasp. 'Don't worry, you'll be fine. I'll be with you and I'm sure the panel will approve your application. So my guess is that by the end of February it should all be passed.'

'Wonderful!' I cried.

I could hardly contain my excitement and could have happily kissed Jill. She'd now taken a pen and notepad from her bag and was writing. I waited patiently until she'd finished.

'I'm going now,' she said, standing. 'I want to get your application moving. I'll phone Stevie and then phone you to confirm the timescale.' She grinned, and I could see she was as happy for me as I was. 'You've made my day,' she said, as I went with her to the front door.

'You've made mine,' I said. 'Thanks again.' I gave her another big hug before she left.

For the rest of that morning and the early afternoon I was on a cloud. I skipped around the house, doing the housework as though on a cushion of air. I knew Adrian and Paula would be overjoyed when I told them, and as for Lucy, well, it was her birthday soon, and what better birthday present was there than a family of her own! I felt the luckiest person alive and I said a silent prayer of thanks. There'd been a time in my life when I'd been told that tests showed I was unlikely to have children, and now here I was with three and still fostering. 'Thank you!' I said out loud.

At two o'clock the landline rang and I rushed to answer it, expecting it to be Jill with the confirmation I'd been anticipating. It was Jill, but as soon as she spoke I knew something was badly wrong.

'Cathy, you'd better sit down.' Her voice was tight and tense. 'I've spoken to Stevie and it's not good news, I'm afraid.' For a second I thought she was going to tell me that Stevie had found a family for Lucy – the match she'd been looking for – which would have been very disappointing, but not the blow Jill now delivered.

'Stevie won't consider your application as a long-term carer for Lucy,' Jill said, 'because she feels you can't meet her needs. I tried to persuade her you could, but she's adamant. She won't put you forward.'

My stomach churned. 'What needs?' I asked, or rather demanded.

'Lucy's cultural needs,' Jill said bluntly.

'So tell me what else I need to do,' I said, sick with fear. 'And I'll do whatever it takes.'

'It's not about what you are doing or not doing,' Jill said. 'I know you're positively reinforcing Lucy's cultural identity, but you can't change who you are.'

'You mean I'm not Thai or part Thai?' I asked, my voice rising.

'That's right. And no one in your extended family is, and neither are any of your close friends.'

My anger flared. 'That's Stevie talking, isn't it?' I said. 'It's racism as well as being ridiculous. We live in a multicultural society, Jill. I have friends from many different cultures. Lucy blends in, she doesn't stand out. You said yourself she'd fitted in perfectly. Yet because my family isn't the same racial mix, we're being ruled out. I think this has more to do with Stevie's hang-ups about cultural identity than what's best for Lucy. That woman's been obsessed with this right from the start. Never mind that we love Lucy and can give her a permanent loving family. All that has been forgotten, sacrificed, because Stevie thinks the right ethnic mix is more important!' I stopped. My breath caught in my throat and tears stung my eyes. I'd probably said too much, but I felt I had nothing to lose.

Jill was very quiet on the other end of the phone and it was a moment before she spoke. 'I'm so sorry, Cathy,' she said gently. 'I really am. I shouldn't have built up your hopes before I'd spoken to Stevie, but I genuinely thought she would be pleased and support your application.'

I sighed. 'It's not your fault.' I said. 'Was that everything? I've got to go now.'

'Yes.'

And without saying a proper goodbye, I put down the phone and wept.

Later that afternoon when the children were home from school they asked me a couple of times if there was anything wrong, as I seemed quiet. I said there wasn't and tried to put on a brave face for their sakes, but it wasn't easy. During the week of our holiday, and when we'd returned, I'd planned what I wanted to say to Jill, and when she'd been so positive I felt elated. All this time I'd been quietly confident that Lucy would stay, and then the blow – the shattering disappointment of Stevie's rejection. I'm normally a very positive, optimistic person; someone who sees their glass as half full, rather than half empty. When I have a setback I console myself that it could have been worse, but at this point all I could come up with was that at least I hadn't shared this with the children, so they'd been spared the disappointment, and that Lucy would be staying until Stevie found her a family, which could take many months.

But while I found some consolation in these thoughts, my anger didn't go away. I genuinely believed that Stevie was misguided in her attitude. I knew political correctness reigned supreme in some areas of the social services, sometimes to the exclusion of other equally important factors and good sense. I was doing all I could to promote Lucy's cultural inheritance, and had she seemed distressed or started saying she didn't fit in with my family then I would have agreed with Stevie and hoped that she would find Lucy a permanent home very soon. But that wasn't the case – far from it. Lucy fitted in and wanted to stay.

I don't give up easily and by the time I went to bed my disappointment and anger had galvanized into action. I decided that the following morning, when I'd returned from taking Paula to school, I'd telephone Jill. And with that thought, I fell asleep, emotionally exhausted.

'Sorry I hung up on you yesterday, Jill,' I began. 'I was very upset.'

'Understandably,' Jill said. 'Look, Cathy, if it's any consolation, I think Stevie is wrong too, but there's nothing we can do about it.'

'That's what I wanted to ask you. Is there anything we can do? I was wondering if I could appeal against Stevie's decision. Maybe take it to her manager?'

Jill paused. I could tell she was choosing her words carefully. 'I discussed this with my manager yesterday,' she said, 'straight after I'd spoken to Stevie. He and I think that to raise this with Stevie's manager would create a lot of bad feeling and wouldn't do any good. Her manager is almost certainly going to uphold Stevie's decision, and furthermore it could result in Lucy being moved early.'

'What do you mean, "moved early"?' I asked, with a sinking feeling. 'They haven't found a suitable family for Lucy, have they?'

'No, but the department might feel that as Lucy's race has become an issue she would be better off in an Asian family. Social services are very sensitive to meeting children's cultural needs.'

'Tell me about it!' I snapped. 'This is political correctness gone mad. Worse than that, it's discrimination! The only person making an issue over this is Stevie. Little wonder the social services get a bad name!' I was fuming, but I meant what I'd said.

Jill allowed me a moment to calm down before she said evenly, 'Cathy, I'm only telling you what my manager and I think. We wouldn't feel comfortable lodging a complaint. I've tried talking to Stevie, but she won't change her mind. As Lucy's social worker, she has every right to make this decision. I wouldn't want to see you hurt more than you already have been by Lucy being suddenly moved.'

'I hear what you're saying,' I said sharply. 'Thanks.' And for the second time in two days I hung up without saying goodbye.

I was trembling as I walked away from the phone, but realistically I knew there was nothing more I could do. Jill was right when she'd said Stevie could make the decision, and that to challenge her could make matters worse. All I could do was hide my disappointment as best I could and concentrate on Lucy's birthday, which was the following week. She wanted a new bike as a present and I was taking her to choose one on Saturday, although she wouldn't be having it until her actual birthday. That evening, when I asked her how she'd like to celebrate her birthday and suggested inviting a few friends from her class to a party, she said: 'There isn't really anyone at school I want to ask. I'd like to spend it with my family. Can we invite Nana and Grandpa, and all go on a family outing? I'd like that.' Which brought tears to my eyes, for reasons Lucy didn't know and I couldn't share with her.

Lucy decided she wanted to go bowling for her birthday outing, at the new leisure centre, which had just opened. She'd heard some of her classmates talking about the new leisure complex and we hadn't been yet. When I telephoned my parents and told Mum that Lucy would like her and Dad to come to her birthday outing, she was as touched as I had been.

'It just shows how much Lucy thinks of us all,' Mum said. 'You know she calls us Nana and Grandpa? And I've heard her calling you Mum sometimes. It just slips out and then she corrects herself and says Cathy.'

'I know,' I said. 'It's difficult. Carers are supposed to discourage their foster children from calling them Mum or Dad. It's considered to be confusing for them, and can also antagonize the natural parents.'

Mum tutted. 'If Lucy feels happy calling you Mum, I don't see a problem. She just wants a proper family of her own, that's all, love.'

And my heart ached again for the family I could never give Lucy.

'We'll see you at twelve o'clock on Sunday then,' I confirmed with Mum. 'After bowling, we'll come back here for a tea party. I've ordered a special birthday cake. Lucy will love it.'

'Shall I make some of my cupcakes too?' Mum asked.

'Oh, yes please. That would be nice. And, Mum, it's fine for Lucy to call you and Dad Nana and Grandpa if she wants. It's just that I have to be careful, as she'll be going to a permanent family before long, with a new "mother".'

'I understand, love.'

I wish I did, I thought.

Both Lucy's actual birthday – the following Wednesday – and her birthday outing were a great success. As Wednesday was a school day, I woke everyone up a little earlier than usual and, still in our nightwear, we gathered around Lucy's bed while she unwrapped her presents and cards. Mum and Dad were bringing their present and card with them on Sunday, and, with nothing arriving from Lucy's mother, Lucy just had our presents and cards to open, plus a card from Jill. There was the bike she'd chosen and a box of chocolates from me, two books from Adrian, some games from Paula and a china ornament in the shape of a cat from Toscha. I think she loved that most of all. Lucy didn't comment that there was nothing from her mother – she didn't seem to expect anything. Once dressed, she had time for a quick ride on her new bike in the garden while I made breakfast, and then after breakfast she had to leave for school.

That afternoon, while everyone was out, I laid the table with a party tablecloth and matching napkins and prepared the meal Lucy had requested. All the children in my house choose what we have for dinner on their birthday, and Lucy wanted chicken casserole with chips. I'd also bought ice cream and a small iced birthday cake. She'd have her proper birthday cake after our outing on Sunday.

When Lucy came home from school she was excited and delighted with the party tableware. She also ate a reasonable amount of the meal. But I think she enjoyed even more all the attention that came with being the 'birthday girl' and being made to feel very special. After dinner she chose some games for us to play, but because it was a school night we couldn't stay up too late.

As I tucked Lucy in and kissed her goodnight, she said, 'Thank you for a nice birthday, Cathy. You've made me feel very special.'

'You are special, love,' I said, giving her a big hug and a kiss. 'Very special indeed. And don't you ever forget that.'

She returned my kiss and then suddenly said, 'I love you all so much! I know I can't stay forever, but I still love you. Will you love me while I'm here?'

'Oh, Lucy, darling,' I said. 'Of course. I love you already. We all do.'

'That's nice,' she said, with a contented smile. 'This is my best birthday ever.' Then turning to Mr Bunny she said, 'There! I told you they loved us, and I was right!'

On Sunday Lucy gave my parents a big hug and a kiss as they arrived. 'I'm so pleased you could come to my party,' she declared.

'We're pleased to be here,' Dad said.

'Thank you for inviting us,' Mum said.

We went through to the living room where my parents gave Lucy her birthday present, and we all watched while she opened it. Lucy had previously told my mother that she wanted to be a famous beautician when she was older and do the make-up for film stars. Now, to Lucy's unimaginable delight, the present from my parents was a large play beauty salon, set in a big red sparkling case. We all admired it. It was fascinating, with rows and rows of little colourful pots containing make-up and nail varnish. There was a mirror, false nails, hair extensions, a battery-operated hairdryer, little bottles of cleanser, toner and perfumes. In fact, everything a girl could possibly need to run a beauty salon for the stars. Lucy was overjoyed, and while she would probably change her mind on a career – many girls go through a phase of wanting to be a beautician – she was happy, which was all that mattered. She read the card from my parents, which contained some lovely words, and then stood it on the mantelpiece next to our card and the one from Jill. Three cards; not many when you think what some children receive, but Lucy had never known anything different. And I knew that previously, before coming into care, her birthday had been completely forgotten and she'd received nothing at all.

Lucy won the bowling – we made sure of it – and when we returned, she, Paula, my father and Adrian played some games while Mum helped me prepare the tea. After we'd eaten, we returned to the living room where Lucy set about practising her skills as a beautician on us all. It was great fun and lasted most of the evening, although I'm not sure the film stars would have been that impressed. Paula had each of her nails painted a different colour to accompany her bright-red lipstick and blue eye shadow. I had a facial and my hair set on rollers. Mum escaped lightly with a foot massage with aromatherapy oil. Adrian had false eyelashes applied and a yellow ribbon clipped into his hair, while Toscha had a pink ribbon loosely tied around her tail. But funniest of all was my father, who'd sat patiently as Lucy applied pink lipstick, luminous silver eye shadow, false nails and blond hair extensions. We were all in fits of laughter and I took lots of photographs.

We'd had one of Mum's cupcakes each at the end of dinner and now that we'd had time to digest our meal it was time for Lucy's surprise birthday cake, which I'd had made. I went into the kitchen where I'd hidden the cake, lit the candles and then carried it into the living room as we sang 'Happy Birthday'. The joy on Lucy's face was indescribable. I could see her eyes glistening as I set down the cake on the coffee table. Made in the shape of a fairy-tale princess's castle, it had four turrets and was in different shades of pink icing.

'Wow!' Lucy and Paula exclaimed together.

'Fantastic,' my parents agreed.

'That's cool,' Adrian added.

Lucy blew out the candles in one go and we clapped and gave three cheers. I then I helped her to cut the cake and she handed out a slice on a party plate to each of us. The cake tasted as good as it looked and we all had seconds, which was a first for Lucy – she'd never had a second helping of anything before.

'This is my best birthday party ever,' she exclaimed to us all.

We smiled, and I put from my mind the thought that this would be Lucy's only birthday party with us, for by next September she would have moved.

Chapter Twenty-One

'No One Wants Me'

On Monday afternoon Stevie telephoned. 'A card has arrived here in the office from Lucy's mother,' she said. 'I'm due to visit you, so I'll bring it with me. I've got a card for Lucy too.' It's usual for social workers to give the children they are responsible for a card, and sometimes they manage a small present too. 'What time is she back from school?' Stevie now asked.

'Half past four.'

'See you later then.'

When Lucy arrived home from school I told her Stevie was coming soon and that she had a birthday card for her, and also one from her mother.

'Tell me when she's gone,' Lucy said, and went straight up to her room.

Lucy remained very hostile towards social workers, as she still held them responsible for not rescuing her when she'd most needed it, and also because they kept moving her and didn't listen to what she wanted. This, of course, was without her knowing that Stevie had stopped my application to keep her.

Before Stevie arrived I checked the house for Toscha, including upstairs and in Lucy's room, but she was nowhere to be seen, so I assumed she was out. Stevie arrived punctually at

4.30 p.m., and as soon as I opened the door she asked, 'Is that cat out?'

'Yes,' I confirmed.

I showed Stevie through to the living room, told her Lucy was in her bedroom and offered her a drink, but she didn't want anything.

'I'll have to see Lucy at some point,' Stevie said, as she always did. Then added: 'To give her the birthday cards and also update her.'

My heart clenched. 'Update her?' I asked. 'Have you found Lucy a permanent family then?' In some ways this would have been good news, as Lucy needed to be settled and for the uncertainty to end.

'No. I need to update her about our search,' Stevie said.

'You mean tell her you're still looking?' I queried.

'Yes.'

'She knows,' I said. 'I told her after the review.'

'Even so, as her social worker I need to tell her. She can't just hear it from the foster carer.'

Stevie had rather a brusque manner sometimes, and even if she hadn't refused my application to keep Lucy I think I would have struggled to like her; but then, as 'the foster carer', I didn't have to like her, just work with her. I thought that updating Lucy when the only update was that they were still looking for a permanent family was unnecessary and unsettling. Wouldn't it have made more sense to wait until a family had been found and then tell her? But I didn't say so.

'Lucy enjoyed her birthday and party,' I said positively.

'Did she invite friends from school?' Stevie asked.

'No. I suggested that, but Lucy said there was no one she wanted to invite, so we had a family outing. It's what she wanted to do. Bowling and then tea here.'

Stevie nodded without a lot of enthusiasm and wrote on her notepad. 'And you're preparing her for moving on?' she asked.

'As much as I can, given that a family hasn't been found yet. Once we know where she's going I'll be able to prepare her better.'

Stevie made another note.

'I'm doing all I can to give Lucy a positive cultural identity,' I continued. 'And she had a good summer holiday, both here and when we went away to the coast. Would you like to see the photographs?'

'Another day,' she said. 'I'm a bit pushed for time right now. Did you buy her the flag?'

'Yes, but she doesn't want it in her bedroom.'

'So put it on the wall in this room then,' Stevie said, glancing around the living room. 'The flag doesn't have to be in Lucy's room. In fact, it's better if it is down here in a communal room. Lucy will feel you are acknowledging and celebrating her culture, rather than shutting it away in her bedroom.'

I heard the criticism and bit my tongue. I knew that nothing I could say or do in respect of Lucy's race would satisfy Stevie. I was white, Stevie was dual heritage, so she had the advantage over me when it came to knowing what was best for Lucy. It wasn't the first time since I'd begun fostering and entered the world of the social services that I felt stigmatized for being white. I knew Stevie didn't approve of me fostering a child with a different ethnic identity, but there hadn't been any choice, and Lucy and I were both very happy with the arrangement.

'I'll find a place for the flag in here,' I said, and continued to update Stevie on the progress Lucy had made since her last visit, as Stevie made notes. I included Lucy's eating, that she was sleeping well, making good progress at school and was generally healthy and happy.

When I'd finished, Stevie said, 'Well, if that's all, I'll go and see Lucy now.'

She tucked her notepad and pen into her bag, stood, and I led the way upstairs to Lucy's room. Lucy's bedroom door was shut, but she knew that Stevie would need to see her at some point. I knocked on the door and then opened it a little. 'Stevie's here,' I said. 'Can she come in?'

Lucy was sitting on the bed flicking through a magazine and, to my surprise, she replied, 'Yes.'

'Good girl,' I said, pleased.

I stood aside to let Stevie in and as I moved away I heard Stevie say, 'Hello, Lucy.' Then I heard Stevie shriek, and both she and Toscha shot out of the room.

'I'm so sorry,' I said, grabbing the cat. 'She must have been hiding.' Or been hidden, I thought.

I carried Toscha downstairs, put her out the back door and returned upstairs. I would speak to Lucy later about hiding Toscha in her room. She'd gone too far this time.

'I've made sure she's out,' I reassured Stevie, as I arrived on the landing where Stevie was still waiting. She wasn't sneezing, so no real harm had been done, other than giving her a shock.

We returned to Lucy's room where the door was still slightly ajar. Stevie went in. Full marks for tenacity, I thought.

'I've bought you a birthday card,' I heard her say. 'And there's one here from your mother.'

There was no reply from Lucy and I hovered on the landing, just to make sure they were all right. I heard Stevie say, 'Cathy tells me you had a nice birthday and you got a new bike,' which was a nice comment to make. Stevie was trying hard and I hoped Lucy would respond, but there was silence.

Then I heard a floorboard creak as Stevie took another step into the room. 'I won't keep you long,' she said. 'But I need to tell you what I've been doing to find you a permanent home. I believe Cathy told you we've ruled out your extended family – your gran, aunt and uncles – so we're now concentrating on finding you a long-term foster family. You'll be able to stay there until you're eighteen and come out of care.'

Stevie didn't get any further. I heard a loud crash as something hit the inside of Lucy's bedroom door. Then Lucy was shouting at the top of her voice: 'Get out! I hate you! Leave me alone!' The vehemence of her anger was frightening.

Stevie rushed from the room as another object hit the inside of Lucy's bedroom door. I went in. Lucy was standing in the middle of the room, her face set hard in anger and her eyes blazing. She had another ornament in her hand and was about to throw it. 'Put it down,' I said firmly. 'You'll be sorry later that you've broken your things.'

'Don't care. Hate you all!' she cried. 'Get out!' She threw the ornament, not at me, but at the door, and it broke in two.

'I'll be going then,' Stevie called from the landing. 'I'll let myself out.'

Lucy screamed, 'I hate you!' I hadn't seen her this angry since the early days, and for a moment I thought she was going to go after Stevie. I stepped forward and, taking a chance, laid my hand lightly on her arm. 'Calm down, Lucy,' I said. 'Take some deep breaths and calm down.'

She pulled her arm away and reached for another ornament. 'Don't!' I said sharply. 'You don't need to do this. I understand why you're upset.'

'I hate you all!' she cried again. 'I wish I'd never been born.' Then she threw the ornament onto the floor and collapsed, sobbing, into my arms.

* * *

'No One Wants Me'

Standing in the middle of the room, I held her and soothed her until her sobbing gradually eased. Once she was calmer, I reached for a tissue from the box and gently wiped her face. 'There, that's better,' I said. I could hear Paula and Adrian on the landing, clearly worried for Lucy. 'It's all right,' I called. 'We'll be with you shortly.'

I drew Lucy to the edge of the bed and we sat side by side. I took her hand gently in mine. 'Feeling a bit better now?'

She gave a small nod. 'I wish I wasn't in care,' she said, her anger now replaced by sorrow. 'I wish I didn't have social workers. I just want to be normal, like other kids. Like Adrian and Paula. I didn't ask to be born. I wish I hadn't been. No one wants me.'

'Oh, love,' I said. Slipping my arm around her, I held her close.

While I felt desperately sorry for Lucy and wanted to say something to help her, I knew I had to be careful in what I said. 'I want you,' I said. 'And so will your permanent family, when Stevie finds them.'

Lucy shrugged. 'Maybe. I just wish she wouldn't keep going on about it. It makes me angry and upset.'

'I understand, love.'

She was quiet for a few moments and then, leaning forward, she picked up one of the two birthday cards that were lying on the floor. 'I've got a card from my mum,' she said, showing me.

'That's lovely,' I said. The card had a pretty picture of a bouquet of flowers on the front, but it didn't say 'To My Daughter' or similar. It was a general birthday card of the type you might send an acquaintance.

'She's written inside,' Lucy said, now opening the card and holding it for me to read.

The printed words in the card said: Happy Birthday. May your day be special. Then underneath Lucy's mother had written: *Have a lovely day. I know you will. I hope you get lots of presents. I'll give you something next time I see you. Love Bonnie (Mum).*

It seemed a distant message from a mother to a daughter, but in some ways appropriate, given the distance I'd previously witnessed between them. Lucy's only comment was: 'She'll forget.'

'Forget what?'

'To buy me a present. She always does. I don't mind. She can't help it.' As with all her mother's other failings and shortcomings, Lucy forgave her mother. I was touched. I doubt I would have been so forgiving in her place.

'You're a lovely person,' I said, and gave her a hug.

She shrugged and I kissed her cheek.

'Shall we put your card on the mantelpiece in the living room with your others?' I suggested.

Lucy nodded and then picked up the card from Stevie, which was still on the floor. 'I'd better put this one on show too,' she said.

'That would be nice.' I smiled.

We went out of Lucy's room. Paula was still on the landing and she came with us downstairs. We both watched Lucy position the two cards beside the others on the mantelpiece, making five in all. It was a nice display. In our house, birthday cards usually stay on show for a couple of weeks after the child's birthday and I then put them safely away.

Lucy and Paula watched some television while I made dinner. We were eating later than usual and I assumed everyone would be hungry. Lucy, however, hardly ate anything – far less than usual – and I thought that, while outwardly she seemed to have recovered from her upset with Stevie, inside she was still hurting and in turmoil. I'd noted before that distress caused Lucy's eating to plummet, and I'd learnt from my reading that this was her way of trying to regain some control in her life.

'I'm really not hungry,' Lucy said, pushing her plate away. So I cleared away and hoped that, as had happened before, her eating would improve when she was completely over the upset. I wondered if Stevie fully appreciated the impact her words would have on Lucy. It was a week before she was eating normally again.

I hung the Thai flag on the wall in the living room as Stevie had suggested, and two weeks later I took it down – at Lucy's insistence. Apart from it looking slightly ridiculous – I mean, how many people have a big flag hanging in their living room? – visitors naturally asked why it was there. I then had to explain that Lucy's father was Thai, which to Lucy – who just wanted to blend in and have a normal family life – singled her out and made her feel conspicuous. Lucy complained, so I took down the flag and continued as I had been doing, by educating Lucy on her cultural heritage in more subtle and, I would say, more meaningful ways.

September gave way to October and autumn arrived. The leaves changed from green to magnificent shades of orange, yellow, red and brown. At the weekends we put on our coats and boots and, bracing ourselves for the chilly air, went for walks in the woods, where we collected pine cones and saw squirrels burying acorns for the winter. The days shortened and the nights drew in, and although I love summer I think there is something cosy and comforting in being at home on a cold, dark evening, when the curtains are drawn, the lights are on and the fire glows, and the family is safely cocooned away from the outside word.

At the end of October we celebrated Halloween. The children dressed up in scary costumes and I went with them to those neighbours who had a pumpkin in their porch, confirming that they welcomed trick or treaters. Then, on Guy Fawkes Night, we went to a fireworks display on the playing fields at Paula's school. As usual there was a huge bonfire built by the parents, staff and pupils, and a dazzling display of fireworks. After the display, while the bonfire crackled in the night air, we stood in small groups and chatted with other families as we ate barbecued hot dogs with fried onions and lashings of tomato ketchup.

Christmas was now fast approaching and by the end of November most of the shops were festively decorated and selling Christmas gifts. Some even had Christmas music playing. I hadn't heard from Stevie since she'd visited us in September, and she was now well overdue for her next visit. It crossed my mind that perhaps Lucy's reaction to her on her last visit had upset Stevie more than she'd shown at the time, although as a social worker she would have had to deal with a lot worse than Lucy throwing a few ornaments and tormenting her with the cat. Lucy only had to see Stevie or hear her name mentioned and she became angry and upset. I hoped Stevie wouldn't make her next visit too close to Christmas, as I didn't want Lucy upset over the festive period. However, when Jill next visited – the first week in December – she said, 'Stevie has left the department and has gone to work for another authority. Her post won't be filled until after Christmas, so if you need to contact the department in the meantime, phone her team manager.'

'All right,' I said.

'Hopefully Lucy will get on better with the new social worker,' Jill added.

'Yes,' I agreed. 'And hopefully her new social worker won't be allergic to cats!'

Chapter Twenty-Two

A New Year, a New Social Worker

I love Christmas, and so does my family. I always make sure the children I look after, as well as my own, have a fantastic Christmas – one they will remember. So many of the children I foster have never had a proper Christmas before, and I can cry at some of the stories they tell me about their Christmases before coming into care. Over the years I've heard of every disappointment and atrocity you can imagine taking place on Christmas day: having no Christmas at all, despite being promised one; having no food in the house and having to beg from neighbours; parents being too drunk, hung over or high on drugs to look after their children, so that they were left to get on with it, as they were every other day of the year; and, worst of all, children being abused on Christmas day. Abuse is evil at any time, but at Christmas – a time of good will and peace – it seems an even viler outrage, and my heart aches. One child I looked after had been badly beaten by his parents on Christmas morning for waking them up early, hoping that Father Christmas had been. He hadn't. The parents locked him in the cellar until they were ready to get up in the afternoon and start drinking again.

Lucy had been in care the previous Christmas, so she knew there was plenty to look forward to. Most foster carers go out of their way to make sure the children they look after have a lovely Christmas, because they know how important it is to them. School broke up four days before Christmas, and Adrian, Paula and Lucy's excitement escalated until Christmas Eve, when they hung their sacks on the front door in anticipation of Father Christmas coming – only, of course, in our house it was Mummy Christmas. They were all so excited they didn't go to sleep until after eleven o'clock, and then I heard them wake with shouts of 'Father Christmas has been!' just before seven o'clock.

Adrian, now fourteen, no longer believed in Father Christmas, but he was happy to keep the magic alive for everyone else's sake. Paula, now aged ten, had her doubts, but put them aside, helped this year by Lucy who, though twelve, had never had the opportunity of believing in Father Christmas as a child and embraced it wholeheartedly, so dispelling Paula's doubts.

As they started unwrapping the presents in their sacks, which had miraculously filled and been placed by their beds during the night, I slipped into my dressing gown and went in and out of their bedrooms to watch them open their gifts. 'Look what Father Christmas has brought me! It's just what I wanted!' Lucy cried over and over again.

'And me!' Adrian and Paula called back from their bedrooms, as they tore the paper from their presents.

Seeing their little faces light up with unbridled joy made all the preparation and hard work that goes into Christmas completely worthwhile. Once they'd finished opening their 'Father Christmas presents', they admired each other's gifts and then, when washed and dressed, we all went downstairs for a light breakfast. I'd set the oven on the timer so the turkey was already cooking, and I now prepared the vegetables while we waited for my parents and my brother and his family to arrive, which they did at eleven o'clock. The happiness and excitement grew as we exchanged gifts and then played games, ate a huge Christmas dinner with all the trimmings and then played more games. The house rang with the sound of laughter – from adults and children – and eventually, when everyone left just before midnight, we agreed it was the best Christmas ever; but then, we always say that.

Adrian and Paula's father took them out the following day (Boxing Day), as arranged. This allowed Lucy and me to spend some one-to-one time together, as on the other Sundays the children saw their father.

'We're not going to do school work today, are we?' Lucy said, pulling a face, as I returned from seeing off the children. Lucy usually did an hour or two of school work when Adrian and Paula were out with their father, as it was a good opportunity for her to have my undivided attention and help.

I laughed. 'No. It's Boxing Day – still part of Christmas,' I said. 'Anyway, you told me you liked doing extra work to catch up.'

'Yes, I don't mind. I'm pleased I'm not bottom of the class any more. I hated that.'

I told Lucy I was going to have to clear up from yesterday before we did anything else.

'Can I help you?' she asked, following me into the kitchen.

'Yes, if you'd like to,' I said. 'Or you can play with your Christmas presents.' I rarely asked Lucy to help in the house, as she'd had far too much responsibility for domestic chores before coming into care.

'I don't mind helping you,' she said, picking up a tea towel as I began washing the first pan. 'I like to help you, you're like a mum. I used to hate doing it for my aunts and Dave.'

'You were made to do far too much,' I said, as I'd told her before. 'It was wrong.'

'But I got through it, and all the other stuff,' Lucy said stoically. 'There's many kids worse off than me.'

I smiled sadly. 'Yes, you're right.' Since Lucy had been with me she'd grown increasingly positive in her outlook, which I thought would serve her well in life.

'Some of my aunts were worse than others,' Lucy said, taking the pan I'd just washed and drying it. 'There was one called Pinky. What a silly name! She was a real cow to me. She used to have men round when Dave wasn't there. They used to drink and smoke stuff. She told me if I took my knickers off and showed my bare bottom to the men they'd give me money. Enough to buy all the sweets I ever wanted.'

My hands froze in the washing-up water and I stopped cleaning the pan. 'And did you show them?' I asked.

'No! I was only little but I knew it was wrong.'

'And they didn't force you?' I asked, hardly daring to look at her.

'I don't think so. It's difficult to remember. There were so many different people in different flats and houses. I remember Pinky kept asking me to take off my knickers. She said she took hers off for the men, so it was OK for me to do it. She also said I shouldn't tell Dave, but he threw her out anyway. Or she left. I don't know which.'

I continued to look at Lucy as she absently dried the pan. 'Have you told anyone about this?' I asked gently. 'One of your social workers or a previous foster carer?'

'No. I'd forgotten all about it until just now. It suddenly popped into my head as I was standing here. Is that normal, Cathy; to forget and then suddenly remember?'

'Yes, perfectly normal,' I said. 'Especially with bad memories. Because you feel safe now your mind is slowly allowing you to remember – only what it feels you can deal with. There may have been a trigger to this memory – possibly being in the kitchen. But suddenly remembering is normal, and when you eventually start therapy the therapist will help you deal with those memories.'

'You help me already,' Lucy said, planting a kiss on my cheek.

I smiled weakly. 'Lucy, what you told me just now is child abuse, and I'll be passing on what you said to your social worker, as I have the other things you've told me. If there is enough evidence, the police will investigate. It's important that people like Pinky and those men are brought to trial, to stop them harming other children. I don't suppose you can remember Pinky's second name? Or the names of the men, or where you were living at that time?'

'No. I don't think I knew,' Lucy said, with a small shrug. 'I remember I didn't have Sammy at that time, and there wasn't a teacher I could talk to. But I don't know how old I was or where we were living.'

'All right, don't worry,' I said. 'You've been through so much; you're doing very well.'

'Much better than you're doing with the washing up,' Lucy said with a laugh. 'You've only done one pan!'

I laughed too and, taking the next pan, began washing it, as Lucy started talking about Christmas: the presents she'd received and the games we'd played, and reliving the highlights. Like many abused and neglected children, Lucy had developed a coping mechanism that allowed her to recount a memory and then return to the present and pick up where she'd left off.

* * *

A New Year, a New Social Worker

No Christmas card or present had arrived via the social services from Lucy's mother, so I assumed none had been sent. Lucy hadn't mentioned not receiving a card or present from her mother and I didn't think she expected one. However, now she suddenly said, 'I hope my mum's all right. I worry about her when I don't hear from her for ages.'

'I'm sure she is all right, love,' I said. 'She can look after herself. But if you're worried, I'll phone the social services when they reopen tomorrow and ask if anyone has heard from her. Or you could phone them yourself, if you like? You're old enough.'

'No, you do it,' she said. Then, taking the next pan, she looked at me thoughtfully. 'Cathy, do you ever make New Year's resolutions? You know, things you're supposed to do or stop doing?'

'Sometimes,' I said.

'Like what?'

'Usually not to eat so much cake and chocolate.'

Lucy laughed loudly. 'You'll break that for sure!'

'I know.'

'I was thinking I should make a New Year's resolution to try and be nice to my new social worker, and to forgive all the people who hurt me. Then I'll be a nicer person, won't I?'

'Oh, love,' I said, turning to her. 'You are a nice person already. I love you just as you are.'

'I love you too,' she said, with another kiss on my cheek. 'And I always will.'

I telephoned the social services the following day, but there was only a skeleton staff in the offices until after the New Year, so as it wasn't an emergency I said I'd phone back in a week. I was aware that the final court hearing had taken place some time in December and I assumed Stevie's manager had represented the social services in court. As the outcome of the hearing didn't directly affect me looking after Lucy, I hadn't been told, but it seemed likely the judge would have granted the social services a Full Care Order, which would give them full parental rights, although it didn't change the care plan. I wondered if Bonnie had attended the court hearing or whether she'd left it to her solicitor and lawyer. All parties in care proceedings have legal representation; if they can't afford the legal costs, then those costs are met by the state through the legal aid scheme.

All too soon the Christmas holidays came to an end and we had to take down the decorations and stow them in the loft for next year. The children were very slow getting up on that first morning back at school, so I had to chivvy them along.

'Six weeks until half-term holiday,' Adrian sighed at breakfast that morning.

Lucy groaned and Paula pulled a sulky face. It wasn't that they didn't like school; it was the wrench of going back after a wonderful Christmas. I felt the same reluctance to start the school routine again.

'I hope it snows like it did last year,' Lucy said, perking up a little at the thought.

'I hope so too!' Paula agreed. 'We had such fun!'

Incredibly, in February Lucy would have been with us for a year. We thought back and remembered how it had snowed on her first weekend with us, and we shared our happy memories.

The following week, on the Tuesday morning, having heard nothing from the social services, I prepared for Lucy's review, which was scheduled to take place at eleven o'clock. Jill had telephoned the department to confirm the review was taking place, and the team manager said that it was and that a new social worker had just taken up the post and would be attending the review. As with Lucy's previous review, it was to be held at my house and Lucy could have attended, but had chosen not to, preferring to go to school instead.

Jill arrived first, ten minutes early. I made us coffee and we took it through to the living room, which I'd previously dusted, vacuumed and tidied as I had the rest of the house. Peter, the reviewing officer, arrived next. I made him a cup of coffee and then joined them in the living room.

'I understand Lucy's new social worker will be attending,' Peter said. 'Have you met her?'

'No,' Jill and I said.

'I'm not expecting many to attend this review,' Peter continued, addressing us both. 'It seems that because no social worker has been in place the invitations to the review haven't been sent out.' Normally, two weeks before a review the social worker sends invitations to all parties involved with the child, but this hadn't happened as Lucy hadn't had a social worker. 'I'm sure you'll be able to tell us what we need to know about Lucy,' Peter added, looking at me.

'Yes, I'm sure I will,' I said. 'I know Lucy very well.'

We sipped our coffees, and Jill and Peter took out their notepads and pens, ready to begin as soon as the new social worker arrived. Five minutes later the doorbell rang and I went straight to answer it. A smartly dressed lady in her forties smiled at me. 'Cathy? Have I got the right address?'

'Yes. Come in.'

'Sorry I'm late,' she said, slightly flustered, offering her hand for shaking. 'I'm Lily, Lucy's new social worker.'

'Nice to meet you,' I said.

'Sorry I didn't have a chance to meet you and Lucy before the review,' Lily now apologized. 'I only took up post yesterday and it's been rather hectic.'

'I can imagine,' I said. But I wondered how much use she was going to be, having just taken up post and not knowing Lucy's case.

'We're through here,' I said, leading the way down the hall and into the living room.

Peter and Jill stood, introduced themselves and shook hands with Lily. I offered her a drink, but she didn't want one. As we settled on the sofa and chairs, Toscha, inquisitive as to who was here, sauntered in.

'What a lovely cat,' Lily said, and immediately rose in my estimation. 'I bet Lucy likes her,' she added.

'She does,' I said. Jill threw me a knowing smile.

Peter now officially opened the review and, as was usual practice, we introduced ourselves. He then spoke to Lily. 'I'm assuming that as the invitations weren't sent there will just be the four of us?'

'Yes, I'm sorry about that,' Lily said, apologizing again.

'It's not your fault,' Peter replied. 'We'll send a copy of the minutes to all parties. Let's make a start then. Cathy, would you like to begin by telling us how Lucy has been doing since her last review?'

I glanced at the sheet of paper I held where I'd listed the key points. Peter wrote as I spoke. 'Lucy is still doing very well at home and school,' I began. 'She has fully integrated into my family and has a lovely relationship with my children, my parents and me. She says she loves us all, and we certainly love her. She celebrated her birthday in September and although she didn't want to invite anyone from school we still had a lovely time.' I then told the review what we'd done for Lucy's birthday and about the presents she'd received.

'Very good,' Peter said as he wrote.

'Lucy is still making good progress at school,' I continued. 'At the start of the new school year in September she went up a year with her class. I am in contact with her new form teacher, Mr Mace, and he is pleased with her progress. I sent a copy of Lucy's end-of-year report, which included her test results, to the social services. She's catching up fast and is now only twelve months behind her peer group.'

'Excellent,' Peter said. Then glancing up at Lily, he asked, 'Do you have a copy of Lucy's school report?'

'Not with me,' she said. 'It will be on file. I'll read it when I return to the office.'

Peter nodded, then looked to me to continue. I said that Lucy was much better at managing her anger and frustration now, and that while her eating had improved I still had concerns, as it didn't take much for her to stop eating after an upset. I said I thought her eating problems were more to do with her emotions and past experiences than any desire to be thin. She didn't ever say she was fat or spend a lot of time in front of the mirror, or purge herself or make herself sick, as some suffering from eating disorders do.

'Well, that's hopeful,' Peter said. 'So, we'll continue to monitor Lucy for the present, without medical intervention?'

'Yes,' I agreed. 'I'm happy with that.' I concluded my report by saying a little about the fantastic Christmas we'd had.

'Thank you very much,' Peter said. 'Did Lucy see her mother at Christmas?'

'No. There hasn't been any face-to-face contact since the last review,' I confirmed. 'Although Bonnie did send her a birthday card via the social services.'

'Oh, that reminds me,' Lily said, dipping her hand into her briefcase. 'There's a Christmas card here for Lucy from Bonnie. It was left on my desk.'

Better late than never, I thought, but didn't say. It wasn't Lily's fault the card was so late.

'I opened it to make sure it was appropriate,' Lily said, handing the card to me. It's usual for the social worker or sometimes the foster carer to open cards and letters from the child's family, to make sure nothing threatening or upsetting has been written inside. This may seem intrusive, but children in care can be easily scared into silence or badly upset by an inappropriate word or comment.

'Thank you,' I said, and laid the card on the sofa beside me.

Peter now asked Jill if she had anything to add to what I'd said.

'Not really,' Jill said. 'As Cathy's support social worker, I visit every month and I'm pleased with the progress Lucy has made under Cathy's care. As far as the agency is concerned, it's been an excellent placement. Lucy has come on in leaps and bounds, and Cathy and her family have found looking after Lucy very rewarding.'

'Thank you,' Peter said, as he finished writing. Then turning to Lily he said, 'I appreciate you've just taken up post, but can you update us as best you can, please?'

'Yes, of course,' Lily said, taking some papers from her briefcase. 'I read as much as I could of the file last night, so I've got a feel for the case and what has been going on, although you'll have to excuse me if I can't answer all your questions. I also had a quick meeting with my manager this morning, and briefly spoke to the family-finding team for their update.' I could see that Peter and Jill were as impressed as I was; Lily had been very diligent and conscientious.

'Let's start with the outcome of the final court hearing,' Peter said, pen poised and ready to write.

Lily nodded. 'The hearing wasn't contested,' she began. 'The social services have been granted a Full Care Order in respect of Lucy. Bonnie was in court, but only spoke through her lawyer. Essentially, she told the judge that she was happy for Lucy to stay in long-term care, as she knew Lucy would have a better life than the one she could give her. Bonnie said she'd like to see Lucy twice a year and also be allowed to send her Christmas and birthday cards, which the social services have agreed to. However, Bonnie complained through her lawyer to the judge about the number of different foster carers Lucy has had since coming into care, and the amount of time it was taking to find Lucy a permanent home. Our lawyer explained that it was because of the matching process – that we were trying to find a permanent family for Lucy to match her cultural heritage. I understand from my manager that Bonnie's lawyer told the judge that Bonnie hadn't a clue what they were talking about, as Lucy was English.'

Jill and I exchanged a meaningful glance, while Peter looked up from his writing. 'The mother has a good point,' he said. 'How long are the social services going to be looking for this family before they widen their search to include other families? It's a pity we haven't anyone from the family-finding team here.'

'I'm sorry,' Lily said. 'When I spoke to the family-finding team this morning they said they were still contacting independent fostering agencies for the best match.'

Peter sighed. 'And Lucy can't possibly stay here with you?' he asked.

It took me a moment to realize he was talking to me.

Chapter Twenty-Three

'she's OK for a Girl'

I was stunned, speechless with shock. Then I began grappling for the words I needed to reply. 'We'd love to have Lucy stay permanently,' I said. 'But we're not allowed to.'

'What do you mean – not allowed to?' Peter asked.

I looked at Jill to help me, and she looked at Peter as she spoke. 'Last September Cathy told me she would like to be considered to look after Lucy long term. I said I would support her application. Lucy had settled in well with Cathy and was making good progress. However, when I approached Stevie she said she wouldn't put Cathy's application forward because she felt she couldn't meet Lucy's cultural needs.'

'I wasn't aware of this,' Peter said, frowning.

'This happened after Lucy's last review,' Jill clarified.

'Are you aware of this?' Peter now asked Lily.

'No,' Lily said.

'Presumably your manager is?'

'I would think so,' Lily said. 'Stevie would have discussed it with him at the time.'

Peter paused and, giving a small cough to clear his throat, looked at us all. 'I would have liked to have been informed at the time. No one has to wait until the next review to advise a reviewing officer of a development in a case or a change in circumstances, especially when it is important. I'm contactable between reviews by phone and email. And if there is something we need to discuss I can bring forward the date of the next review.' None of which I knew, and I doubted many other foster carers knew either.

'I'm sorry you weren't informed,' Lily said, although of course she hadn't been responsible for this.

Peter looked thoughtful and then said to Lily: 'I appreciate you've only recently joined the team, but what is your view on supporting Cathy's application, assuming she still wants to keep Lucy long term?'

'I do,' I said, before Lily had a chance to reply. I felt my pulse quicken and my cheeks flush. I looked at Lily and waited, as Peter and Jill were doing.

'I don't know,' Lily said after a moment, shifting uncomfortably in her chair. 'I'm not familiar with Lucy's case, and I haven't even met Lucy yet. I'd have to discuss it with my manager and the family-finding team. It wouldn't just be my decision.'

'No, I appreciate that,' Peter said.

Jill was looking as though she was bursting to say something, but was wisely waiting to hear what else Peter had to say, for clearly he hadn't finished yet.

'It's not my decision either,' Peter continued, mainly addressing Lily. 'But I have an opinion, and having been Lucy's reviewing officer for two years I know the case well. I shall be including my view in the record of this review. I would like to see Cathy's application given full consideration; indeed, I don't really understand why it wasn't before. If Lucy's mother isn't asking for a family for Lucy that matches her daughter's dual heritage, then I don't see why the social services should continue in their search and prolong the uncertainty for Lucy. First and foremost, Lucy needs a permanent home and a loving family, which Cathy can offer. When you return to your office, I should like you to set up a meeting with your manager and the other professionals involved in Lucy's case, to consider the possibility of Lucy staying here as a long-term fostering placement.'

'Yes, Sir,' Lily said. 'Sir' didn't seem out of place, given Peter's now very authoritative manner. 'I will,' she said, and made a note.

Peter also wrote and then looked up. 'Is there anything else we need to discuss?' he asked, looking at us all.

Stunned into silence, Lily and I shook our heads. 'No, I think we've covered everything,' Jill said.

'In that case I'll set the date for the next review; not in six months' time, but in a month, so we can see what progress has been made. But, Cathy,' he said, now turning to me, 'you can expect to hear from the social services well before the next review – within the next couple of days, and certainly by the end of the week.'

Lily nodded in agreement and made another note while I looked again at Jill. She was clearly as taken aback by this sudden development as I was, but I could also see caution in her gaze, warning me not to get my hopes up yet. It was the first time I'd been at a review when the reviewing officer had been as proactive as Peter. Usually they just recorded and reviewed. I thought it was fantastic that Peter was making full use of his role.

Having set a date for the next review for the second week in February, Peter thanked us all for attending and closed the meeting. He stood to leave, said goodbye and I saw him out. When I returned to the living room Lily was packing her papers into her briefcase. The poor woman looked quite shocked, and I wasn't surprised, given what had happened.

'I'll need to see Lucy as soon as possible,' she said, standing. 'Can I visit you on Friday after school? I'll have had a chance to talk to my manager by then.'

'Yes, of course,' I said.

'What do you think your manager will say?' Jill now asked.

'I don't know,' Lily said. 'I haven't discussed it with him before.'

'He may have had a change of heart after Bonnie's complaint in court and now the reviewing officer's comments.'

'I really don't know,' Lily said again, clearly flustered. 'I'll do as the reviewing officer said, I'll speak to him and set up a meeting. I'll phone you when I have any news.'

'Thank you,' I said.

Lily said goodbye to Jill and I saw her to the door. 'I'll phone,' Lily said again, as she disappeared down the path towards her car.

I closed the front door and returned to the living room. My mouth was dry and my thoughts were whizzing. 'Well, well! What a turn of events,' I said, as I flopped down onto the sofa with a heartfelt sigh.

Jill was looking at me and was clearly as bemused as I was, but I could see that her expression was also serious. 'Cathy, I don't want you disappointed twice. Please don't raise your hopes yet, and don't say a word to the children. This could all come to nothing if the department still feels that Lucy's needs would be better met by another family.'

'I know,' I said. 'But I can hope.'

Which is what I did. I spent the rest of the day wishing, hoping and praying that Lucy would be allowed to stay.

* * *

Will You Love Me?

When Lucy came home from school that afternoon, while omitting any reference to permanency, I told her about the review, which as her foster carer I was expected to do. She wasn't really interested, but I told her who was present and that everyone was very pleased with her progress. I said that her new social worker was very pleasant, and I gave Lucy the Christmas card from her mother. 'It was sent before Christmas,' I said. 'Unfortunately it got overlooked.'

Lucy didn't comment that it was late, nor that the card had been opened. I guessed that, having been in care for some time, she was used to having her post opened. As she slid the card from the envelope, her whole face lit up. 'Mr Bunny!' she exclaimed. 'Thank you, Mum.'

I moved closer so I could see the card. On the front was a traditional snow scene, but sitting on the pile of snow in the middle was a picture of a toy rabbit, the image of Mr Bunny.

'How lovely!' I cried. 'I wonder where your mother managed to find that card. She must have spent a long time looking.' I didn't know if Bonnie had spent time looking for the card or if she'd just stumbled across it, but it was a thoughtful gesture and clearly meant a lot to Lucy. She opened the card and, still smiling, read the words inside. Then she passed the card to me to read. The printed words said simply: Merry Christmas and A Happy New Year. Bonnie had added … *to you and Mr Bunny. I hope you all have a lovely Christmas. See you in the New Year. Love Bonnie (Mum) xxx.*

'That's lovely,' I said. 'You'll have to put it somewhere safe.'

'I'll put it in my drawer with my other cards and my special book,' Lucy said.

I handed her back the card and she disappeared upstairs to her room to put the card safely away. It didn't matter to Lucy that her mother hadn't sent her a present, or that she hadn't seen her over Christmas. Lucy accepted her mother's behaviour and had realistic expectations of what her mother could and could not do. It was enough that her mother had sent a card, which reassured Lucy that she was safe and well.

I heard nothing from Lily or Jill on the Wednesday or Thursday of that week, but I knew they would phone if there was any news. Although I continued as best I could with the weekday routine, what was going on at the social services was never far from my mind. I regularly imagined the discussions that were taking place, hypothesizing on what was being said and the various outcomes. This included everything from the positive – it had been decided that I could apply to keep Lucy – to the negative – my application still wouldn't be upheld. So by the time Friday arrived, I thought I could handle any news; that was, until Lily phoned. I'd just returned from taking Paula to school and was in the hall taking off my coat and shoes when the phone rang. 'Hello,' I said, picking up the handset.

'Cathy.' As soon as I heard Lily's voice my legs trembled and I sat on the chair beside the phone. 'Sorry I haven't been in touch sooner. It's been constant meetings here since I saw you on Tuesday, mainly about Lucy. I'm due to see Lucy after school tonight, but I wanted to speak to you first. The department has reviewed Lucy's case and we have come to the conclusion that, assuming Lucy wants to, we would support an application by you to keep her long term.'

I opened my mouth, but no words came out, as Lily continued talking in the background, explaining procedure. Had I heard her correctly? Had they changed their minds? Was Lily saying that Lucy didn't have to move and could stay and be part of my family?'

'So you'll support my application?' I asked.

'Yes. Assuming Lucy wants to stay, which from what I know I'm sure she will. When I see Lucy tonight I'll explain what permanency will mean for her. I'll phone Jill when we've finished. We're too late for the February permanency panel so I'd like to take this to the March panel. We should be able to manage that if we get a move on.' There was a pause and then she said: 'You've gone very quiet. Are you OK?'

'Yes, I'm fine,' I said, my eyes filling. 'Just trying to take it all in.'

'Well, I'll leave you to it then. I'll see you and Lucy after school, at about half past four.'

'Can I tell Lucy?' I thought to ask.

'Yes, if you'd like to.'

'Thank you. See you later.'

I put down the phone and remained sitting in the hall. Sometimes monumental news – good or bad – is so overwhelming that we are unable to process it all in one go, and have to digest it piecemeal to fully understand what we've been told. So it was with Lucy. I'd heard what Lily had said and gradually I understood. Lucy could stay for good. Tears of relief and overwhelming happiness rolled down my cheeks as I cried and laughed, and Toscha looked at me as though I'd gone completely mad.

During the rest of the day, while I was going about my chores, I quietly rejoiced in the news and pictured telling the children. At first, I thought I would gather the three of them together and tell them all at once, but then I decided they should be told separately, taking into account their individual needs and levels of understanding. Paula, I would tell as we walked home from school – we often spoke of important matters then, when there was just the two of us. I'd tell Adrian and Lucy separately as they arrived home. My eyes filled each time I pictured telling them the wonderful news, and also my parents, who I knew would be as pleased as I was.

Jill telephoned during the afternoon, having spoken to Lily. 'Congratulations!' she said, as soon as I answered.

'Thank you, Jill. I still can't believe it.'

'I'm so pleased for you. We all are.' Homefinders was a small fostering agency, and I knew they all shared in the good news of their foster carers. 'I hope someone has thought to tell Peter the department's decision,' Jill added with a laugh. 'I'll remind Lily the next time I speak to her, or there'll be another telling-off at the next review.'

'Yes.' I smiled. 'Jill, did Lily tell you what prompted the department to change their minds and support my application?' I asked.

'Not exactly. But reading between the lines, I think it was a combination of Bonnie's complaint in court, the reviewing officer's comments and the change of social worker. Lily was 100 per cent behind you and supported your application. She didn't have the same reservations as Stevie.'

'Thank goodness,' I said. 'But I do wonder how many other children are in the same position as Lucy and have had to wait years for a permanent family with the "right" ethnic match.'

'Too many,' Jill said bluntly. 'Attitudes are changing, but gradually. There is still a long way to go. Of course, cultural identity is important, but more important to a child is having a loving family. Anyway, at least Lucy's wait is over. She's got her family. I'll prepare the documents we need and then I'll come and see you. And, Cathy?'

'Yes?'

'It's essential that Lily sees Lucy tonight when she visits. Lucy can't hide in her bedroom as she has been doing. As her social worker, Lily needs to hear from Lucy herself that she wants to stay.'

'I understand,' I said.

'Well, there's no need to say "have a happy weekend". I know you will. I'll phone to arrange a visit as soon as I have the paperwork ready.'

'Thank you, Jill,' I said again. 'Thanks for everything.'

'You're welcome. I couldn't be happier for you all.'

Later that afternoon, wrapped up against the cold, I stood in the playground chatting to other mothers as I waited for school to finish. I was bursting to tell Paula the good news. As soon as the bell rang I stepped forward, away from the other mothers, with my gaze concentrated on the door she would come out of. She saw me straight away, smiled, and ran over.

'Hello, love,' I said, giving her a kiss, as I always do. 'Have you had a good day?'

'We had fish fingers, mashed potato and baked beans for lunch,' she said. 'My favourite.'

'Good. And did you remember to change your reading book?'

'Yes, and we've got comprehension and maths homework.' She pulled a face. 'It's difficult.'

'Don't worry, I'll help you over the weekend,' I said, helping her do up the top button on her coat.

Paula slipped her gloved hand into mine and called goodbye to her friends as we crossed the playground. I wanted to be away from the crowd so that no one could hear us when I told Paula our news. On Monday she could tell her friends, but for now this was private and personal – just for us. Once we were the other side of the congestion at the school gates, I gave Paula's hand a little squeeze and began: 'Paula, you know you've told me in the past how much you like having Lucy living with us, and that you look upon her as a sister?'

'Yes,' she said. 'She's like family and I wish she could stay.'

'Well, love, I have some very good news. Lucy's new social worker phoned me today and the social services have decided that Lucy *can* stay with us, if she wants to.'

'She will!' Paula cried. Then, thinking this might be too good to be true, she asked, 'Really? Are you sure?'

I smiled. 'Absolutely positive. Lucy can stay and be part of our family for good.'

'Yippee!' Paula cried, giving a little skip. 'I'm so pleased. I love Lucy, and I love you and Adrian, and all my family!'

Which was enough to make me emotional again, and it was a few moments before I could talk. 'I love you too,' I said. 'Very, very much.'

As we continued to walk home, I reminded Paula that Lucy's social worker was coming to see her after school and that she would want to talk to Lucy alone. 'I understand,' Paula said, in her grown-up way. 'Will Lucy still have to see social workers now she's staying with us? And have all those reviews, when you spend ages cleaning the house and get out the best mugs?'

I smiled at her. 'Yes, but after permanency has been granted the reviews will happen less often, although Lucy will still see her social worker regularly.' This was because, as a long-term foster placement, Lucy would technically still be in the care system.

When we arrived home, Paula wanted to wait in the front room and watch at the window for Lucy to arrive, but I told her I thought it was best if she carried on as normal, and that I would like to speak to Lucy alone first.

'All right, Mummy,' she said sweetly, and barely able to contain her excitement she ran off to play.

I went into the kitchen to begin the preparations for dinner so that it would be ready for when Lily had gone. Presently, as I worked, I heard Adrian let himself in the front door. 'I'm home, Mum!' he called, as he did every afternoon on arriving home.

'Hi, love. I'm in the kitchen,' I returned.

Following his usual routine, Adrian dumped his school bag in the hall, together with his shoes and coat, and then came into the kitchen to find himself a snack to see him through to dinner.

'Have you had a good day?' I asked.

'Yes, thanks. What's for dinner?' He peered into the pans and then started rummaging in the fridge.

'Adrian, I need to talk to you about something important,' I said.

He paused and met my gaze. 'Yes?'

'You know how well you get along with Lucy? Am I right in thinking you would be happy if she stayed?' But as soon as I said the words, I realized I'd phrased it badly. Supposing he said no?

To my utter relief he said, 'Yeah, sure. She's OK for a girl. I'll miss her when she's gone.'

'That's what I thought. I'm pleased, because the social services are going to allow Lucy to stay, assuming she wants to.'

'She will,' he said. 'She likes it here. She's told me.'

'And what about you, Adrian? Are you completely happy with her staying? It's a big commitment for us all.'

'Yes, of course,' he said, tearing off a lump of crusty bread to go with the piece of cheese he'd cut. 'I'm happy for her to stay. But two sisters!' He pulled a face. 'How could you, Mum!'

'And one amazing son,' I said, kissing him on the cheek. 'Love you.'

'Love you more!'

Now all I had to do was tell Lucy.

Chapter Twenty-Four
Special Day

When I heard the doorbell ring I was immediately in the hall to answer it. I hadn't given Lucy a front-door key yet, but now she was twelve and was staying for good I would give her a key. Paula was in the living room and Adrian was in his bedroom. I felt a heady mixture of excitement and nervousness as I opened the front door.

'Hi, love. How are you?' I said, as she stepped inside. As usual, she offered her cheek for kissing.

'I'm not seeing that social worker,' Lucy said straight away. 'I know you said she was nice, but I'm still not seeing her. Sorry. I'm going to my room.' She kicked off her shoes, dumped her coat on the hall stand and began upstairs.

'Lucy!' I called after her. 'There's something I need to tell you. You have to see your social worker. She has good news.'

'I doubt it,' Lucy replied glumly, and continued upstairs. 'You can tell me later what I need to know.'

'She has to speak to you!' I cried, going after her. This wasn't how I'd visualized telling Lucy, not at all; and she *had* to see her social worker. 'They're letting you stay!' I shouted, as I ran upstairs.

'I know, you told me,' she retorted. 'Until they find another family.'

'No! For good!'

She paused on the top step, with her back to me, then turned and stared at me. 'What do you mean, for good? What are you saying?'

I joined her on the landing and took her hand. 'Lucy, your new social worker phoned me today. She said that if you wanted to stay here permanently, the department will support my application to keep you. So you won't have to move ever again; we'll be your forever family.'

Lucy stared at me completely bewildered, and I knew how she felt. This had all come so quickly and was a shock after a year of believing she was going. 'Why?' she asked, her brow furrowing. 'I don't understand.'

'Because I asked for you to stay, love. I knew you wanted to, and we love you. You do want to stay, don't you?'

She nodded dumbly, still unable to take it in. 'Let's go and sit in your room and I'll explain what's happened,' I said.

I led her along the landing to her room where we sat side by side on the bed, as we had done many times in the past for our chats. I held her hand and gave it a reassuring squeeze. She looked at me, so lost and out of her depth, it reminded me of when she'd first arrived, adrift and very afraid.

'Lucy,' I began, 'halfway through last year I realized how settled you were here and that you'd grown to love us, as we had you. More than once, you asked me if you could stay and I always had to tell you that Stevie was looking for a permanent family for you – to match your cultural identity.' Lucy frowned.

'I know, love. I felt as you did, and thought you should stay. You were happy here and looked upon us as your family. When we returned from our lovely summer holiday I asked Jill if she thought I could apply to have you permanently, and she thought it was a good idea. She told me not to say anything to you,

271

Adrian or Paula until she'd spoken to Stevie, because she didn't want you to be disappointed. It was just as well I didn't tell you, because Stevie believed she should keep looking for the right family for you.' Lucy scowled again.

'But since then, things have happened that have made the social services change their minds. Your mother told the judge in court that she was worried about how many moves you'd had and how long it was taking the social services to find you a permanent family. Then you had a change of social worker, and your new social worker is happy to back my application. Lily will explain all about this when she comes, and she will need to see you. She has to ask you if you want to stay.'

'Of course I do!' Lucy cried. 'Oh my God, I'm staying! I'll see her and tell her, of course I will.' Her face had lost its fearful hunted look and she was grinning from ear to ear. 'Oh, is this really happening? I can't believe it. I'm so happy.' Then she frowned. 'They won't change their minds, will they? I couldn't bear it if they did.'

'No, although it will have to be approved by the permanency panel, but you don't have to worry about that.'

'Oh, Cathy!' Lucy cried again, finally accepting that she could stay for good. 'I've nothing more to worry about. Thank you. I love you all so much.' Slipping her arms around my waist, she laid her head against my chest and I held her close as she quietly cried. 'I'll be normal now,' she said. 'Like all the other kids at school. I'll be able to invite a friend home for tea, now I have a family of my own.'

It's often the little comments that take you unaware and make you well up, and so it was with what Lucy had just said. I realized how much she must have been craving what most children took for granted – a family – and tears sprang to my eyes.

Special Day

'Invite your friend as soon as you like,' I said, when I was able to speak.

We didn't have time to talk further as the doorbell rang. 'That'll be Lily,' I said. 'Come with me and we'll answer it together.'

Lucy wiped her eyes and, without offering any objection to seeing her new social worker, she stood and, holding my hand, came with me downstairs. Paula appeared from the living room and skipped down the hall to us. 'Are you happy?' she asked Lucy. 'I am!'

'Very,' Lucy said, smiling.

I opened the door with Lucy on one side of me and Paula on the other. 'What a welcoming party!' Lily said.

'This is Lucy and this is Paula,' I said, introducing them, as Lily hadn't met either of them before.

'Hello ladies,' she said, shaking their hands. 'How are you both?'

Paula smiled sheepishly while Lucy said, 'I'm good, thank you.'

Lily flashed me a knowing smile as she came in. I hung her coat on the stand and then we went into the sitting room. Adrian was still in his room, so rather than interrupt him now I'd tell him later what Lily had said.

'As you can guess from all the happy faces, I've told the children the good news,' I said to Lily. 'Do you want to speak to Lucy alone first?'

'Yes, I think that would be best, then I'll have a chat with you after.'

Paula and I left the living room as Lily and Lucy sat on the sofa. It was nearly half an hour before Lucy came to find us, now completely relaxed and smiling. 'You can come in,' she said. 'Lily had to make sure I understood what was happening, and ask me if I wanted to stay. I told her yes, yes, yes!' She picked Paula up, gave her a big hug and then swung her round, which made Paula laugh loudly.

We returned to the living room. Paula sat on my lap while Lucy sat on the sofa next to Lily. 'I've explained to Lucy what permanency will mean for her,' Lily said, addressing me. 'And she's happy for us to go ahead. I've also explained that she will still be in care and I will be visiting her to make sure she's all right.'

'I don't mind now,' Lucy said. 'I like Lily.'

Paula shot Lucy a quizzical glance, clearly taken aback by her sudden change of attitude towards social workers, having previously refused to see any. I could understand why Lucy felt differently. Now she was no longer living under the constant threat of being moved again, her social worker had changed from being her enemy to her ally.

'I've also spoken to Bonnie,' Lily continued, addressing me. 'She's confirmed she's happy for Lucy to stay with you, and, as you know, she would like to see Lucy a couple of times a year. It's over six months since she last saw her and she's back in town for a while, so I'm going to set up contact for next week. I'm thinking of Wednesday. Are you able to collect Lucy from school and take her to contact?'

'Yes,' I said.

Lily made a note. 'Bonnie has asked if she can have your telephone number so she can phone Lucy on special occasions – Christmas and birthdays. Before I give her your number, I wanted to confirm it was all right with you first.'

'Yes, that's fine with me. It'll be nice for Lucy to speak to her mother between seeing her.' If there are safeguarding concerns, then the parents of a child in care are not given the foster carer's contact details, but there were no such concerns here.

Special Day

'Well, I think that's all for now,' Lily said, as she finished writing. 'Do you have any questions?'

'I can't think of any,' I said. I looked at Lucy, who shook her head.

'Phone me if you think of anything,' Lily said to us.

She packed away her notepad and pen and stood. 'I'll let you get on with your dinner then – something smells good!'

'It's casserole,' Paula said, finally brave enough to speak.

'Hmmm, my favourite,' Lily said.

'You're welcome to stay and have some, if you'd like to,' I offered. 'There's plenty.'

'That's kind of you, but I need to be going now. Thanks anyway.'

We all stood and then, to Lily's surprise, Lucy went over and threw her arms around her. 'That's for letting me stay,' she said. 'And thank your manager. I'm very happy.' From which I guessed that Lily had explained her manager's role in the decision.

'I'm very pleased for you,' Lily said. 'It's at times like this that I know why I became a social worker.' She kissed Lucy on the head.

The girls and I saw Lily to the front door and said goodbye. Once she'd gone, Paula went upstairs to fetch Adrian for dinner while Lucy helped me serve. Lucy ate well, and after we'd eaten I telephoned my parents and told them the good news. They were of course delighted.

'Will you continue fostering now Lucy is staying?' Mum asked.

'Oh yes. We have the room and it worked out well with the children we looked after on respite.'

'As long as you don't overdo it,' Mum cautioned, as she had before.

'Don't worry. Adrian, Lucy and Paula are a big help. In fact, I couldn't manage without them.' Which was very true. Fostering is a whole family commitment.

The children stayed up later than usual, and by way of a little celebration we had microwave popcorn and lemonade while watching a DVD. We would have another celebration in March when the permanency panel passed my application and Lucy staying became official. But for now, this marked the day when our lives changed forever – although in practice nothing changed, as Lucy was already part of my family.

That night Lucy's second wish was granted – it snowed. We woke on Saturday morning to find the world outside had been transformed into a winter wonderland, as we had done almost a year before. I didn't need to provide entertainment for the children that weekend; it was ready-made. We spent the mornings in the garden building a snowman and having snowball fights, and then in the afternoons we dragged our toboggans to the park nearby, which had a hill ideal for tobogganing and was very popular when it snowed. We saw friends and neighbours there; children of all ages and their parents, gliding down the slippery snow-covered hill on anything they had available, including tea trays. The four of us took turns using our two toboggans, climbing to the top and then flying down the shiny slope, over and over again. It was great fun and we didn't notice the cold. We only started for home in the late afternoon, when the air chilled and the sun began to sink, turning the white snow a magical, glistening icy pink.

Monday was a normal school day, as there wasn't enough snow to keep people at home. At school, Paula told most of her friends that Lucy was staying, so she now had a sister. I didn't know if Adrian told his friends – he's a very private person and doesn't always share news – but when Lucy arrived home she had told at least one friend, for she said, 'Can my friend Josette come to tea on Friday?'

'Yes, of course,' I said, delighted.

'And Cathy, I'm seeing my mum on Wednesday. I'm sure it's her birthday soon. I want to get her something, but I won't have a chance to go into town. Can you get me a card and present for her, please?'

'Yes. I'll go tomorrow, and we need to make a note of the date for next year.'

'Don't get her one of those sloppy cards, though,' Lucy added matter-of-factly. 'The ones that say things about being a wonderful mother. She knows she's been crap. You've been more of a mother to me than she ever was.'

I couldn't find it in my heart to tell her off for saying 'crap'. That Lucy could accept her mother for what she was, and still care about her, touched me deeply.

'I'll find something suitable,' I said.

The following day, after I'd taken Paula to school, I drove into town, and after much deliberation found a birthday card I thought would be appropriate. I bought a present for Lucy to give to her mother: a silver photograph frame in which I would put a photograph of Lucy, a box of chocolates and a box of toiletries. I also had another front-door key cut, which I gave to Lucy when she arrived home from school.

'And when do I have my own front-door key?' Paula demanded haughtily, with her hands on her hips.

'When you start secondary school,' I said. 'That's when Adrian had his key.'

'And suppose I'm home before you, how will I get in?'

'Paula, you're ten. I meet you from school and you're never home alone.'

'I suppose I'll just have to accept that then,' she said with the same air, and with her hands still on her hips she marched off theatrically.

I'm sure the youngest child in a family grows up faster than the older ones.

I showed Lucy the presents and card I'd bought for her mother. She was pleased. 'The card's good,' she said, and I was relieved. On the front were printed the words: To Someone Special. Inside there was a short verse, which ended: '... although we can't be together, I'll be thinking of you on your special day. Happy Birthday'. I didn't know what Lucy wrote in the card – she took it to her room to sign, and I didn't ask. What she wrote was personal, between her and her mother.

Jill telephoned the next day and said she needed to see me. She had the paperwork ready for me to read and sign as part of my application to the permanency panel.

'That was quick,' I said, aware of how many forms needed to be completed.

'I started completing the forms last September,' Jill said. 'Then, when your application didn't go ahead, I filed them away. I've completed the agency's part, but there are some boxes on the forms for you to fill in.' We made an appointment for Jill to visit on Thursday at half past ten.

On Wednesday, the day Lucy was having contact with her mother, I arranged for Paula to go to a friend's house after school, rather than spend over an hour in the car on a cold winter's night. Adrian would let himself in as usual. It also meant that I didn't have so much rushing around to do, and I arrived at Lucy's school in plenty of time. The wrapped presents and card were in a gift bag on the back seat. I parked in one of the visitors' bays in the school's car park, where I'd arranged to meet Lucy. While I waited for school to finish, I listened to the radio. I wasn't anxious at the thought of meeting Bonnie again, just sad that life hadn't been kind to her and had resulted in her having to give up her daughter. I thought it said a lot about Bonnie that she had been able to put her daughter's best interests first. Knowing her mother had accepted that she would be better off in care had without doubt helped Lucy settle in and fully integrate into my family.

Lucy was one of the first to come out of school. She saw my car, ran over and, jumping into the passenger seat, kissed my cheek.

'Hi, love,' I said. 'Have you had a good day?'

'Yep!' she said, and fastened her seat belt. 'Josette's mother says Josette can come to tea on Friday, but she wanted your address and telephone number, so I wrote it down and gave it to Josette. I hope that's OK?'

'Yes. Absolutely. Parents need to know where their children are and that they are safe, no matter how old they are. I'd do the same.'

'Josette's already asked if I can go to her house the following Friday,' Lucy said, excited. 'Is that OK? I'll get her address.'

'Yes, of course.'

'And her mum said to say thank you for offering to take Josette home afterwards.'

'She's welcome,' I said. 'They sound a nice family.'

'Yes, they are.'

Lucy continued chatting as I drove, mostly about Josette and another girl she was making friends with. We arrived at the contact centre with ten minutes to spare. I parked the car and we got out, with Lucy carrying the gift bag. Inside the centre we gave our names to the receptionist and then signed the visitors' book. The receptionist said that Bonnie had already arrived and was in Red Room. 'Go on in,' she said. 'The contact supervisor will be with you shortly.'

Now that the care proceedings had finished and as there were no safeguarding issues, having a contact supervisor present wasn't so critical and was really only to monitor contact and make sure it was a positive experience for Lucy. It was quite possible that future contact would take place away from the centre – in the community, as it is known – and without a supervisor, which would make the time Lucy spent with her mother more relaxed and natural. The door to Red Room was ajar and I followed Lucy in. Bonnie was sitting on the sofa flicking through a magazine, which she returned to the magazine rack as we entered.

'Hello,' she said to Lucy, standing and taking a step towards her.

'Hi,' Lucy said. Going over, she kissed her mother's cheek.

I saw that Bonnie was surprised. She drew back slightly. She didn't return the kiss or hug her daughter. I don't think she could.

'Hello, Bonnie,' I said, going over. 'Nice to see you again.'

'And you,' she said softly, with a small smile.

'Happy Birthday,' Lucy said, handing her mother the gift bag.

'For me?' Bonnie said, genuinely amazed. 'How did you know it was my birthday?'

'I thought it was about now,' Lucy said. 'But I didn't know the exact date.'

'It's tomorrow,' Bonnie said. 'Thank you so much. How lovely of you to remember.'

Special Day

My heart went out to her; she was so pleased, I wondered if she'd ever had a present and card on her birthday before. As I looked at Bonnie, I saw that, although it was only a little over six months since I'd last seen her, she'd aged. She looked as though she'd lost weight and was very pale. She was again dressed fashionably in jeans and a zip-up top and even had on a little make-up, but there was a remoteness about her. Her eyes looked distant and slightly glazed. I remembered reading in the paperwork that she'd been on anti-depressants at various times in her life, and I wondered if she was on them now, to help her cope.

The supervisor came into the room, introduced herself and sat at the table. 'I'll go now,' I said.

'You can stay if you like,' Bonnie said.

The supervisor was as surprised as I was by this offer; usually the natural parents can't wait for the foster carer to leave.

'No, this is your special time, for you and your daughter,' I said to Bonnie. 'I'll come back in an hour at the end of contact.'

'Open your presents, Mum,' Lucy said, sitting on the sofa.

'Yes, I will,' Bonnie said, sitting beside her daughter. 'I'll open my card first, and then my presents. I've got three presents!' she exclaimed, peering into the bag. There was a touching child-like naivety in her enthusiasm and, as I left, I thought that if there was ever a case of a mother in need of looking after as much as her child, it was Bonnie. I wished I could have taken her home and looked after her too.

Chapter Twenty-Five
Thunderstorm

I went for a short walk while Lucy saw her mother, but the evening was so cold I soon returned to the contact centre, where I sat in the waiting room and flicked through a couple of old magazines someone had left there. My thoughts returned to Bonnie and Lucy, now in Red Room. A lot had happened in the interim since they'd last seen each other and I wondered if Bonnie would talk to Lucy about the court case and why Lucy was staying with me. I felt I should say something to Bonnie, perhaps to reassure her that I would take good care of Lucy, and thereby acknowledge the responsibility I felt for looking after her long term. I decided to see what Bonnie said and to take my cue from her.

The hour's contact came to a close and, leaving the waiting room, I went to Red Room where I knocked on the door and went in. The room was unusually quiet for the end of a contact, as I remembered it had been the last time Lucy had seen her mother. Bonnie and Lucy were sitting side by side on the sofa, close, but not touching, just like the last time. I smiled as they looked up, and then the contact supervisor said to them: 'Time to pack away now.' Although the only item that needed putting away was the pack of playing cards Lucy held in her hand. There were no other games or toys out.

Thunderstorm

Lucy stood and crossed to the toy cupboard and put away the cards.

'What have you been playing?' I asked, filling the silence.

'Snap,' Lucy said.

'It's the only card game I know,' Bonnie said, with an embarrassed laugh.

'It's a fun game,' I said. 'We play it at home.' Although in truth it was a game for much younger children, and we only played it when we had small children visiting us.

The room fell silent again, and Lucy returned to the sofa and took her coat from the arm of the chair. Bonnie stood and picked up her jacket too. 'Thank you for the presents,' she said to me.

'You're welcome,' I said. 'Did the social worker give you my telephone number, as you asked?'

'Yes. Thank you,' Bonnie said quietly. 'It will be nice to talk to Lucy sometimes. But don't worry, I won't make a nuisance of myself and keep phoning.'

Once again my heart went out to her. 'Phone whenever you want,' I said. I knew I was taking a chance, as Bonnie might have phoned continuously, which would have been very unsettling for Lucy, but from what I knew of Bonnie I didn't think she would.

'I'll take good care of Lucy,' I added.

'I know you will,' Bonnie said. 'Lucy's told me how happy she is with you. I can't thank you enough for looking after her. She's had so many moves, and not everyone has been as kind to her as you have.'

A lump immediately rose in my throat. Bonnie's self-effacing manner, with no hint of resentment that I had stolen her role as parent, made me want to reach out and hug her. I didn't, because I knew she would find that very difficult.

'There's no need to thank me,' I said. 'We are all very pleased Lucy can stay. Hopefully one time you'll be able to meet Adrian and Paula.'

'Yes, I'd like that,' Bonnie said. 'Thank you. Well, goodbye then, love,' she said, turning to Lucy. 'Take care, and be good for Cathy.'

'Goodbye,' Lucy said.

There was something so very sad and a little strange in this emotionless farewell, especially as Lucy was always so tactile with us at home. I didn't offer my hand to Bonnie for shaking – I doubted she would have accepted it – so I said simply, 'Look after yourself then, Bonnie. Phone when you're ready.'

'I will,' she said, with a small smile.

I felt I had missed an opportunity to say more to Bonnie, but I didn't know what else I could say. Anything I considered sounded trite and even patronizing. Bonnie picked up the gift bag and returned to sit on the sofa to wait until we had left the building.

'Bye, Mum!' Lucy called, as we went.

'Bye, love,' Bonnie replied.

As we went through the door, I turned and smiled a final goodbye. Bonnie was sitting on the sofa with the gift bag clutched protectively to her chest, as if it was her most treasured possession, and perhaps it was. She reminded me of one of those child refugees you see in photographs, who have all their possessions in a bag that they hold close, in case anyone should try to snatch it.

Lucy linked her arm through mine as we left the contact centre. In some respects it was a relief that there hadn't been a big emotional scene when Lucy had parted from her mother. It can take days or even weeks for a child to fully recover from the upset of saying goodbye at the end of an emotionally charged contact. I hoped Bonnie had some good friends whom she could confide in and who would support her, for she seemed so alone in the world, and we all need at least one shoulder to cry on.

Jill visited the following morning as arranged and asked me how the contact had gone. I told her, and then I shared my concerns for Bonnie.

'Will the social services offer Bonnie counselling?' I asked. I knew they did for some parents with children in long-term care.

'I'm sure Lily would have offered it,' Jill said. 'Although from what I know of Bonnie's lifestyle, she doesn't stay in one place long enough to access counselling or support services.' Which I had to accept. 'Did Bonnie give Lucy the birthday present she mentioned in her card?' Jill asked.

'No, and Lucy didn't expect it, so she wasn't disappointed.'

'Just as well,' Jill said dryly. 'But it's best not to make a promise if you can't keep it.'

'I don't suppose Bonnie has the money to buy presents,' I said.

'No,' Jill agreed sadly. 'I don't suppose she has.'

Jill now took a file of papers from her large bag, which doubled as a briefcase. 'Your application to the permanency panel,' she said, tapping the file. 'Because you're already fostering Lucy, we've been able to streamline the process. If she wasn't here already, your application would have been far more complex and lengthy. Don't worry, I'll go through this with you now.'

I moved closer so I could see the papers and Jill opened the file. 'The application begins with the basic stuff, your essential information, which I've taken from our records,' she said, referring to the top pages. 'I've checked it all and it's current.' I nodded and ran my eyes down the pages as Jill turned them.

'Then we have your fostering history,' she said. 'And what you learnt from looking after those children. This was all included in your last review, which you read and signed at the time.' I nodded and skimmed the pages. 'Then we go on to information about your family,' Jill said, 'including family interests, and that you are all aware of the implications of fostering long term. There is a paragraph on your motivation for offering a long-term placement to Lucy, how well you handle contact and how you support Lucy. All of which you do admirably, of course,' Jill added, as I read. She paused while I finished reading and then turned the page again. 'Here we have your children's views about fostering Lucy long term, which are of course very positive, followed by Lucy's views on staying here – again, all positive – which I wrote after speaking to you and Lily.' Jill paused again as I finished reading these pages.

'Thank you,' I said.

'The next question is standard, so don't take it personally,' Jill said. My gaze fell to the next box on the form which asked: 'Do the carers and their family understand the impact of racism, and what do they do to support the child's ethnic origin?'

I read Jill's reply and nodded. 'Thank you,' I said again.

'I'm almost certain there will be a question along these lines at the permanency panel too,' Jill said. 'So be prepared.'

'I will,' I said.

'Your references,' Jill continued, turning the next few pages. 'All positive, of course. Then your police checks and medical, which are current and always included. And a copy of your last fostering review, which you've already read.' This alone was twelve pages long. 'And, finally,' Jill said, 'my conclusion, with my recommendation to the panel that they should grant your application to foster Lucy long term.'

Jill waited while I read this section.

'What lovely words,' I said.

'You deserve it. So if you're happy with all of this, sign here, and I'll send it with Lily's part of the application for the March panel.'

I picked up my pen, signed on the dotted line and returned the file to Jill. She then told me a bit about what to expect at the panel hearing, after which she read and signed my log notes.

'You know, you'll still have to keep your log notes going, even after permanency,' Jill said.

'Yes, I know.'

'Well, if there's nothing else, I'll be off. See you at the review next week,' Jill said. 'Ask Lucy if she would like to attend her review. She might feel differently now.'

'I will,' I said.

When Lucy arrived home from school that afternoon, I told her Jill had visited and the reason why. But when I asked her if she'd like to attend her review, she said, 'Maybe next time. I don't want to miss school.' Which was reasonable.

'Perhaps I could ask for your next review to be held during a school holiday?' I suggested. 'So you won't have to miss school.'

'OK,' Lucy said amicably, and went off to listen to her music, which was far more interesting than discussing her review.

That evening, when I went upstairs to say goodnight to Lucy, she was sitting in bed, with Mr Bunny on the pillow beside her. Her hands were beneath the duvet and there was a lump in the covers, as though she was concealing something, something she'd possibly hidden when she'd heard me approaching.

'Is everything all right?' I asked.

'Yes, but there's something I want to show you,' she said. 'It's a secret and I haven't shown anyone before.'

I sat on the bed, puzzled and a little apprehensive as to what it could be. I thought I knew Lucy well and I couldn't think of anything she might have wanted to hide from me all this time. She was sharing her worries and past experiences more easily now.

'It's this,' she said, producing the object from under the duvet. 'I think you call it my Life Story Book, but I call it my diary.'

'Oh, yes,' I said, surprised and relieved. 'That's right. I remember Paula and I had to close our eyes when you unpacked it when you first arrived.'

Lucy smiled. 'Now I'd like you to see it, and you can read some of the writing, but I'll tell you what you can and can't read.'

'Thank you, love,' I said. That Lucy wanted to share this with me now was not only very touching, but also highly significant: she was, in effect, entrusting me with her past. And although it was her bedtime, I knew I needed to give her all the time she needed.

'That's a photograph of me on the front,' Lucy said, tilting the book so I could see. 'I'm three years old there.'

'What a lovely dress you're wearing,' I said.

'It was my party dress,' Lucy announced proudly. 'Do you know how I know I was three?'

'No.'

'There are more photographs like this inside. I'm wearing my best dress because it was my third birthday.' Lucy opened the book to reveal a double page of photographs showing her at the same age and in the same dress. The top of the page was neatly labelled: 'Lucy's Third Birthday'.

'I had a little party,' Lucy said, happy at the recollection. 'There's my cake, and look at all those presents! I can remember unwrapping them and playing games. That lady was my foster carer.' She pointed to an adult in one of the photographs. 'She was called Annie,' Lucy said. 'She's written all the names of the people in the photographs underneath. Mum was there too.'

I looked at the photographs. Bonnie was sitting on the sofa watching Lucy unwrap her presents. So much younger and with different coloured hair, I wouldn't have easily recognized her.

'I had a lovely day,' Lucy said, with a satisfied sigh. 'I was happy living at Annie's. Here I am in the garden,' she said, turning the pages. 'And here it's Christmas.'

I smiled as I looked at the pictures. 'Presumably Annie started this book for you?'

'Yes, one of my social workers told me she did. The social worker said she'd asked Mum for some photographs of me when I was a baby to put in it, but it never happened.'

'I'll ask Lily,' I said. 'It's important you have some photographs of when you were very little. I'm sure Bonnie must have taken some.'

'Thanks,' Lucy said, and turned the page. 'Here are some more of me with Annie and her family. We did lots of things. Look at me at the farm stroking the rabbit, and here I am on the swings in the park. I don't really remember all of those things, but I can tell I was happy because I'm smiling in all the photographs. I look happy, don't I?'

'You certainly do, love.'

Lucy turned the page again and the photographs taken at Annie's suddenly stopped. Lucy's face grew serious. 'I think Mum must have taken me away then, because that's Dave,' she said, pointing to a passport-size photo. 'I was going to tear it up, but I kept it to remind me what he looked like, in case I ever meet him again. He was horrible to me. He looks horrible, doesn't he?'

'Yes,' I agreed. With a shaved head, one earring, a scar running through one eyebrow and cold, grey, staring eyes, he looked the epitome of a thug. I wondered what Bonnie had seen in him and how she could ever have entrusted her daughter to him.

'There he is with Mum,' Lucy said, pointing to the photograph beneath. It was another passport-size photo, presumably taken in a booth, and showed Bonnie and Dave with their heads pressed together and lips pursed towards the camera.

'Who gave you these photographs?' I asked.

'Mum,' Lucy said. 'I think she was proud of Dave.'

I didn't comment. Lucy turned the page. 'And there's me again,' she said, brightening very slightly. 'I'm at school.' But I could tell as soon as I looked at the photograph she hadn't been happy at that time.

'My teacher gave me the photo,' Lucy said. 'All the children in the school had their photographs taken. We were supposed to pay for them, but Mum didn't have the money, so my teacher said I could keep it anyway. She was a nice lady. She was called Mrs Bridges.'

I looked at the posed school photograph. Lucy's skin was pale and her hair hung lankly around her shoulders. Even though she was trying to smile for the photographer, it was a hollow smile. Her gaze was lifeless, and it was clear to me not only that she was hurting inside, but she wasn't being well looked after.

'I think I was six then,' Lucy said sombrely. 'But there's so much I can't remember. It's very confusing.'

'It might help if we ask Lily to tell us what she knows about your past. As your social worker, she'll be able to look back in the files.'

'Yes, please,' Lucy said, and turned the page. 'I started to write in this book then,' she said. 'Mum and Dave didn't know I had this book. I kept it hidden and only wrote in it when they were in bed or out. I had two things that were mine – this book and Mr Bunny.' She gave Mr Bunny a little kiss before continuing.

I looked at the page Lucy now showed me, with its childish scrawled handwriting – more like that of a three- or four-year-old than a child of six.

'I tried to write my name here and draw a picture,' Lucy said. 'I know it's not very good. I didn't go to school much then, so I couldn't write or draw well. That's supposed to be me and Sammy. He was my friend. When I was unhappy at home and wasn't allowed to go and see Sammy, I used to look at his picture instead.'

The image of Lucy taking comfort from this childish drawing was so sad and pathetic I could have cried. I put my arm around her and gave her a hug. Sometimes a hug can say more than words.

Lucy turned the page again and I was now looking at a number of stick drawings of a lady. 'They are all of Mrs Bridges,' Lucy said.

'I might have struggled to recognize her,' I said with a smile.

'So would I!' Lucy said, laughing. Then her face grew serious. 'I can't remember all that happened at that time, but I know my mum wasn't around, and Dave had lots of girlfriends who I had to call aunt.' She turned the page and I now looked at rows of childishly drawn faces with their mouths wide open.

'Those were my "aunts",' Lucy said. 'They were always angry with me, so I drew them shouting. I've tried to write some of their names underneath, but I couldn't spell.'

The 'names' were really only jumbles of letters, indecipherable as words, until we got to the picture at the bottom of the page, which showed two people shouting, one with hair and the other without. Underneath Lucy had written clearly 'Mum' and 'Dave'. 'That's when Mum came back to Dave. There was a big argument and she left again. Then I had another aunt. That's her,' Lucy said, pointing to the next drawing. 'She stayed for a while, then suddenly I had to leave Mrs Bridges and Sammy and go and live with Dave and a strange woman. I was very unhappy. I didn't know anyone in the new school and I couldn't make friends. No one wanted to play with me. Look at all these pictures of me crying.'

Lucy turned the page and I now looked at a double page of childishly drawn faces that were supposed to be Lucy. There must have been twenty or more, all looking unbelievably miserable, with large tears falling from their eyes. The overall impression was of devastating sadness.

'You were so unhappy then,' I said quietly, shocked.

'I was,' Lucy said. She turned the page and the whole of the next side was covered in dark-grey crayon. 'That's a thunderstorm,' she said. 'I pinched the crayons from school. We didn't have any at home. I don't know why I drew a thunderstorm, perhaps it was raining at the time.'

'Or perhaps it was your way of showing how unhappy you were,' I said. 'All that dark grey is how you felt inside. Children can sometimes show their feelings in art when they can't put them into words.'

'You could be right,' Lucy said. 'I hadn't thought of it that way before.' She paused and then said, 'I didn't see Mum for ages, then suddenly she came and took me away. I was seven. I know because I wrote the number seven here so I would remember.' She turned the page. 'That's my drawing of Mum and her new boyfriend arguing.'

Her drawings were maturing now and it was obvious the picture was of two very angry people; their fists were raised as though they were about to hit each other. Lucy had drawn a balloon coming out of their mouths, which contained the words: 'I hate you!'

I didn't say anything. Lucy was turning the page again and suddenly the drawings had gone, replaced by photographs, and I knew immediately that Lucy was in foster care again.

'I wouldn't let the foster carer see this book,' Lucy said. 'So she gave me the photos and a gluestick and I stuck them in. That's why some of them are wonky and coming loose.'

'Don't worry. We can soon stick those in again,' I said.

Lucy nodded. 'That's the carer, and those are her other foster children,' she said, pointing to the photographs. 'The kids didn't like me and I got blamed for everything that went wrong. Perhaps it was my fault. I wasn't happy there, but it was better than at Dave's. I saw Mum a lot to begin with, and then she stopped visiting. Some time later I had to leave. The foster kids said it was because I was so horrible no one wanted me.'

'That was a cruel thing to say,' I said. 'Of course you weren't horrible. Just very confused and upset.'

Lucy gave a little shrug and turned the page. We were now looking at some photographs of another carer. 'She was called Angie,' Lucy said. 'That's her daughter, Shelly. They were kind to me and I liked being with them, but I was only allowed to stay for a little while, then Mum took me away again. I would have liked to have stayed longer,' Lucy added wistfully.

There were no photographs on the next two pages. Lucy had written the number nine at the top and had ruled some lines beneath it, where she'd written in dates with a few short sentences, like diary entries. 'I don't want you to read this,' she said, covering the writing with her hand and then turning the page. 'I wrote horrible things about Mum and her new boyfriend. I feel guilty now, but at the time I was very upset and angry.'

'I understand, love,' I said. 'You'd been through so much, of course you were hurt and angry.'

As Lucy turned the page again, more photographs appeared and I knew she was in foster care again. All foster carers are expected to keep a Life Story Book for the child with photographs and memorabilia.

'That's the carer, Heather,' Lucy said. 'That's her husband and two daughters. It was OK there, but I had to change schools again and I wasn't doing well in any subjects. I spent Christmas with them. I did my best to fit in and I think they liked me a little, but they had to move house. They told me they wanted to take me with them, but my social worker said I couldn't go. Maybe that's true or maybe they just wanted to be rid of me, I don't know. I then had to go and live with Pat and Terry. You met them.'

'Yes,' I said. Pat and Terry were the couple Lucy had stayed with prior to coming to me.

'I knew when I went there I couldn't stay,' Lucy said. 'Stevie told me it was because they only looked after babies. I thought that was just an excuse and that, like all the others I'd lived with, they didn't want me around for long. I was eleven, and a couple of months after I arrived I had to go to secondary school. The building was huge and I kept getting lost. I couldn't do my work or make friends and I stopped eating. I felt so alone, I really didn't think life was worth living. I knew Mum couldn't look after me, but no one else wanted me either. Then one afternoon, when I got home from school, Pat said Stevie was coming to tell me she'd found me another foster carer and I'd be moving at the weekend. Something seemed to snap inside me. I couldn't take any more. I screamed and shouted and then locked myself in the bathroom. Pat kept trying to talk to me through the bath-room door, but I wasn't listening. Nothing mattered any more. When Terry came home, he broke down the door and got me out. So I ran to my bedroom. They left me alone. I don't think they knew what to do. I planned on staying in my room until I starved to death. I wanted to die, I really did. Then in the even-ing Pat came in with the phone and left it on the bed. Your voice came through. I tried not to listen, but you kept on and there was something in your voice that told me I should pick up the phone. The rest you know,' Lucy finished quietly.

We both sat in silence for some time, subdued by the events Lucy had relived. 'Thank goodness you did pick up the phone,' I said at last, taking her hand between mine.

'You can be very persuasive,' Lucy said, with small smile.

'Good.'

Yet I saw that Lucy's Life Story Book had ended with the photographs of her stay at Pat and Terry's. I wondered why she hadn't stuck in the photographs I'd been giving her. I'd taken plenty and had always given Lucy a copy, but there wasn't one in her book.

'Where are all the photographs of us?' I asked presently.

'In my drawer,' Lucy said. 'I haven't added them because in the past every time I put the photographs in the book I had to leave. I didn't want to leave here, so I didn't stick them in, and it worked. I'm staying!'

My heart melted. 'It's safe for you to stick them in now, love,' I said. 'You won't be tempting fate. Trust me, you're staying. I'm certain the panel will approve it.'

Lucy smiled and, leaving the bed, she returned her Life Story Book to the drawer and closed it. Climbing back into bed she snuggled beneath the duvet. Mr Bunny was tucked in beside her. I kissed her goodnight. 'Thank you for sharing your special book with me,' I said. 'I'm so pleased you were able to pick up Pat's phone.' For without doubt that had been crucial in Lucy coming to me.

'I'm pleased I was able to,' Lucy said.

I kissed her goodnight again and came out, aware of just how close I'd come to being another entry in Lucy's Life Story Book. Had I not pursued my application to keep Lucy, had we not had a change of social worker, had Peter not been so proactive, my family and I would have simply become yet another photograph. If ever there was a story showing the failings of the care system, it was in Lucy's book. All those years of missed opportunities, where everyone involved had played their part and inadvertently contributed to her life of rejection, insecurity and isolation ... I felt the collective responsibility, and hoped that in time I could make it up to Lucy and undo some of the harm done.

Chapter Twenty-Six
'I'll Try My Best'

On Friday, Lucy's friend Josette came to dinner. They used the bus to come home and Lucy let them in with her front-door key. I went into the hall to greet them.

'Mum, this is Josette,' Lucy said, introducing me.

'Come on in and make yourself at home,' I said.

Josette smiled and offered her hand for shaking. 'Lovely to meet you,' she said, with a strong French accent. 'Thank you for inviting me.'

'You're welcome. It's nice to meet you too.'

'We'll get ourselves a drink and then go up to my room,' Lucy said, hanging their coats on the hall stand.

On the way to the kitchen Lucy took Josette into the living room to introduce her to Paula. I kept out of their way while Lucy and Josette were in the kitchen making themselves a drink, and when they went up to Lucy's room I continued with the preparation of the evening meal. It wasn't long before Paula appeared in the kitchen.

'Can I go and play with Lucy and her friend?' she asked.

'Perhaps later,' I said. 'I think they're listening to music and chatting now.' I thought that girls of Lucy's age needed some privacy when spending time with a similar-aged friend. 'How about helping me with the meal?' I suggested. But it didn't hold the same appeal to Paula, so she skipped off to amuse herself until I called everyone for dinner.

As the children arrived at the meal table, Lucy introduced Adrian to Josette, and I could see he was a little taken aback when Josette offered her hand for shaking. But the French shake hands easily, it's part of their custom and charm, and Adrian responded with a charm of his own. I could see he was quite taken with her. They sat down and I brought in the serving dishes and placed them on the table and we all helped ourselves. After an initial awkwardness everyone relaxed and started chatting as they ate. Listening to Josette with her delightful French accent was captivating, and I could see Adrian and Paula were very impressed that she could speak a second language so fluently. Josette told us that her father's work had brought her family to England. They'd arrived four months previously and would be staying for at least three years. I wondered if being the new girl in the school had encouraged Lucy to make friends with her, for, having moved herself so many times, Lucy knew what it felt like to arrive in a new class and not know anyone.

When I took Josette home in the car that evening, she invited me in to meet her parents and elder brother. They were all as delightful as Josette, although we didn't stay long as it was getting late and Paula was with me. Josette's mother thanked me for inviting Josette to dinner and bringing her home in the car, and then confirmed that Lucy was invited there for dinner the following Friday and she would bring Lucy home afterwards. I didn't know if Lucy had told Josette I was her foster mother or if she'd let her assume I was her natural mother, but it didn't matter. It was up to Lucy what she told her friends, and I knew she'd tell them whatever she felt comfortable with. Clearly my old friends knew Lucy was my foster daughter who was now staying permanently, but what Lucy told her new friends was her decision, and I would go along with it.

The following Tuesday, Lucy's review was held as scheduled at my house. It was relatively short and consisted mainly of Lily updating Peter on all that had happened since Lucy's last review the month before. Lily told him that she'd taken Lucy's case back to her manager and the family-finding team, and that they'd decided to support my application to keep Lucy permanently.

'Good,' Peter said, without any surprise. So I guessed he was already aware of the decision, having been in contact with Lily since the last review.

'I've spoken to Lucy,' Lily continued. 'She confirmed to me that she wants to stay with Cathy long term. The social services are now of the opinion that Cathy can meet Lucy's needs. I've submitted the application to the permanency panel, including the matching report, and it will be heard at the March panel.'

'Excellent,' Peter said. 'And you've given Cathy the date of the panel meeting?'

'Yes,' Lily confirmed.

'You know you have to attend the panel hearing?' Peter said to me.

'Yes, it's in my diary,' I said.

'So how does Lucy feel about staying?' he asked me.

'She's over the moon,' I said. 'It's what she's wanted for a long time. We all have.' Lily and Jill nodded.

'And you've advised Bonnie of the decision?' Peter now asked Lily.

'Yes,' Lily confirmed.

'I understand Lucy has seen her mother since the last review?' Peter now said to Lily.

'Yes,' Lily said. 'The contact went as well as could be expected.'

'And contact will remain at twice a year?' he said, making a note.

'Yes, that's the department's recommendation,' Lily said. 'Although it will largely depend on Bonnie keeping in touch.'

'And how was Lucy after the last contact?' Peter asked me.

'She took it in her stride,' I said. 'I think she was helped by knowing she's settled now and that her mother is happy with the arrangement.'

Peter nodded as he wrote. Then he raised a couple of questions with Lily about procedure and, satisfied, asked Jill if she had anything to add. Jill said only that she was pleased with the outcome and thought it was a good match, and Peter agreed.

I then asked if it would be possible for Lily to go through some of Lucy's history with her. 'We have been looking at her Life Story Book,' I explained. 'Lucy is rather confused about some episodes in her life and the decisions that were made at the time. I think it would help if you could fill in the gaps and explain what happened. I don't know enough of her past to help her.'

'I'll pull out the files and see what I can find,' Lily said helpfully. 'There's been social services involvement since Lucy was a baby, so it may take me a while to piece it all together.'

'Thank you,' I said, as Peter and Lily wrote. 'Also, Lucy would like some photographs of when she was a baby and a toddler,' I said. 'The first photographs she has in her life-story book are of her aged three, when she first went into care.'

'You will need to ask Bonnie for those,' Peter said to Lily.

Lily nodded and made a note.

'And, finally,' I said with a smile, 'can I have a copy of Lucy's birth certificate, please, so I can set up a savings account for her, and also apply for a passport for her.'

Peter looked at Lily again, as this would be for her to initiate. 'Yes, I'll apply for one,' Lily said. 'Lucy should be saving. Have you got any plans to go abroad on holiday?'

'Not straight away,' I said. 'But I would like the passport ready for when we do.'

Peter nodded, finished writing and, with no further business on the agenda, he took out his diary to arrange the date for Lucy's next review. 'April,' he said. 'In two months' time. After that we'll go to six-monthly reviews.'

Perfect, I thought. Easter was in April. 'Can we schedule the review for the Easter holidays?' I asked. 'So Lucy can attend.'

'Yes, of course,' Peter said, slightly amused. 'I take it Lucy's feeling a bit happier with us all if she wants to attend her review?'

'Yes. A lot happier,' I said.

Three weeks later I attended the permanency panel hearing, which was held in a conference room at the local government offices. As a foster carer, I had to attend a similar panel hearing every three years to renew my registration to foster, so I knew it would be quite daunting. Knowing, however, didn't help. As Lily came out of the conference room, having given her report to the panel and answered the panel's questions, Jill and I went in. A sea of faces looked up at us: ten panel members sitting along three sides of a huge rectangular oak table. My stomach churned. Two chairs had been left empty facing the other panel members, so Jill and I sat down. I took a very deep breath and thought I heard Jill do the same. I guess it was daunting for her too. Each panel member had a bundle of papers in front of them – copies of my application, with all the supporting documentation. They would have received these a week before the hearing so that they had time to read them and compose their questions.

The chairperson began by saying good morning and introducing himself by name and explaining that he was the chairperson, after which all the other panel members introduced themselves. Going round the table, they gave their name and position. The panel was comprised of two social workers, a doctor, a foster carer, one local authority elected member, two parents who'd adopted and a teacher, none of whom I knew. Jill and I then introduced ourselves: Jill, as my support social worker; me as Lucy's foster carer. The chairperson thanked us, and then said a few words about why we were here: to consider my application to foster Lucy long term. Jill was then asked to speak and gave a brief résumé of my fostering history, the composition of my family and the reasons why she supported my application to look after Lucy permanently. The chairperson thanked Jill and then looked to me.

'We've all read your application thoroughly,' he said. 'Your fostering history is very impressive. I should like to start the questions by asking you to tell us what Lucy is like to live with on a daily basis. Then I'll pass to the other panel members so that they can ask their questions.'

Here goes, I thought. I took another deep breath before I began. I'd anticipated this question or something similar, and gained confidence from being able to answer – describing Lucy, and what she was like to live with, all of which was of course positive. The chairperson nodded and thanked me, and then one of the two social workers asked me what impact I thought looking after Lucy had had on my children, positive and negative. I said that she'd fitted into my family very easily and was like a sister to Adrian and Paula. I described how she played with Paula and helped her out. I said that Lucy had taught us humility and forgiveness, because despite everything that had happened to her she wasn't bitter. I said that she and Adrian teased each other sometimes, as siblings do. That was the only negative comment I could think of.

The other social worker then asked me to describe Lucy's routine, which I did, although it overlapped with the first question and I repeated myself a little. Then, one of the adoptive parents asked what Lucy's interests and talents were. I elaborated on points I'd mentioned in response to the first question, adding that she wanted to be a beautician when she was older, although of course that might change. Then the elected member from the local authority, obviously a veteran at these panels, asked: 'Can you tell us about Lucy's ability to make and sustain friendships?'

I certainly could, and I spoke at some length on the huge improvement Lucy had made since coming to live with us – from not being able to make friends to having a number of school friends, including one best friend whom she also saw regularly out of school.

'Excellent,' he said. 'Thank you.'

The doctor then asked: 'As an experienced foster carer, how do you see Lucy's ability to form attachments to significant people in her life?'

This wasn't a question I'd prepared, but having attended many training sessions on attachment issues I knew the significance of the question and how to answer. I said that despite Lucy's early experiences, once she trusted an adult she was able to form an appropriate attachment to them, and had done so with all members of my family, including my parents. I nearly added 'and the cat', but thought that might have sounded flippant. The doctor then asked if I was aware that sometimes abuse and deprivation in early life didn't surface until much later, and I said I was. Then suddenly I found the questions had stopped and the chairperson was thanking me. So the question that Jill and I had been convinced would come up – in respect of Lucy's cultural needs – hadn't, possibly because it had been covered extensively in my application. Whatever the reason, I breathed a sigh of relief.

'If you and your support social worker would like to wait outside the room, we'll conclude our discussion,' the chairperson said. 'I'll invite you to return when we have made our decision.' I knew this to be normal practice.

Jill and I stood and the panel members waited until we'd left before commencing their discussion. I'd been answering questions for half an hour, but it didn't seem that long. Once outside the room I flopped into one of the chairs in the waiting area. High on adrenalin, my cheeks were flushed and my heart was racing.

'You did well,' Jill said, sitting in the chair beside me.

'I hope so,' I said. 'I answered their questions as best I could. I just hope it was good enough.'

'Don't worry. You'll be fine,' she said. Yet, while it was almost certain the panel would approve my application, there was a slim chance they might not, and I wouldn't relax until I officially had their approval.

Fifteen minutes later, the door to the conference room opened and a member of the panel asked us to return. My heart started pounding again and my mouth went dry. As we entered the room the panel members looked at us, but I couldn't read anything in their expressions. Once Jill and I were seated, the chairperson looked directly at me as he spoke.

'We've now concluded our discussion,' he said. 'I'm pleased to be able to tell you that the panel unanimously endorses your application to foster Lucy long term. Congratulations.'

'Thank you,' I said, grinning. 'Thank you very much.'

'Well done,' Jill said to me.

Other panel members also added their own 'congratulations' and 'well dones'. Jill then thanked the chairperson and pushed back her chair, ready to leave. It suddenly hit me that it was all over and I stood too. If I'm honest, it seemed a bit of an anti-climax: hearing the chairperson's words and then just walking from the room after all those anxious months of hoping, planning and waiting. I would have liked a fanfare with thousands of congratulatory balloons released into the sky. Instead, I heard the door to the conference room close behind us and a little voice in my head offering a silent prayer of thanks for the outcome.

'Come on,' Jill said, touching my arm. 'Let's go and get a coffee.'

'Good idea,' I said.

'And there's something I need to ask you,' she added.

'Oh yes?'

I'd seen that look on Jill's face before.

'I've been thinking, now Lucy is settled and we've got the panel hearing out of the way', she said, as we made our way downstairs, 'that you might like to start fostering again properly, rather than just doing respite?'

'Yes,' I said. 'I've been thinking that too.'

'Good,' Jill said. 'Because I've had a referral through for a four-year-old girl.'

'Jill, you're incorrigible!' I exclaimed with a smile.

'I know. What would you do without me?'

'I honestly don't know.'

Over coffee, Jill explained that the referral was for a little girl called Alice. Her social worker was applying to court the following morning for an Interim Care Order. 'I understand she's a real sweetie,' Jill said. 'She's been staying with her grandparents for the last few months, as her mother has mental-health issues. They're in court at ten o'clock tomorrow so, assuming the order is granted, she'll be with you about one o'clock. I have a copy of the referral in my bag.'

That afternoon, when Lucy, Adrian and Paula returned home from school, I had a lot to tell them. First and foremost was that the panel had said Lucy could stay permanently, so it was official. Everyone clapped and whooped for joy. Then I told them about Alice and their responses were:

'Goody, a little one to play with,' from Paula;

'She'll be very upset, so I'll help settle her in,' from Lucy;

'Not another girl!' from Adrian.

I tell Alice's story in my book *I Miss Mummy*, so I won't say any more about her now, or anything about the very worrying circumstances of her arrival, which didn't go to plan, not at all. Instead, I want to move on ten months to when Alice was about to leave us. It was a cold night in January. Paula was in bed asleep, Adrian was in bed reading and I went upstairs to say goodnight to Lucy.

We spent a few moments talking about various things, as we often did last thing at night before she went to sleep. Mr Bunny was on the pillow beside her as usual and, once we'd finished talking, I kissed them both goodnight. I stood, ready to go, but as I did I had the feeling Lucy had something on her mind.

'Is everything all right?' I asked. 'There's nothing worrying you, is there?'

She paused, toying with the edge of the duvet, and I knew there *was* something on her mind. I sat on the bed again. 'Yes?' I asked gently. 'What is it?'

'I'll Try My Best'

'I need to ask you something,' Lucy said quietly and avoiding eye contact. 'You can say no if you like. I'll understand. I won't be hurt or disappointed. Well – I will be, but I'll try not to show it.'

'Yes?' I prompted, wondering what on earth it could be that Lucy was finding so difficult to tell me. She didn't normally have this much trouble talking to me.

'Well, it's this,' she said, looking very serious and fiddling with the duvet. 'You know I think of all of you as my proper family?'

I nodded. 'Yes, we are.'

'And you know I sometimes call you Mum?'

'Yes.'

'Well, I've been doing some research, reading books in the school library, and online, about adoption. And I was wondering if you could adopt me? I love you all so much, and I promise I won't be any trouble. You can say no if you want.'

My eyes immediately filled and I took Lucy in my arms and held her close. I was too choked up to speak. She was quiet, but I felt the warmth of her love and the trust she was putting in me in her embrace. After a few moments I drew slightly away and looked at her. I knew what I would like to say, but I had to be realistic.

'Lucy, love,' I said, 'I already look upon you as my daughter, and I couldn't love you more. While I would be very happy to adopt you, it wouldn't be my decision.'

'I know,' Lucy said. 'I understand.'

'I'll speak to Lily tomorrow and see what she says. You still have some contact with your mother and her views will be taken into account. It may be that she won't want you to be adopted. I can ask, but if it doesn't happen we don't need a piece of paper to say we're mother and daughter, do we?'

Lucy smiled sadly. 'I guess not, but it would make me very happy.'

'I know, love, I understand. I'll try my best.'

Chapter Twenty-Seven
Special Love

The following morning, as soon as I returned home from taking Paula to school, I telephoned Lily and told her of the discussion Lucy and I had had in respect of me adopting her. Lily said she would need to consult her team manager, but she thought that if Lucy and I wanted adoption, then the department would support my application. However, as I expected, she added a note of caution: she would need to speak to Bonnie to ascertain her view. We both knew that most parents of children in care, while agreeing to a long-term foster placement for their child, would strongly oppose adoption, as it took away all their legal status as parents. Even the birth certificate of an adopted child can be changed to show the adopted parents' names, replacing those of the child's birth parents.

That evening I told Lucy that Lily was looking into our request, but that it might take some time before we knew anything for definite.

It was three months before Lily was able to contact Bonnie, and Lily told me that to begin with Bonnie had reservations about me adopting Lucy, as she thought she wouldn't be able to see Lucy again. Once Lily had reassured her that I was happy to continue with the present contact arrangements, Bonnie said she wouldn't oppose the adoption, as she wanted whatever Lucy wanted. Not only was Bonnie's attitude completely selfless, it was also very unusual. Needless to say, Lucy was overjoyed, and I began the application process.

A year later, when Lucy had been with me for two years, the adoption order was granted and Lucy officially became my daughter. At Lucy's request, we changed her surname to our family name, and I applied for a savings account and passport in her new name. An added bonus for Lucy that came with being adopted was that there was no more social services involvement – no more reviews or visits from social workers – as she was no longer in care.

We celebrated Lucy's adoption with a party at home, where my parents, my brother and his family, Lily, Jill, Josette and Vicky (now another good friend of Lucy's) all came for the evening and I made a buffet tea. Lucy had told Josette and Vicky about her adoption, but, apart from her teacher, no one else at school knew.

Although the social services' involvement had finished with the granting of the adoption order, Lily offered to continue to arrange and supervise contact if I wished. As I had a good working relationship with Bonnie, I felt there was no need for supervised contact, so it was left to Bonnie and me to organize between us. This arrangement worked well and Bonnie continued to see Lucy twice a year and phoned occasionally – usually on birthdays and at Christmas. Sometimes Lucy saw Bonnie at my house, and on those occasions she met Adrian and Paula. Other times, Bonnie and Lucy went out, and I always gave Lucy extra money so they could have some lunch and do something fun – go to the cinema, for example – as Bonnie was permanently broke. I often wished Bonnie would change her lifestyle and get off whatever she was on, but I didn't say anything to her or Lucy. Bonnie clearly struggled with life, and telling her she needed to change wouldn't have helped. I was sure she would change if she could, and hoped that one day she would.

Lucy was always slightly pensive and quiet when she returned from seeing her mother. Often she didn't want any dinner or just picked at her meal. While her eating had improved drastically, if she was upset or worried it showed in a loss of appetite. I was still keeping an eye on Lucy's eating, but I didn't have the same concerns as I'd had when she'd first arrived. She'd put on some weight and was within the normal weight range for her age and height, but she's naturally petite and slim, so she'll never be very big. Lucy was offered counselling just before the adoption, but she refused. Entering counselling or therapy is a personal choice and the time has to be right. She knows she can go into it when she feels ready. Very touchingly, when it was mentioned she said, 'Having my own family is my best therapy.' Which made me tear up.

One day, when Lucy was sixteen and had been out with Bonnie, she returned home and went straight to her room. I gave her some time and then went up after her. I knocked on the door and went in. She was sitting on her bed cuddling Mr Bunny, a sure sign she had something on her mind.

'Are you all right, love?' I asked, going further into the room.

'Sort of,' she said quietly, glancing up at me.

'Sort of isn't good enough,' I said, sitting on the bed. 'I need to know you're completely all right. Please tell me what's wrong.'

She threw me a small sad smile and then, looking down, concentrated on Mr Bunny. 'It's difficult,' she said, after a moment. 'I'm not sure you'd understand.'

'Try me,' I said, touching her arm reassuringly.

She paused again and then said, 'When I'm out with Bonnie I feel guilty that I can't love her more. She's my birth mother, but I don't feel for her what I feel for you. I can't love her as I love you, and that makes me feel guilty and unhappy sometimes.'

'Oh love, I do understand,' I said. 'Perfectly. Let me try and explain something. We are not born loving our parents. We bond with those who look after us, and loving someone is part of that bond. I love you and you love me because of the time we've spent together and all the things we've done and been through together. I've been a mother to you and you've been a daughter to me, so we love each other as mother and daughter. Sadly, Bonnie was never able to give you that special mother–daughter relationship, so it's natural that you feel differently towards her, although I know she loves you.'

'But I feel like I've always been your daughter,' Lucy said, as she'd said before. 'Like you had me.'

'I know. I feel the same. I couldn't love you more if I had given birth to you. That's how strong our bond is. But in your heart, even though you might not know it, there is a special place for Bonnie, separate from the love you feel for me. It will be different, but it will be there, so there's no need for you to feel guilty. Bonnie understands and just wants you to be happy. That's a very selfless love.'

Lucy was silent for a moment, and then looked at me, her expression brightening. 'Yes, that helps. I understand,' she said, and kissed my cheek. 'I've got two mothers and it's OK to love them differently. Thanks, Mum. I love you.'

'I love you too.'

Cathy Glass

———

One remarkable woman, more
than **100** foster children cared for.

Learn more about the many
lives Cathy has touched.

Another Forgotten Child

Eight-year-old Aimee was on the child-protection register at birth

Cathy is determined to give her the happy home she deserves.

A Baby's Cry

A newborn, only hours old, taken into care

Cathy protects tiny Harrison from the potentially fatal secrets that surround his existence.

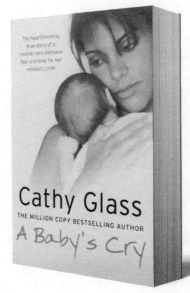

The Night the Angels Came

A little boy on the brink of bereavement

Cathy and her family make sure Michael is never alone.

Mummy Told Me Not to Tell

A troubled boy sworn to secrecy

After his dark past has been revealed, Cathy helps Reece to rebuild his life.

I Miss Mummy

Four-year-old Alice doesn't understand why she's in care

Cathy fights for her to have the happy home she deserves.

The true story of a frightened young girl who is desperate to go home

Cathy Glass
THE MILLION COPY BESTSELLING AUTHOR

I Miss Mummy

Cathy Glass
THE MILLION COPY BESTSELLING AUTHOR

The Saddest Girl in the World

The true story of a neglected and isolated little girl who just wanted to be loved

The Saddest Girl in the World

A haunted child who refuses to speak

Do Donna's scars run too deep for Cathy to help?

Cut

Dawn is desperate to be loved

Abused and abandoned, this vulnerable child pushes Cathy and her family to their limits.

Hidden

The boy with no past

Can Cathy help Tayo to feel like he belongs again?

Damaged

A forgotten child

Cathy is Jodie's last hope. For the first time, this abused young girl has found someone she can trust.

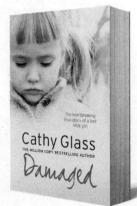

Inspired by true stories...

Run, Mummy, Run

The gripping story of a
woman caught in a horrific
cycle of abuse, and the
desperate measures she
must take to escape.

Cathy Glass
THE MILLION COPY BESTSELLING AUTHOR
Run, Mummy, Run
A novel inspired by a true story

My Dad's a Policeman

The dramatic short story about a young boy's desperate bid to keep his family together.

A shocking story about one boy's desperate efforts to keep his family together

The Girl in the Mirror

Trying to piece together her past, Mandy uncovers a dreadful family secret that has been blanked from her memory for years.

Sharing her expertise...

Happy Kids

A clear and concise guide to raising confident, well-behaved and happy children.

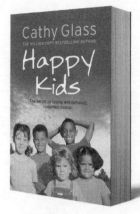

Happy Adults

A practical guide to achieving lasting happiness, contentment and success. The essential manual for getting the best out of life.

Happy Mealtimes For Kids

A guide to healthy eating with simple recipes that children love.

Be amazed
Be moved
Be inspired

———

Discover more about Cathy Glass
visit www.cathyglass.co.uk